INSIDE AUSTRONESIAN HOUSES

PERSPECTIVES ON DOMESTIC DESIGNS FOR LIVING

INSIDE AUSTRONESIAN HOUSES

PERSPECTIVES ON DOMESTIC DESIGNS FOR LIVING

Edited by James J. Fox

A publication of the Department of Anthropology
as part of the Comparative Austronesian Project,
Research School of Pacific Studies
The Australian National University
Canberra ACT Australia

E PRESS

Published by ANU E Press
The Australian National University
Canberra ACT 0200, Australia
Email: anuepress@anu.edu.au
Web: http://epress.anu.edu.au

Previously published in Australia by the Department of Anthropology in association with the Comparative Austronesian Project, Research School of Pacific Studies, The Australian National University, Canberra 1993.

National Library of Australia
Cataloguing-in-Publication entry

Inside Austronesian Houses

Bibliography.
ISBN 0 731515 95 1 (print)
ISBN 1 920942 84 X (online)

1. Dwellings - Asia, Southeastern. 2. Dwellings - Oceania. 3. Asia, Southeastern - Social life and customs. 4. Oceania - Social life and customs. I. Fox, James J., 1940-   . II. Australian National University. Dept. of Anthropology. III. Comparative Austronesian Project.

392.360095

All rights reserved. No part of this publication may be reproduced, stored in a retrieval system or transmitted in any form or by any means, electronic, mechanical, photocopying or otherwise, without the prior permission of the publisher.

Typesetting and drawings by Margaret Tyrie
Cover design by Adrian Young

© The several authors, each in respect of the paper presented, 1993
This edition © 2006 ANU E Press

DEDICATED TO THE MEMORIES OF:

Anthony Forge
and
Hedda Morrison

Building a new longhouse (photo by Hedda Morrison)

Table of Contents

Acknowledgements	xi
Chapter 1. Comparative Perspectives on Austronesian Houses: An Introductory Essay *James J. Fox*	1
The Comparative Austronesian Focus	5
The House as a Topic of Study	6
Austronesian House Terms	9
Ordered Structures and Their Orientation	14
Structures of Origin Within Austronesian Houses	16
Time and Memory in Austronesian Houses	20
Concluding Remarks	23
References	24
Notes	28
Chapter 2. The Lahanan Longhouse *Jennifer Alexander*	31
Balui Longhouses	32
The Levu	33
The Tilung	37
Tilung Composition	39
Continuity of the Tilung	40
References	41
Notes	42
Chapter 3. Good Walls Make Bad Neighbours: The Dayak Longhouse as a Community of Voices *Christine Helliwell*	45
Lawang Construction and Lawang Space	50
Lawang Behaviour: Public or Private?	55
Concluding Remarks	59
References	60
Notes	62
Chapter 4. Posts, Hearths and Thresholds: The Iban Longhouse as a Ritual Structure *Clifford Sather*	67
The Iban Longhouse	68
Sources and Elders	70
Hearths and Posts	72
Upriver, Downriver, Parts and Wholes	76
Trunk, Base and Tip	77
East and West	80
The Longhouse Bathing Place	81
Interior Architecture	83

The Ritual Use of Longhouse Space	85
Rites of Birth	86
Rites of Death	89
The Gawai Antu	95
Conclusion	106
References	110
Notes	113

Chapter 5. Raising the House Post and Feeding the Husband-Givers: The spatial categories of social reproduction among the Minangkabau *Cecilia Ng* — 121

Introduction	121
Spatial Organization in the House	123
Use of Space in Ceremonies	131
Food	136
Conclusion	140
References	141
Notes	142

Chapter 6. Memories of Ridge-Poles and Cross-Beams: The categorical foundations of a Rotinese cultural design *James J. Fox* — 145

Introduction	145
Two Forms of Knowledge: Ndolu and Lelak	147
The Origin of the Rotinese House: Textual Foundations	149
Orientation and Exegesis	153
The Internal Structure of the Rotinese House	156
Internal Structures and the Performance of Rituals in the House	165
The House as Oriented Structure and Inner Space	170
The Rotinese House as a Memory Palace	172
Points of Comparison Between Houses on Roti and on Timor	174
The Atoni Pah Meto of West Timor	175
The Ema of North Central Timor	178
References	181
Notes	182

Chapter 7. The Kalauna House of Secrets *Michael W. Young* — 185

References	196
Notes	197

Chapter 8. Maori Meeting-Houses in and Over Time *Toon van Meijl* — 201

The Marae	202
The Meeting-House Described	203
Social and Political Aspects	205
Symbolic Representation	207

Spatial Orientation	209
Temporal Implications of Spatial Orientation	213
Transformation of the Meeting-House Over Time	215
The Influence of Pakeha Patronage	217
Concluding Remarks	219
References	221
Notes	223

Chapter 9. Houses and the Built Environment in Island South-East Asia:
Tracing some shared themes in the uses of space *Roxana Waterson*   227

Structures and Functions	227
The House as an Animate Entity	229
Houses as Units of Kinship	230
Social Relationships and the Uses of Space	231
Trunk and Tip, Centre and Periphery: Images of Growth and Power	236
References	237
Notes	242

Contributors   243

Acknowledgements

Putting together this volume has taken both time and effort. The starting point for the volume was a wide-ranging seminar on House and Household held 19–20 May 1989 as part of the Comparative Austronesian Project. At this seminar there were sixteen presenters whose purpose was to stimulate discussion on the topic. Most of the papers in this volume began as short presentations at that seminar.

The volume is dedicated to the memory of Anthony Forge and of Hedda Morrison. Professor Forge gave a presentation on 'Ritual Space: Austronesia and Non-Austronesia' at the House and Household seminar and, had he not fallen seriously ill, he might have prepared a paper for the volume. His death has been a great loss to our community in Canberra.

So, too, was the death of Hedda Morrison whose magnificient photographs are ethnographic documents of the first order. Three of her photographs of domestic life among Iban have been used to enhance the presentation of this volume. These photographs have been reproduced with the kind permission of her husband Alistair Morrison. They originally appeared in *Vanishing world: the Ibans of Borneo* by L. Wright, H. Morrison and K.F. Wong (1972, New York: Weatherhill/Serasia). The photograph on the cover appeared on page 57 of *Vanishing world* with the title 'Family lunch in the bilek'; the frontispiece photograph appeared on page 44 with the equally simple title 'Building a new longhouse'; the photograph at the opening of Clifford Sather's paper appeared on page 31 and was entitled 'The *ruai*, or communal area of the longhouse, where meetings are held and ceremonies take place'.

The photographs at the opening of Michael Young's paper are prints of glass plate photographs taken by Diamond Jenness and are reproduced here with the permission of the Pitt-Rivers Museum, Oxford. Other photographs were provided by the authors of the papers in this volume.

For reproduction of the Iban cloth that forms the cover design for the volume, we wish to thank the National Gallery of Australia and the curator of Asian Textiles Robyn Maxwell, who supplied the photograph of a *pua' kumbu'* to match the Iban textile in Hedda Morrison's photograph. The photograph is of a textile that was originally collected in 1950 by Professor Derek Freeman and his wife, Monica, at Rumah Nyala on the Sut River. Both the cloth and photograph of the Iban household date from approximately the same period. The cloth now forms part of the National Gallery's superb collection of Iban textiles.

Christine Helliwell's paper, originally presented at the House and Household seminar, was published in *Oceania* 62, 1992 and is now reproduced with permission of the Editors.

The editing of this volume has been carried out, in various stages, with great care by Paula Harris and Katy Bellingham. Despite numerous interruptions, Margaret Tyrie managed to prepare the text and most of the figures in the volume with skill and attention. They deserve a special word of thanks for their quiet perseverance in the long preparation of this volume.

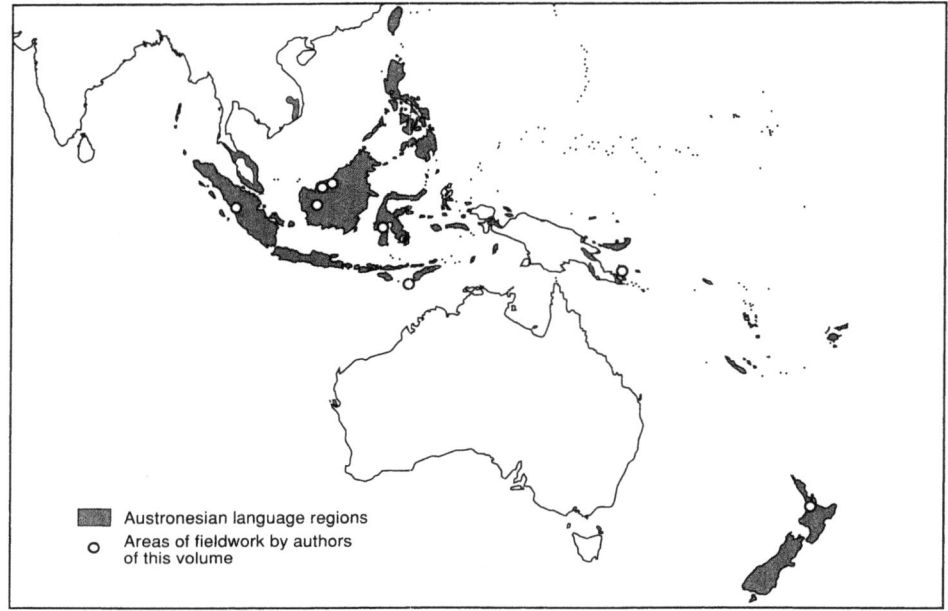

Chapter 1. Comparative Perspectives on Austronesian Houses: An Introductory Essay

James J. Fox

The eight papers that comprise this volume share a common objective. Their purpose is to examine the spatial organization of a variety of Austronesian houses and to relate the domestic design of these houses to the social and ritual practices of the specific groups who reside within them.

Throughout the Austronesian-speaking world, houses are given great prominence. Many houses are stunning architectural creations. Their construction is a subject of notable study. Such houses — as well as those that are far less striking — are invariably more than they appear to be, and certainly more than simple physical residences. Although a house has a physical referent, the category of 'house' may be used abstractly to distinguish, not just households, but social groups of varying sizes. The 'house' in this sense is a cultural category of fundamental importance. It defines a social group, which is not necessarily the same as the house's residential group.

The house, as a physical entity and as a cultural category, has the capacity to provide social continuity. The memory of a succession of houses, or of a succession within one house, can be an index of important events in the past. Equally important is the role of the house as a repository of ancestral objects that provide physical evidence of a specific continuity with the past. It is these objects stored within the house that are a particular focus in asserting continuity with the past.

Most Austronesian houses also possess what may be called their particular 'ritual attractor'. This ritual attractor is part of the structure of the house. It may be a specific post, beam, platform, niche, altar or enclosure that has a pre-eminence among the other parts of the house and, as such, represents, in a concentrated form, the house as a whole. The rituals of the houses acknowledge this attractor, generally from the moment of construction.

The house itself, and not just the objects and elements within it, can also constitute a ritually ordered structure. As such, this order can be conceived of as a representation of a cosmological order. In some Austronesian societies, the house is regarded as the ancestral 'embodiment' of the group it represents. As either representation or embodiment, the house may become a centre — a combination of theatre and temple — for the performance of the ceremonies of social life.

Thus, in a complex way, the house is culturally emblematic: it has a clear, concrete representation but relates to and embodies abstract social ideals and a variety of culturally specific values. From a physical structure — a particular arrangement of posts and beams — one can begin to trace the ideals and social values of a society. To do this is to view a society from 'inside' its houses. All of the essays in this volume adopt this perspective, hence the title of this volume: *Inside Austronesian houses*.

The houses considered in this volume range from longhouses in Borneo to Maori meeting-houses in New Zealand and from the magnificent houses of the Minangkabau of Sumatra to the simple, somewhat ramshackle dwellings of the population of Goodenough Island. An examination of the diversity of these houses gives some indication of the variety of Austronesian houses through island South-East Asia to Melanesia and the Pacific. The intention is to relate these various examples of domestic design to social activities and ritual practice and thereby to consider both commonalities and differences in the use of domestic space in different regions of the Austronesian-speaking world.

Of the three papers on Borneo houses, Jennifer Alexander's considers the Lahanan longhouse, a massive structure of hardwoods that can be virtually coterminous with an entire village settlement. The Lahanan are a core group of the Kajang in the Belaga region of Sarawak's Seventh Division. Alexander examines the layout of these Lahanan houses and their division into separate apartments along an extended common gallery.

Each longhouse is associated with its headman and the Lahanan aristocrats who constitute a 'house-owning group' and trace their origin to a founding ancestor. Alexander's paper examines the composition of apartments, and their differentiation, continuity and role in the organization of labour. The Lahanan case makes an excellent contrast with both the Gerai longhouses studied by Christine Helliwell and the Iban longhouses studied by Clifford Sather.

The Gerai are a Dayak community in Kabupaten Ketapang in Kalimantan Barat. Several longhouses make up one village. Increasingly, however, these longhouses are giving way to free-standing dwellings of individual families. The Gerai house, like the Lahanan house, is divided into an 'inner division' consisting of individual apartments and an outer public gallery. Gerai longhouses, however, are not 'owned' by a particular aristocratic house-owning group. 'Each individual household owns the nails, planks, strips of bamboo, lengths of rattan, units of thatch and so on which together comprise its longhouse apartment.' Helliwell argues that to consider such a longhouse as a collection of individual apartments neglects 'the relationships that flow from one apartment to another, tying them together into a community'. She points to a permeability of partitions and the flow of sound and light that foster an 'uninterrupted sociability from one end of the longhouse to the other'.

Clifford Sather provides a detailed examination of the Iban longhouse, drawing on specific ethnographic material from the Saribas Iban along the Paku River in lower Second Division of Sarawak. Like the Lahanan and Gerai houses, the Iban longhouse consists of a series of apartments that front onto an unpartitioned gallery available for communal use. Every Iban house is identified with a territorial domain in which individual families grow crops and observe the customary rules and ritual interdictions of the community. Each house has its headman and elders but neither of these constitutes an aristocracy as they do among the Lahanan. Complementing these elders is a custodial figure associated with the origin of the house whose ritual role is to preserve the well-being of the longhouse community. The longhouse itself provides a physical representation of its origin structure in the arrangement of its houseposts. Within the defined structure, Sather examines the performance of Iban rituals and the 'multiple "orders" of meaning' that they generate.

Cecilia Ng's paper is concerned with principles of domestic spatial organization among the Minangkabau of Sumatra. Based on fieldwork in Nagari Koto nan Gadang in the district of Lima Puluh Kota in West Sumatra, this paper focuses on use of space within the house and on the role of women as organizers and participants in the performance of ceremonies whose enactment is carefully set out within the house. Houses, in this case, are associated with core groups of women who provide the 'source of continuity' in society, whereas men circulate as 'agents of continuity'. Men's lives are defined by a series of outward movements while women's lives are marked by movement within the house. Generations of women move through the house reproducing lineage continuity. Thus, in Ng's words, the allocation of space inside the house is 'a template of the key definitions of male and female identity'.

The Rotinese house presents yet another form of the Austronesian house. Although certain houses, by their history, ancestral associations or by common agreement become the ceremonial focus of much larger social groups, most houses in eastern Indonesia tend to be single or extended family residences. Houses may thus be distinguished by their ancestry as well as by the group with which they are identified, and are categorized accordingly. Among the Rotinese, who number over 100 000 and who now live on both the island of Roti and on the neighbouring island of Timor, there exists a strong ethic to distinguish among the traditions of the eighteen historically recognized, former domains of the island. The traditions of the house follow the traditions of the domains.

The paper on the Rotinese house is concerned primarily with the traditions of the house in the domain of Termanu, a domain of the central north coast of the island. It focuses on the narrative origin of the house and on the house's physical layout as an oriented structure and as a 'memory palace' — a mnemonic cultural design for the remembrance of the past. Like longhouses in Borneo or the houses of the Minangkabau, Rotinese houses are a locus for the performance of rituals but these houses do not provide the same scope for ceremonial enactment. Sections within the house are markers of significance rather than fully-fledged performance sites. Much of the house consists of an inner sanctum that is closed to outsiders. Large ceremonial gatherings spill out to surround the house where rituals are performed, leaving always a portion of the house as a place of 'inner mystery'.

Similar features can be seen in the houses in Melanesia and in the Pacific. Writing of Goodenough Island in the D'Entrecasteaux Group at the eastern end of Papua New Guinea, Michael Young describes the Kalauna house as a 'house of secrets'. Architecturally simple structures, Kalauna houses are the repositories of their owners' magical paraphernalia that constitute the secret heirlooms of the house. Kept well away from visitors, these heirlooms include locked boxes of shell valuables, baskets of bone relics and yam stones and, most importantly, fist-sized black stones that are considered to be inhabited by ancestral spirits.

As is the case with houses in many parts of eastern Indonesia, the Kalauna house has to be considered within a wider spatial setting and in relation to points of orientation within this space. Thus Kalauna hamlets are marked out by various stone 'sitting platforms' (*atuaha*) that are built and identified with groups of lineally related men (*unuma*). The houses of particular groups in a hamlet are aligned to face their associated lithic monument. Whereas in South-East Asia the dead are often layed out in a specific area within the house, the dead in a Kalauna hamlet are made 'to sit up' on their *atuaha* in front of house (Young 1971:22–23). The rituals of the house must be taken to include the rituals of the *atuaha* with which it forms an integral part.

Toon van Meijl's paper on the Maori of New Zealand highlights a similar relationship between the meeting-house and the ceremonial courtyard (*marae*) for which the meeting-house forms the focal point. Meeting-houses and *marae* are seen as 'going together' and are commonly invoked by visiting orators in parallel phrases:

House standing here, I greet you;

Marae lying here, I greet you.

More cryptically expressed in ritual language, *marae* and meeting-house are associated with the Maori gods of war (Tuu-matauenga) and peace (Rongo-ma-tane) who are represented as outside and inside:

Tuu outside, Rongo inside.

Meeting-houses are generally named after an ancestor and usually linked to a *haapu* or 'subtribe' group. Van Meijl's paper examines contemporary meeting-houses, their symbolism and the notion of timelessness evoked through the ceremonies within these houses. The spatial coordinates of the house are linked to coordinates of time and both are condensed in the performance of ceremonies. Van Meijl contrasts this sense of time with the evidence of the historical changes that houses have undergone since the arrival of the Europeans and speculates on how these changes may continue.

The concluding paper in this collection is provided by Roxana Waterson who has written a major comparative study of the house entitled *The living house: an anthropology of architecture in South-East Asia* (1990). She is also a noted authority on the *tongkonan* or family houses of origin among the Toraja of Sulawesi among whom she has done considerable ethnographic research. In her paper, Waterson considers many of the 'shared themes in the uses of space' touched on by other papers in the volume. These include the idea of the house as an animate entity, as a kinship unit, as a forum for the expression of social relationships and as an image of power and growth. The paper offers a broad perspective on the traditions among the Austronesians and an appropriate conclusion to the volume.

The Comparative Austronesian Focus

Versions of these papers were initially presented at a Workshop on House and Household held in the Research School of Pacific Studies of The Australian National University as part of its Comparative Austronesian Project. This Comparative Austronesian Project was established, as an interdisciplinary project, to focus research on the Austronesian-speaking populations as a whole. Its goals were (1) to develop a historically-based understanding of the Austronesian-speaking populations, (2) to fashion a general framework and common vocabulary with which to define the distinguishing features of an Austronesian heritage and (3) to make comparisons not just between closely related regional groups but between cultures and societies from the entire Austronesian world.

The Austronesian language family is possibly the largest language family in the world. Native speakers of distinct Austronesian languages can be found from the island of Mayotte off the western coast of Madagascar to Easter Island in the Pacific, a distance of some 15 000 kilometres. From Taiwan through the Philippines and Indonesia, westward to Madagascar, and eastward along the coast of New Guinea through the islands of Melanesia to Micronesia and the whole of the Pacific, the Austronesian languages extend over an enormous geographical area. Pockets of these languages are also found in southern Vietnam and Cambodia, on the island of Hainan, and in the Mergui archipelago off the coast of Burma. It is estimated that there are around 1200 Austronesian languages currently spoken by approximately 270 million people (see Tryon 1993). The time-depth for the spread of the languages of the Austronesian family from a likely homeland on the south coast of China and/or Formosa is of the order of 6000–7000 years. The migrations of the Austronesian speakers, their changing modes of subsistence, their means of voyaging, their trade and their relations among themselves and with populations speaking other languages are all the subject of considerable research.

For anthropology as well as for linguistics, the Austronesians constitute a major field of study. How one approaches this study is a matter of critical importance. For the Comparative Austronesian Project, a linguistically attuned, historical perspective was deemed essential to an anthropological understanding of these cultures and to a comparative examination of them (see Bellwood, Fox and Tryon n.d.). Given the large number of Austronesian cultures, however, the papers in this volume represent a rather limited sample. A collection of papers of this kind can hardly be considered to constitute a systematic investigation. The purpose of this volume is quite different. Its intention is to identify a variety of resemblances and, at least implicitly, to point to several significant differences within the Austronesian field of study.

Each paper presents a detailed discussion of the cultural design and social usages of domestic space in a particular culture. These discussions taken together point to aspects of domestic cultural design that appear to be similar among different, in some cases widely separated, Austronesian populations. They also touch on a range of differences that may be of considerable importance to understanding the historical transformations that have occurred among the Austronesian populations. Thus even with this small collection of papers it is possible to pose a number of comparative questions, which in turn may open new directions for further analysis.

The House as a Topic of Study

A major impetus for the current study of the house as a focus of social organization and ritual activity has been the work of Claude Lévi-Strauss. In a series of lectures at the Collège de France from 1976 through 1981, Lévi-Strauss examined the concept of the 'house' in a survey of the social organization of societies ranging from the Canadian north-west coast through Indonesia, Melanesia, Polynesia, New Zealand, Madagascar and Micronesia. The summaries of these lectures were published in French in 1984 and in English in 1987.

Lévi-Strauss' intention, in his lectures, was to introduce the concept of 'house' as another 'type of social structure' — an intermediate structure between the elementary and complex structures which he had previously distinguished (Lévi-Strauss 1949, English translation 1969). Lévi-Strauss' inspiration for his analysis was derived from his understanding of the noble 'houses' of medieval

Europe. The characteristics of such 'houses' were critically defined by: possession of a 'domain' consisting of material and immaterial wealth or honours; the extensive use of fictive kinship in alliance and adoption; and the transmission of the 'domain' — titles, prerogatives, and wealth — via women as well as men. These characteristics serve to undermine a simple reliance on principles of descent and exogamy for the perpetuation of social groups. As Lévi-Strauss (1987) remarks, one purpose in introducing the concept of 'house' was to address the weakness afflicting theoretical debates that are 'haunted by the idea of descent' (p.165). The 'house' can be seen as a forum in which a tension between conflicting principles of descent and alliance, property and residence, exogamy and endogamy are expressed and seemingly resolved. This resolution is, for Lévi-Strauss, unstable and illusory and is thus, borrowing Marxist terminology, a kind of 'fetishism'. From this perspective, therefore, the 'house' may serve as both an institution and an illusion.

In his lecture summaries, Lévi-Strauss makes two kinds of comments. The first relate his views (in a condensed, somewhat cryptic format) on 'house societies' as a type of structure. These comments are of particular relevance in terms of his earlier dichotomy between elementary and complex forms of social structures. His other comments consist of a variety of observations on societies selected mainly from among Austronesian-speaking populations in Indonesia, Melanesia, Madagascar and the Pacific. Rather than combine these observations as a set of specific Austronesian comparisons, Lévi-Strauss takes the opportunity to compare various examples of these Austronesian 'house societies' with others in North America and elsewhere. Many of his general remarks nonetheless pertain directly to comparisons among Austronesian societies.

In his examination of 'house societies', Lévi-Strauss was in effect reverting to an older tradition in anthropology that began with Lewis Henry Morgan in his classic study of *Houses and house-life of the American aborigines* (Morgan 1881, reprinted 1965) and was given theoretical sophistication in Marcel Mauss and Henri Beuchat's *Seasonal variations of the Eskimo: a study in social morphology*, which originally appeared in the *Année Sociologique* (1904–5, English translation 1979). These two major studies, although developed from differing theoretical perspectives, established the initial foundation for the anthropological study of houses and their relation to social life.

Morgan's (1881) work is a continuation of his *Ancient society* (1877, reprinted 1964) and was originally intended to form part of that study. As such, it is a systematic work developed within a social evolutionary framework that endeavours to trace the forms of social organization associated with the stages of human progress. In Morgan's view, each of these stages from Savagery through Barbarism to Civilization was marked by a new technological development: the development of bow and arrow, the invention of pottery, the domestication of animals, the invention of smelting and eventually the establishment of an alphabet. The basis for virtually all forms of social organization was a lineal descent group which he termed the *gens*. This *gens* passed through successive stages of development but throughout its development was characterized by practice of hospitality and communalism (what Morgan called 'communism in living').

In retrospect, most of Morgan's comparative framework may seem a crude and cumbersome approach to an analysis of domestic architecture but for its time, it was a work of considerable sociological discernment. Morgan's bequest to anthropology has been profound. His work contributed, as a foundation work, to what seems to be an abiding obsession with descent and descent systems in anthropology. Even Morgan's evolutionary perceptions have, in various forms, continued to be of influence. It is by no means insignificant that Lévi-Strauss dedicated his first major book, *The elementary structures of kinship*, to Lewis H. Morgan. There would even appear to be a parallel between the way Morgan focuses on different communal house types in his developmental schema and the way Lévi-Strauss invokes the house as a type of social structure in the transition from elementary to complex structures of society.

Mauss and Beuchat's early study of domestic design is of a different order. It forms part of an extensive examination of the seasonal variations that Eskimo society undergoes in the course of a year. The change from dispersed summer dwellings to collective winter houses is taken as important evidence of social transformations which, in Mauss and Beuchat's argument, are considered within an ecological perspective. The floor plans and cross-sections of a variety of distinctive winter houses, each built with different materials, are examined to identify a common prototype. Different environmental conditions are taken into account as important factors influencing physical design. Mauss and Beuchat's argument is, however, that despite these differences, a common cultural design can be discerned and this design reflects a collective social pattern.

If Morgan was the first to examine, within an evolutionary framework, a wide range of house structures among different populations, Mauss and Beuchat were among the first to note ecological and historical factors affecting house structures among related populations with a similar culture. Subsequent research on the house, including that of Lévi-Strauss, can be situated within and among these differing perspectives.

Apart from Roxana Waterson's *The living house*, the most important recent work to address these issues from a predominantly Austronesian perspective is the collection of essays edited by Charles Macdonald, *De la hutte au palais: sociétés "àmaison" en Asie du Sud-Est insulaire* (1987). In this work Charles Macdonald considers the appropriateness of Lévi-Strauss' concept of the house in relation to the societies of the Philippines as does Bernard Sellato in relation to the societies of Borneo. Both researchers adopt a similar approach by ordering the societies of these areas in terms of a scale of development from simple non-stratified societies through to elaborately stratified societies. On this basis, both Macdonald and Sellato reach similar conclusions, namely that Lévi-Strauss' concept of house is of minimal analytic relevance to relatively unstratified societies and only seems relevant to those societies that are stratified and possess a quasi-feudal structure organized around a nobility. These conclusions would seem to follow from the way in which Lévi-Strauss defined his notion of the house. The result is, as Macdonald notes, that a large majority of these Austronesian societies cannot be considered 'house-societies' as designated by Lévi-Strauss (Fox 1987:172).

Sellato, for his part, recognizes 'levels' of 'house societies' in Borneo. Whereas many societies with longhouses would not meet the defining criteria for a 'house society', other societies, such as the Kenyah, whose longhouses are organized according to a chiefly and aristocratic order would indeed qualify. Two other essays in the Macdonald volume, by Antonio Guerreiro and Ghislaine Loyré, take up this notion and examine the 'house societies' of this more restricted classification. Guerreiro compares the houses of the Kayan, Kenyah and Modang while Loyré examines the houses of Mindanao, particularly the Maranao and Maguindanao.

None of the essays in the Macdonald volume are concerned to examine the organization of the house as a cultural design nor do they consider aspects of this cultural design among societies with different levels of stratification. The papers in the present volume represent societies with different levels of stratification, even in the case of those papers that deal with Borneo. Moreover they are not specifically concerned with the notion of house as posed by Lévi-Strauss. Rather they examine the house as it is internally defined and thereby suggest elements of a concept of house that are more broadly applicable among the Austronesians.

Austronesian House Terms

All the papers in this volume deal with Austronesian-speaking populations and, as a collection, they point to a range of similarities and differences in Austronesian cultural traditions associated with the house. Some of these similarities may be attributed to cultural borrowings, especially among neighbouring or near-neighbouring populations. More significant, however, are those similarities that reflect a common linguistic derivation. Comparative linguistics offers evidence of these common derivations that is of considerable value as background to the papers that comprise this volume.

Linguist Robert Blust (1976, 1980, 1987) has written extensively on the house and the principal elements of its design as they pertain to Austronesian cultural history. Blust (1987) has compiled a list of the principal terms that signify some kind of 'house' among the different linguistic subgroups of Austronesians and has examined these terms in detail. The lexically reconstructed forms of these various house terms are (1) * *Rumaq*, (2) * *balay*, (3) * *lepaw*, (4) * *kamaliR*, (5) * *banua*. (All such lexical reconstructions are conventionally designated by *.)

Although the higher order subgrouping of the Austronesian language family is still the subject of controversy, Blust's subgroup classification is widely used as a working hypothesis for current research (Pawley and Ross in press). According to this classification, the Austronesian language family divides into two major divisions: Formosan and Malayo-Polynesian. Malayo-Polynesian is in turn divided into a Western Malayo-Polynesian subgroup and an even larger and more diverse Central-Eastern Malayo-Polynesian subgroup (CEMP). This large CEMP subgroup is again divided into a Central Malayo-Polynesian and an Eastern Malayo-Polynesian subgroup. Differentiating still further, the Eastern Malayo-Polynesian subgroup is divided into a South Halmahera-West New Guinea subgroup and an Oceanic subgroup. This classification yields five higher order subgroups: (1) Formosan (F) which can in fact be further subdivided; (2) Western Malayo-Polynesian (WMP); (3) Central Malayo-Polynesian (CMP); (4) South Halmahera-West New Guinea (SHWNG) and (5) Oceanic (OC). Although the constituent status within this classification of both WMP and CMP requires further investigation, the distribution of various house terms among Blust's subgroups can be used to examine the current evidence concerning the history of the house among the Austronesians.

The first of the principal Austronesian house terms, * *Rumaq*, shows reflexes in all five subgroups of Austronesian. It is the most widely distributed term for 'house' and its usage among Austronesian populations is often given a metaphoric sense to define an associated social group claiming some kind of common derivation or ritual unity (Fox 1980). In terms of this volume, the Iban, Gerai and Minangkabau (whose languages are classified as Western Malayo-Polynesian) all reflect *rumah*, whereas the Rotinese (whose language belongs with the Central Malayo-Polynesian languages) use the cognate *uma*. Similar forms are widely distributed among Central Malayo-Polynesian languages: Rindi, *uma*; Savu, *àmu*; Atoni, *ume*; Tetun, *uma*; Ema, *umar*; Babar, *em*; Buru, *huma*; Nuaulu, *numa*.

Although the term * *balay* has no known reflexes in Formosan languages, it does take a variety of forms in both Western Malayo-Polynesian and Oceanic languages. In the Philippines, reflexes of this term (Isneg, *baláy*; Cebuano, *baláy*) may refer to a 'house' while in many Malayic languages, Minangkabau included, *balai* denotes a 'public meeting-house'. This is also the meaning of the Palauan *bai*. Other reflexes refer to a 'raised platform' or a kind of pavilion which may have a roof and walls on one or two sides, as is the case with the Balinese *bale*. Such structures are to be found in household compounds as well as in temples and other public places. In her paper, Alexander notes a seemingly similar structure that forms an adjunct to each apartment in a Lahanan longhouse. This structure called *baleh*, which Alexander glosses as 'kitchen' is separated from the apartment proper (*tilung*) by an open washing and drying platform.

In Melanesia, reflexes of * *balay* may refer to 'a shed for yams' or 'a garden house' (Arosi, *hare*) or 'a house of retirement for women during menstruation and childbirth' (Are'are, *hare*). In the Pacific, however, reflexes of * *balay* generally refer to the house proper as they do in the Philippines (Fijian, *vale*; Samoan, *fale*; Hawaiian, *hale*). Blust proposes an original primary gloss for this term as 'village meeting house' suggesting that the general Malayic language forms retain the original meaning, whereas those in Oceania indicate a transformation in the use of this structure.

The third term, * *lepaw*, has at least one identifiable reflex in a Formosan language where it refers to a 'house' (Kuvalan, *lêppaw*). Reflexes of this term, however, are predominantly found in Western Malayo-Polynesian languages where they have a variety of meanings. Blust (1987:91) reports three instances of this term, each with a somewhat different meaning: 'storehouse for grain' (Ngaju, *lepau*), 'hut, building other than longhouse' (Uma Juman, *lêpo*) and 'back verandah or kitchen verandah of a Malay house; booth or shop' (Malay, *lepau*). Alexander, in her paper, interestingly identifies the *lepau* among the Lahanan as a 'farmhouse' which may be either a simple shelter or a solid dwelling where families 'may spend up to a month during peaks in the swidden rice cultivation cycle'. Whittier (1978:107) reports a similar term, *lepau*, meaning 'field hut' among the Kenyah, and Rousseau (1978:80) the term *lepo'* meaning 'single family farmhouse' among the Kayan.[1] Although Blust proposes an original meaning as 'granary', it would seem more appropriate to suggest a general meaning that would subsume the notion of an 'alternative dwelling', one that could be used for a variety of purposes such as hunting, gardening, marketing and even fishing.

The Samal-speaking Bajau Laut have houses (*luma'*) raised on poles along the seashore but they also have family houseboats, known as *lepa*, in which they regularly spend a great deal of time fishing (Sather 1985:191–195). Such boats constitute the alternative, sea-based houses of the Bajau. As Sather explains,

> a young man was outfitted with a boat at the time of his marriage. This was done so that he and his wife would be able to begin married life as an independent boat crew with their own source of income separate from the control of their parents and other kin ... [F]rom marriage onwards, nearly all men remained boat-owners for as long as they were economically active (1985:195).

Whether Bajau *lepa* is a reflex of * *lepaw* remains to be established. This usage may, however, link 'house' and 'boat' in a way that reflects earlier, more common

Austronesian practices. Cognates of this term for boat are widely distributed among speakers of various languages of South Sulawesi (Grimes and Grimes 1987:172–173).

A fourth term for house * *kalamiR*, like * *balay*, has no recognizable reflexes among Formosan languages but has numerous reflexes in Western Malayo-Polynesian languages. In the Philippines, these reflexes generally refer to a 'granary, storehouse or barn' whereas in the Oceanic subgroup, a range of reflexes of this same term denote special 'men's houses'. Blust proposes the gloss 'men's house' for * *kalamiR*, having previously assigned the gloss of 'granary' to the term * *lepaw*. This designation assumes, however, the existence of Melanesian type men's houses among the early Austronesians prior to their contact with the non-Austronesian populations of New Guinea. *The comparative Austronesian dictionary* (Tryon 1993), assigns * *kalamiR* the gloss, 'granary, shed'. It might therefore be appropriate to see the widespread Western Malayo-Polynesian reflexes as a retention and the usages found in Oceania as an innovation.

The final house term with wide generality is * *banua*. Since no reflexes are to be found in Formosa, this term also has to be considered a Malayo-Polynesian construct. Reflexes occur in all subgroups of Malayo-Polynesian, but only in a scatter of languages does the term refer to the 'house' (Toraja, *banua*; Banggai, *bonua*; Wolio, *banua*; Molima, *vanua*; Wusi-Mana, *wanua*). Far more often reflexes of * *banua* denote an area that may be glossed as 'land, country, place, settlement, inhabited territory, village'. Both usages of * *banua* occur in different societies considered in this volume. Thus, for example, the Iban *menoa rumah* is the 'territorial domain' of a longhouse; *manua*, on Goodenough Island, refers to the 'house', but as Young (1983) notes elsewhere, *manua* 'also connotes "village" in the sense of dwelling place or home'. Young in fact glosses the reduplicated form of *manua*, *manumanua*, as 'staying at home' (p.55). Given the preponderant distribution of the wider meaning of * *banua*, there seems to be ample reason to assign the gloss of 'country, inhabited territory' to this term.

Overall the evidence of these house terms suggests that the Western Malayo-Polynesian groups retain somewhat more of the earlier traditions of the house, whereas these traditions among Central-Eastern Malayo-Polynesians have undergone transformations. As the Austronesian-speaking populations expanded, they encountered significant populations of non-Austronesian speakers in Halmahera, along the coast of New Guinea, and on many of the islands of western Melanesia. The evidence suggests that early contact and, in many areas, continuing relations between Austronesian and non-Austronesian populations was indeed of critical importance.

In addition to his examination of house terms, Blust (1976) has also endeavoured to construct the terms for some of the basic elements of the

Malayo-Polynesian house. His linguistic evidence points to a raised structure built on 'posts' (* *SaDiRi*), entered by means of a 'notched log ladder' (* *SaReZaSan*), with a hearth (* *dapuR*), a 'storage rack above the hearth' (* *paRa*), 'rafters' (* *kasaw*), and a 'ridge-pole' (* *bu(qS)ungbu(qS)ung*) covered in 'thatch' (* *qatep*). The structure defined by these elements is a familiar one through much of South-East Asia. As an architectural entity this structure is certainly not confined to the Austronesians (Izikowitz and Sorensen 1982). Henriksen (1982) reports on a neolithic house excavated at Nong Chae Sao in Thailand that could well fit this same structure. One must therefore assume that the early Austronesians and their descendants shared broadly similar South-East Asian architectural traditions and in the course of their history adapted a variety of other traditions from eastern Asia, India, the Middle East and Europe in developing their current construction techniques. Both Dumarçay (1987), succinctly in his excellent summary volume *The house in South-East Asia*, and Waterson (1990), at considerable length in *The living house*, document the remarkable *mélange* of architectural techniques that have influenced the construction of Austronesian houses. It is interesting to note, however, how the Austronesians transmitted elements of a South-East Asian architectural tradition to New Guinea, Melanesia and the Pacific. Brigitta Hauser-Schäublin concludes her massive two-volume study *Kulthäuser in Nordneuguinea* with important historical observations:

> The hut on piles with supports carrying both the roof and the built-in floor seems to belong to Austronesian cultures. On the North Coast [of New Guinea] both elements are combined: the first floor platform is supported by its own poles, whereas the upper floors are slotted into the horizontal beams. In areas settled by non-Austronesian groups, all parts of the building are traditionally lashed with lianas. The Middle Sepik cultures are masterpieces of this highly developed binding technique. Pin and peg techniques are only known in those regions where Austronesian languages are spoken. The Middle Sepik cultures took over the idea of buildings with projecting gables from the Austronesians who settled at certain places on the North Coast. They adapted it to their own technology and architectural experience, giving it a new expression (Hauser-Schäublin 1989:618).

Perhaps the most significant aspect of the terms for the house that can be reconstructed for Proto-Malayo-Polynesian is their saliency for defining prominent features of the house among the Austronesians. Posts and ladder, ridge-pole and hearth within an encompassing roof are the elements of the house most frequently marked as the foci of rituals for the house. They are the principal ritual attractors in the house. The papers in this volume direct attention to this important aspect of Austronesian houses.

Ordered Structures and Their Orientation

One common feature of traditional Austronesian houses is their ordered structure. For many houses, this structure consists of a formal orientation. The spatial coordinates of this orientation vary considerably from one Austronesian society to the next. Such coordinates may be either external or internal to the house itself or, in fact, both. Where they are external, they represent a wider orienting framework — often a cosmological orientation — within which the house must be positioned. Where, however, links to a wider cosmological orientation have been severed or are no longer considered relevant, houses may still be ordered in terms of a set of internal orienting principles. The pattern of building may follow a fixed order and certain features of the houses — certain beams, posts, corners — may constitute points of reference. These points of reference act as ritual attractors around which critical activities are organized.

The house may be complete unto itself in creating its internal structure without reference to external coordinates. In some instances, however, the application of similar coordinates, differentially applied, may distinguish the internal orientation of the house from the external system (see Fox, Comparative Postscript on Houses on Roti and on Timor, pp.170–177 this volume). Yet, however it is constituted, this ordered structure is critical to the activities, particularly the ceremonial activities, conducted within the house. A variety of the ways in which Austronesian houses constitute ordered structures are illustrated in this volume.

The Lahanan longhouse, for example, follows a common Borneo pattern, one that sets the house in a wider orientation. The Lahanan longhouse is always built parallel to a river with its veranda or gallery facing the river. The longhouse is thus oriented in terms of the coordinates of 'upriver' (*naju*) and 'downriver' (*nava*). In relation to the river, one 'goes up' (*baguai*) to the house and 'down to work' (*ba'ai nyadui*) toward the river. In the settlement described by Alexander, the longhouse was built along a main river or 'trunk' (*batang*) and the headman's apartment, whose gallery is 'the locus of religious and social activity', was located on the 'downriver' end of the house.

The Iban longhouse has a similar orientation which Sather, in his paper, presents as fundamental:

> As riparian settlements, Iban longhouses are built along rivers and streams with their long axis ideally oriented parallel to the main river course. Consequently, the two ends of a longhouse are normally distinguished as the 'upriver' (*ulu*) and 'downriver' (*ili*) ends ... This orientation, as well as the presence of a centralizing 'source', is basic and is evoked constantly in everyday speech.

To this is added another set of coordinates, as Sather also notes:

A second basic orientation of the longhouse is in terms of the sun's movement through the sky, from east to west ... The gallery side of the house should thus ideally face eastward, in the direction of the rising sun.

A further set of coordinates involves a relationship between 'base' and 'tip'. Both the main river and the longhouse are described as a 'trunk' (*batang*) and this trunk is conceived of with its 'base' (*pun*) as 'downriver'. Thus the apartment of the ritual custodian of the longhouse (*pun rumah*), like that of the Lahanan headman, is positioned 'downriver' from the central post (*tiang pemun*) of the house.

The Rotinese house, like many traditional houses in eastern Indonesia, is based upon a set of external spatial coordinates. For the Rotinese, these coordinates are the directional coordinates of the island and are considered to represent a basic cosmological order. Houses are supposed to have their 'head' (*langa*) to the east (*dulu*) and their 'tail' (*iko*) to the west. This axis is recognized as the path of the sun. Entrances to the house may be either from north or south, directions which are synonymous in Rotinese with 'left' (*ki*) and 'right' (*kona*). (The further coordinates of 'up' or 'skyward' (*lai*) and 'down' or 'earthward' (*dae*) differentiate levels within the house.) The internal spatial layout of the house is based on the directional coordinates but is specially marked in terms of a single post known as the 'right post' (*di kona*) whose invariant position is in the south-eastern corner of the house. This entire structure is conceived of as a creature with its head to the east and its tail to the west; the rafters of the house are its ribs and the ridge-pole its spine.

Van Meijl describes virtually the same kind of structure for the Maori meeting-house: 'Meeting-houses are not only named after an ancestor. Their structure represents the body of an eponymous ancestor too'. The ridge-pole is the spine, the rafters are the ribs, the bargeboards the arms, the front window the eye, and the juncture of the eaves of the veranda represents the face. The interior of the house is the chest. Unlike the Rotinese house, however, this ancestral body is not reported to be oriented in any particular direction, yet internally, within this body, van Meijl describes various areas on the right and left sides of the house and in the front and rear that are complementary to one another and considered to be relatively 'sacred' (*tapu*) or 'common' (*noa*).

The definition of 'inside' is a relative notion within traditional Austronesian houses. Although 'inside' may include everything beneath the roof, more often the category of 'inside' (Proto-Austronesian, * *Dalem*) is specifically defined. In the Rotinese house, the 'inner house' (*uma dalek*) refers to the 'female' precinct on the western side of the house. In the Gerai house, *lem uma* is the 'inside of the apartment' defined by the door (*lawang*) as opposed to the gallery (*ruang*) which is described as 'outside' (*sawah*). Helliwell's description of the Gerai house concentrates on this orientation within the house and its implications in distinguishing between 'we' and 'other'. By contrast, the *rumah dalam* in the Minangkabau house is an enclosed space under the house set aside for women to weave in. From Ng's description, it would appear that, unlike other sections of the house, this space is not open for use on ceremonial occasions.

All of these differently defined sections of the house have 'female' associations as, indeed, does the house as a whole in many contexts. The Javanese term *dalem* epitomizes these various senses. *Dalem* is 'house' (*omah*) in the highest Javanese speech register; in a lower register, however, it may refer to the inner family room(s) of an ordinary house or to the inner precinct of a palace, which is not considered to be the place of the ruler but rather the most private abode of the women of the palace. Some Javanese see this *dalem* as the sacred resort of a female goddess (see Mangunwijaya 1991:13).

Of all the houses described in this volume, the Kalauna house appears at first to be anomalous. Young remarks that the 'Kalauna house has no particular orientation, no symbolically salient "sides" or halves, no interior demarcations'. Yet all Kalauna houses are aligned to face particular *atuaha* platforms associated with specific descent groups. As places for work and gossip as well as being sites for ritual, these platforms must be considered as an essential extension of the house itself. Although houses have 'mouths' (*awana*) as doorways and 'eyes' (*matana*) as windows, such symbolism is not, as Young points out, systematically developed. The house is predominately defined as 'inside'. Thus Young notes that 'the house's interior (*vetawana*) is symbolically salient itself: as concealed interiority, a domain of *nafone*, "inside" or "within-ness" '. The house is both a repository for ancestral relics and magic paraphernalia and an abode for the spirits of the ancestral dead. Key components of the house — the ridge-pole and even the walls — are believed to be occupied by these spirits of the dead. In this sense, the Kalauna house is considered to be 'animated' as an ancestral embodiment.

Structures of Origin Within Austronesian Houses

Among the Austronesians, a concern with 'origins' is of paramount social importance. This concern with 'origins' is more than a concern with 'descent'. Indeed, in many Austronesian societies, the concern with 'descent' (as it has been generally defined) is of minor significance. By contrast, the concern with 'origins' constitutes a fundamental epistemological orientation and takes on a remarkable variety of forms (Fox 1971, 1980a:14, 1988:14–15, n.d.a). This concern is manifest in complex origin narratives — elaborate accounts of the emergence and/or the arrival of predecessors; traditions of the migration and journeying of groups and individuals; tales of the founding of settlements, of houses, or of ancestral shrines; accounts of contests to establish priority, to secure the rightful transmission of ancestral relics, to assert the often disputed ordering of succession to office or, in some areas, to establish precedence in affinal relations. This concern with 'origins' is essential for social identity and social differentiation.

It is particularly interesting to note the way in which the idea of 'origin' is commonly designated in a large number of Austronesian languages. One such category for designating 'origin' refers to the 'base' or 'trunk' of a tree thus connoting and conflating ideas of 'base', 'trunk', 'cause', 'beginning', 'source' and 'origin'. The idea of origin is thus conceived of, in a botanic idiom, as a kind of epistemic development from a 'base' to a 'tip' or, more divergently, to a myriad of separate 'tips' (Fox 1971).

Houses, by the nature of their construction, lend themselves to the expression of this botanic metaphor of origin. Waterson in her paper explicitly notes this use: 'botanic metaphors of "trunk" and "tip" occur not only in rules about the correct "planting" of house posts but as ways of talking about kinship' (see also Waterson 1990:124–129). Houses may thus express critical relationships among groups based on locally defined concepts of origin and derivation.

In terms of these conceptions of origin, Lévi-Strauss' comments on the layout of the traditional Karo Batak house, as described by Masri Singarimbun (1975) in his monograph *Kinship, descent and alliance among the Karo Batak*, take on special significance. Lévi-Strauss (1987) notes two critical features of Karo society: that wife-givers are superior to wife-takers and that the foundation of a village requires the participation of wife-givers with subordinate wife-takers. Traditional houses, consisting of as many as eight resident families living juxtaposed to one another, also reflect these fundamental relationships. Thus, as Lévi-Strauss indicates,

> the family of the dominant lineage occupies the so-called 'base' apartment and its wife-taking family occupies the so-called 'summit' apartment, inferior as such (because the base is larger and stronger), but favoured because it is situated on the eastern side, from whence comes the fresh morning breeze, which is more agreeable to the inhabitants than the oppressive heat of the afternoon, which has a negative connotation, and which the dominant family faces in order to protect the other apartments (1987:157).

Although Lévi-Strauss sees in this situation a contradiction between the Karo system of marriage alliances and its political and residential rules, his description closely follows Singarimbun, who sees no evident difficulties in these household arrangements:

> The social organization of the house is related to this organization of its internal space because the apartment called 'the base of the tree' is the place of the chief of the house (*pengulu rumah*), and opposite to him, occupying the apartment called 'the top of the tree', is his deputy who

is one of his jurally inferior *anakberu* [wife-takers] ...the Karo house has an east-west orientation and the apartment of the head of the house is located at the west end, facing the heat of the afternoon sun, because he is regarded as one who is able to confront 'heat' or in other words, 'evil' (Singarimbun 1975:61–62).

Singarimbun's examination of the Karo house is in fact more complex than is indicated by Lévi-Strauss in that it distinguishes a set of shared household arrangements based on a contrast not just between 'base of the tree' (*benakayu*) and 'top of tree' (*ujungkayu*) but also those households 'opposite' (*lépar*) the 'base' and 'top'. Critical to all of these relationships within the house is the sharing of kitchen cooking fires. Households divide according to whether they 'share a kitchen' with the 'base' or 'top' or with households opposite to the 'base' or 'top'. Although related as wife-giver to wife-taker or as 'chief' and 'deputy', the families of the 'base' and 'top' are set furthest from one another in their cooking arrangements.

Although his purpose was to draw conclusions about the nature of affinal relations, Lévi-Strauss does highlight a feature of the traditional Karo house that is common to a wide variety of Austronesian houses and is well exemplified, for example, in this volume by the Minangkabau and Borneo cases.

Cecilia Ng notes the use of a similar metaphor to distinguish social and ritual positions in the Minangkabau house. The traditional Minangkabau house is built as a women's domain where men, as husbands, are received as 'guests'. Within this structure, the *pangkalan* (from *pangkal* meaning 'base', 'beginning', 'origin') defines a specific area on one end of the house. The *pangkalan* is the section of the house that adjoins the kitchen and the area through which all guests enter the *ruang*. Between these two areas is the central post of the house. Set lower than the elevated *anjuang* at the opposite end of the house, the *pangkalan* is opposed to the *anjuang*. In her analysis of women's life cycles within the house, Ng points to the fact that women move from sleeping near the central post into the *anjuang* when they marry and then through separate apartments until they end their reproductive life and come to sleep in the *pangkalan* on the opposite side of the central post. Here 'base' and 'pinnacle' describe not a set of affinal relationships, as in the case of the Karo Batak house, but rather a sequence of reproduction and its celebration within the matrilineal Minangkabau group.

Clifford Sather also devotes a considerable portion of his paper to the careful examination of the categories of 'base' and 'tip', of the use of these categories in defining spatial arrangements within the Iban house and of their fundamental association with ideas of origin and continuity. His analysis, like that of Ng's, is too extensive and detailed to be simply summarized. Its comparative significance, however, is worth noting. The Iban term for 'base', 'source' or 'origin' is *pun*, which derives from the Proto-Austronesian term *puqun meaning 'tree', 'trunk', 'base' or 'source'. With the insertion of an infix, *pun* gives rise to *pemun*, which is the term applied to the 'source post' (*tiang pemun*) of the Iban longhouse. The central source post is the first post of the house to be erected; then the building of the house proceeds, first downriver, then upriver, with each apartment given its own *tiang pemun* that is ritually subordinate to the central source post. The term *pun* is applied not just to the posts of the house but refers equally to persons and directions. When applied to persons, *pun* also has the sense of 'initiator' or 'founder' but implies a continuity with the past generations. Each longhouse has one *pun rumah* who is the custodian of the central *tiang pemun* of the house and is required to maintain the ritual welfare of the house as a whole. Each apartment has its own *pun bilik* who is the caretaker of the family's *tiang pemun* and of its ancestral sacra, which include its ritual whetstones and special 'source rice' (*padi pun*). In all of these usages, the metaphor of 'base' and 'tip' defines a direction of life and growth as indeed it defines precedence among groups within the longhouse.

The Lahanan, like the Iban, rely on the notion of 'base' as origin and use this concept to distinguish groups within the longhouse. Most apartments (*tilung*) in a Lahanan longhouse consist of single households, generally organized as stem families. Those who reside in an apartment are known as the 'people of the apartment' (*linau tilung*). However, as Jennifer Alexander makes clear, the ownership of the apartment and its contents, its heirlooms and all rights to land are not vested in this circumscribed residential group but rather in what is called the *tilung pu'un* or *tilung asen* — the '*tilung* of origin'. Alexander describes the *tilung pu'un* as 'a kinship group comprising all persons with consanguineal links to the *tilung*, irrespective of where they may be living'. Heirlooms provide the symbolic focus for this *tilung pu'un*. Rights to these heirlooms and to land belong to all members of the group; the custodial role is given to the senior member of the residence group. Since, as Alexander goes on to point out, 90 per cent of married couples live in the wife's apartment, female lines provide the continuity of this group and most custodians of property are women.[2]

Houses in eastern Indonesia are often explicitly designated according to 'origin', using the same metaphor of 'base' as in Borneo or Sumatra. The continuity implied by these origins, which in some societies is defined lineally and in others affinally, may be traced through houses but is not defined exclusively by them. On Timor, such designations are applied among affinally related groups that are identified as 'houses'. Thus among the Ema, 'houses' that bestow women on other 'houses' are known as the *uma mane pun*, 'the base houses of the wife-givers' (Clamagirand 1980:142); among the Mambai, houses in similar relationships are designated as *umaen fun*, 'wife-givers of origin' (Traube 1980:353 n.10). Such houses are regarded as established life-giving progenitors.

Among the Rotinese such progenitor designations are not applied to houses but to persons. Instead of *uma mane pun* or *umaen fun*, the Rotinese identify lines of former wife-givers as *to'o-huk*, 'mother's brother of origin', and the *bai-huk*, 'mother's mother's brother of origin' (*pun, fun* and *huk* all deriving from Proto-Austronesian * *puqun*). Rotinese houses, however, figure prominently in the ritual display of these relationships. On either side of the ladder, *heda-huk* (which was formerly a notched tree trunk), leading up into the house itself are two specially named positions: the *sosoi dulu* and the *sosoi muli*. These are the recognized ritual positions for the 'mother's brother of origin' and the 'mother's mother's brother of origin'. At mortuary rituals, only the progenitors in the maternal line of origin have the right to sit at these places and to be fed before all other guests. These positions are at the entrance to the house and are not associated with the ritually most important post in the house, the 'right post' (*di kona*) which is located in the south-eastern quadrant of the house.

Maori define 'origins' using a combination of terms for 'growth' (*tupu*), for 'ancestor' (*tupuna* or *tipuna*) and for 'base', 'origin', 'cause', 'source' (*puu*) (Salmond 1991:344–345). The term *hapuu* (from *puu*), often translated as 'sub-tribe' or clan, can in fact refer to groups of varying size who trace their origin from a particular ancestor (*tupuna*). Maori meeting-houses (*whare hui*) are also considered to be 'ancestral houses' (*whare tupuna*) and as such, they are the focal point for particular local groups (*taangata whenua: whenua > *banua*). As van Meijl explains in this volume,

> [i]n meeting-houses owner groups, usually subtribes, symbolize their unity and their distinction from other subtribes ... Meeting-houses are not only named after an ancestor. Their structure represents the body of the eponymous ancestor too ... The ridge-pole (*taahuhu*) is regarded as his spine representing the main line of descent from the apex of the (sub)tribe's genealogy. The rafters (*heke*) are his ribs representing junior descent lines derived from the senior line or *taahuhu*.

These ancestral representations as well as those carved on the 'face' of the house, combined with the 'old portraits of ancestors' and 'photographs of recent forbears' that hang on the walls make the Maori meeting-house a pre-eminent structure for the display of origins.

Time and Memory in Austronesian Houses

In recounting the oral histories of the Ilongot, a small population of shifting cultivators in northern Luzon, Renato Rosaldo (1980) explains that the Ilongot 'readily listed in succession the names of the places where they had "erected their houseposts" and "cleared the forest"' (p.42).[3] Remembering the bamboo, once planted near a house, serves as another icon of the previous occupation of a site.

Using lists of place names, crude sketches and more detailed contour maps, Rosaldo was able to reconstruct a remembered past among the Ilongot — a past that was structured on a chronology of changing household residence: 'to coordinate one household history with others was vexing because clusters of houses split, then joined and split, then joined again' (Rosaldo 1980:42). In all of these bewildering shifts, one constant is the rule of residence that a man reside with his wife. Although the man is described as the 'source' (*rapu*) of courtship, he 'goes into' the house of the woman (p.179). A further rule that the youngest married daughter reside with and care for her aged parents provides the basis for continuity across generations.

Among the Ilongot, houses are shifted every four or five years and it is noteworthy that in tracing these shifts, the Ilongot allude to their houses, not as entire structures, but in terms of the memory of the erection of houseposts. This focus on the posts of the house is a significant feature of many Austronesian houses. The papers in this volume make clear the ritual significance associated with the 'central post' (*tonggak tuo*) in the Minangkabau house, the 'source posts' (*tiang pemun*) in the Iban longhouse, and the 'right post' (*di kona*) in the Rotinese house. All of these posts are ritual attractors within the house. Not only are these posts given special prominence in the ceremonies associated with the building process, they are also preserved, if possible, when an older house is dismantled, and used to form a (ritual) part of the new structure. The authors of the beautifully illustrated volume *Banua Toraja: changing patterns in architecture and symbolism among the Sa'dan Toraja, Sulawesi-Indonesia* emphasize this point in their discussion of the 'navel post' (*a'riri posi'*) of the Torajan house:

> During the rebuilding of a *tongkonan*, the erection of the new *a'risi posi'*, or of the original pillar saved from the old house, takes place during the three great feastdays of the house's consecration ... The pillar is decorated with a sacred *maa'* cloth, the young, yellow leaves of the sugar palm, and the red leaves of the *Cordyline terminalis* (Kis-Jovak et al. 1988: 40).

The housepost expresses an idea of botanic continuity that is consistent with the overall imagery of the house. Sather, for example, notes in this volume that 'the ordering of the *tiang pemuns* creates the image of the longhouse as an upright tree'. The same observation can be made of the Torajan house. Waterson observes that

> those who trace their descent from a common pair of founding ancestors, man and woman, are called *pa'rapuan* or *rapu*. *Rapu tallang* in Torajan means 'a stool of bamboo'. The family is compared to the bamboo whose many stems sprout from a single clump. The *tongkonan*, especially when being referred to in the most general sense of an origin-house, regardless of rank, is often called the *banua 1 pa'rapuan* or 'house of the *pa'rapuan*'.

From the same root is derived an adjective, *marapuan*, which means 'having a great many descendants' (1986:97).

The authors of *Banua Toraja* make this image of the tree explict: 'The house itself, the centre for the *rapu*, is often compared to a tree' (Kis-Jovak et al. 1988:39).

A tree with many branches emanating from a single base or a stand of bamboo with multiple stems sprouting from one clump are two among many botanic icons that, among Austronesians, translate spatial imagery into a temporal sequence. The 'base' is prior and takes precedence.

A set of categories that effects a similar translation consists of the opposed terms for 'front' and 'rear' which may equally be applied to 'that which comes before' and 'that which comes after' in a temporal as well as a physical sense. In his paper, van Meijl considers the use of these categories in the Maori meeting. In Maori, the past is referred to in terms of *mua*, 'that which has gone before', *ngaa raa o mua*, 'the days in front', in constrast with what follows after, *kei muri*. Following Salmond (1978), van Meijl notes that

> the place of the seniors (past) in the front and the more junior (future) towards the rear of the house, corresponds with the temporal succession from the remote past to the more recent past, toward the future.

A similar set of categories are applied to the Rotinese house. These categories are *dulu/muli*. *Dulu* is the term for 'east', the 'direction of the rising sun'; *muli* for 'west', the direction of the setting sun. Since the house is oriented on an east–west axis, the 'outer' section of the house is to the east and the 'inner' section to the west. This context creates a series of associations that contrast the first-born (*uluk*) who is elder and foremost but who must go 'out' from the house with the last-born (*mulik*) who is junior but who will stay 'in' the house and inherit it. The categories combine to interrelate temporal and spatial orders. Essentially, however, they establish different relationships of precedence. These different relationships are not, however, coincident nor are they simple reflections of one another. Thus in assigning ritual positions to the 'mother's brother of origin' and 'mother's mother's brother of origin', it is the (later) progenitor relationship of the mother's brother that is given precedence at the eastern position (*sosoi dulu*) in the house. As is discussed in this volume, in the case of the Minangkabau house and of the Iban house, this categorization of the Rotinese house creates a ritual arena within which the temporal sequence of ceremonies from birth to death can be carefully conducted.

From Roman times to the Renaissance, Western scholars cultivated, as a formal technique of the art of rhetoric, a tradition that assigned to particular locations within an imagined house a sequence of ideas or objects that were to be memorized. The house, in this tradition, was made to serve as a structure for remembering. One of the arguments in the paper on the Rotinese house is that this association of ideas with locations within the house is an implicit feature of many Austronesian cultures. It is in the rituals of the house that these ideas are recollected and enacted, thus making the house not just a 'memory palace' but a 'theatre of memories'.

Concluding Remarks

It is probably wise to conclude this introduction on a cautionary note. In a recent paper, Roy Ellen (1986) has provided a remarkable examination of the Nuaulu house on the island of Seram in eastern Indonesia. His description of the Nuaulu house is exemplary in its detail. Houses (*numa*) are occupied by extended family groups or households (also termed *numa*) which form the minimal corporate units of Nuaulu society. Houses are built on posts (*hini*) that are always ritually 'planted' in their 'natural orientation' with their 'roots' in the ground. Such properly planted houses are generally referred to as 'sacred houses' (*numa mone*) and are the depositories for ancestral objects. Most of them are clan section houses and are associated with elaborate ritual activities. These houses are also ordered structures. They are oriented according to intersecting coordinate axes (mountain/sea :: north/south; sunrise/sunset :: east/west) and these axes are given gender associations as male and female. The north-east corner of the house (identified as male and defined by the intersection of mountain/sunrise) is considered as the 'most sacredly charged' point in the house. Ellen describes the inner layout of the house and relates this structure to the layout of the village and central position of the village ritual house (*suane*). Having systematically constructed this complex analysis of the house in Nuaulu social life, Ellen argues against the tendency to conflate different levels, categories and metaphoric expressions in a total symbolic conflation: 'To compress all symbolic domains together in a totality is artificial and certainly does not reflect "local models", or symbolic consciousness' (p.23). This is a view shared by all the contributors to this volume and is most clearly and emphatically articulated by Clifford Sather who argues that the Iban longhouse represents 'a plurality of symbolic orders' — orders that are not only multiple but also constantly 'created and re-created in ritual'.

By necessity, each of the papers in this volume can only provide a glimpse inside a particular Austronesian house. The intention is not, however, just to point to the complexity of these structures as designs for living and the plurality of the symbolic orders that are created within them, but to indicate an important comparative dimension to this complexity and plurality. One only has to read these papers to get a sense of the family resemblances that exist among Austronesian houses, not just in physical structures but, more importantly, in the fundamental categories by which these structures are culturally ordered. It is hoped therefore that this volume will prompt the further comparative study of Austronesian houses while it is still possible to do so and before these remarkable dwellings give way to new residential units.

References

Bellwood, Peter, James J. Fox and Darrell Tryon

n.d. *The Austronesians in history* (forthcoming).

Blust, Robert

1976 Austronesian culture history: some linguistic inferences and their relations to the archaeological record. *World Archaeology* 8(1):19–43. Reprinted in P. van de Velde (ed.) *Prehistoric Indonesia: a reader* (Verhandelingen van het Koninklijk Instituut voor Taal-, Land- en Volkenkunde 104), pp.218–241. Dordrecht: Foris Publications (1984).

1980 Early Austronesian social organization: the evidence of language. *Current Anthropology* 21:205–247.

1987 Lexical reconstruction and semantic reconstruction: the case of Austronesian 'house' words. In *Diachronica* IV(1/2):79–106.

Clamagirand, Brigitte

1980 The social organization of the Ema of Timor. In J.J. Fox (ed.) *The flow of life: essays on eastern Indonesia*, pp.134–151. Cambridge: Harvard University Press.

Dumarçay, Jacques

1987 *The house in South-East Asia* (M. Smithies trans. and ed.). Singapore: Oxford University Press.

Ellen, Roy

1986 Microcosm, macrocosm and the Nuaulu house: concerning the reductionist fallacy as applied to metaphorical levels. *Bijdragen tot de Taal-, Land- en Volkenkunde* 142(1):1–30.

Fox, James J.

1971 Sister's child as plant: metaphors in an idiom of consanguinity. In R. Needham (ed.) *Rethinking kinship and marriage*, pp.219–252. London: Tavistock.

1980a Introduction. In J.J. Fox (ed.) *The flow of life: essays on eastern Indonesia*, pp.1–18. Cambridge: Harvard University Press.

1980b Comment on Blust: 'Early Austronesian social organization'. *Current Anthropology* 21:233–235.

1987 The house as a type of social organization on the island of Roti, Indonesia. In C. Macdonald and members of l'ECASE (eds) *De la hutte au palais:*

sociétés "àmaison" en Asie du Sud-Est insulaire, pp.215–224. Paris: CNRS Press.

1988   Origin, descent and precedence in the study of Austronesian societies. Public lecture, in connection with De Wisselleerstoel Indonesische Studien, 17 March 1988, Leiden University.

n.d.a Origin structures and systems of precedence in the comparative study of Austronesian societies. Forthcoming in P.J.K. Li (ed.) *Proceedings of the international symposium on Austronesian studies relating to Taiwan*. Taipei: Academia Sinica.

n.d.b Genealogy and topogeny: toward an ethnography of Rotinese ritual place names. Forthcoming in J.J. Fox (ed.) *The poetic power of place*. Canberra: Department of Anthropology, Research School of Pacific Studies, The Australian National University.

Grimes, Charles E. and Barbara D. Grimes

1987   *Languages of South Sulawesi* (Materials in Languages of Indonesia No. 38; Pacific Linguistic Series D No. 78) Canberra: Department of Linguistics, Research School of Pacific Studies, The Australian National University.

Guerreiro, Antonio

1987   "Longue maison" et "grande maison", considérations sur l'ordre social dans le centre de Bornéo. In C. Macdonald and members of l'ECASE (eds) *De la hutte au palais: sociétés "àmaison" en Asie du Sud-Est insulaire*, pp.45–66. Paris: CNRS Press.

Hauser-Schäublin, Brigitta

1989   *Kulthäuser in Nordneuguinea*, 2 vols (Abhandlungen und Berichte des Staatlichen Museums für Völkerkunde Dresden No. 43). Berlin: Akademie-Verlag.

Henriksen, Merete Aagaard

1982   The first excavated prehistoric house site in Southeast Asia. In K.G. Izikowitz and P. Sorensen (eds) *The house in East and Southeast Asia: anthropological and architectural aspects* (Scandinavian Institute of Asian Studies Monograph Series No. 30), pp.17–24. London: Curzon Press.

Hudson, A.B. and Judith M. Hudson

1978   The Ma'anyan of Paju Empat. In V.T. King (ed.) *Essays on Borneo societies* (Hull Monograph on Southeast Asia No. 7), pp.215–232. Oxford: Oxford University Press.

Izikowitz, Karl G. and P. Sorensen (eds)

1982 *The house in East and Southeast Asia: anthropological and architectural aspects* (Scandinavian Institute of Asian Studies Monograph Series No. 30). London: Curzon Press.

Kis-Jovak, Jowe Imre, Hetty Nooy-Palm, Reimer Schefold and Ursula Schulz-Dornburg

1988 *Banua Toraja: changing patterns in architecture and symbolism among the Sa'dan Toraja, Sulawesi-Indonesia*. Amsterdam: Royal Tropical Institute.

Lévi-Strauss, Claude

1969 *The elementary structures of kinship* (translated by J.H. Bell, J.R. von Sturmer and R. Needham (ed.)). Boston: Beacon Press. (Orig. pub. as *Les structures élémentaires de la parenté*. Paris: Presses Universitaires de France, 1949.)

1987 *Anthropology and myth: lectures* 1951–1982. Oxford: Basil Blackwell. (Orig. pub. as *Paroles données*. Paris: Libraire Plon, 1984.)

Loyré, Ghislaine

1987 Les maison de Mindanao. In C. Macdonald and members of l'ECASE (eds) *De la hutte au palais: sociétés "àmaison" en Asie du Sud-Est insulaire*, pp.89–107. Paris: CNRS Press.

Macdonald, Charles

1987 Sociétés "àmaison" et types d'organization sociale aux Philippines. In C. Macdonald and members of l'ECASE (eds) *De la hutte au palais: sociétés "àmaison" en Asie du Sud-Est insulaire*, pp.67–87. Paris: CNRS Press.

Mangunwijaya, Y.B.

1991 *The weaverbirds* (translated by Thomas M. Hunter). Jakarta: The Lontar Foundation. (Orig. pub. as *Burung-burung manyar*. Jakarta: Penerbit Djambatan, 1981.)

Mauss, Marcel with H. Beuchat

1979 *Seasonal variations of the Eskimo: a study in social morphology* (translated with a foreword by James J. Fox). London: Routledge and Kegan Paul. (Orig. pub. as 'Essai sur les variations saisonnières des sociétés Eskimos: étude de morphologie sociale' in *Année Sociologique* 1904–5, 9:39–132.)

Morgan, Lewis H.

1964 *Ancient society; or researches in the lines of human progress from savagery through barbarism to civilization* (L.A. White (ed.)). Cambridge: Harvard University Press. (Orig. pub. 1877.)

1965   *Houses and house-life of the American aborigines.* Chicago: University of Chicago Press. (Orig. pub. in Contributions to North American Ethnology, Vol. 4. Washington: Government Printing Office, 1881.)

Morris, H.S.

1978   The Coastal Melanau. In V.T. King (ed.) *Essays on Borneo societies* (Hull Monograph on Southeast Asia No. 7), pp.37–58. Oxford: Oxford University Press.

Pawley, Andrew and Malcolm Ross

In press Austronesian historical linguistics and culture history. *Annual Review of Anthropology* 22.

Rosaldo, Renato

1980   *Ilongot headhunting 1883–1974: a study in society and history.* Stanford: Stanford University Press.

Rousseau, Jérôme

1978   The Kayan. In V.T. King (ed.) *Essays on Borneo societies* (Hull Monographs on Southeast Asia No. 7), pp. 78–91. Oxford: Oxford University Press.

Salmond, Anne

1978   Te Ao Tawhito: a semantic approach to the traditional Maori cosmos. *The Journal of the Polynesian Society* 17:5–28.

1991   Tipuna-ancestors: aspects of Maori cognatic descent. In A. Pawley (ed.) *Man and a half: essays in Pacific anthropology and ethnobiology in honour of Ralph Bulmer*, pp.343–356. Auckland: The Polynesian Society.

Sather, Clifford

1985   Boat crews and fishing fleets: the social organization of maritime labour among the Bajau Laut of southeastern Sabah. *Contributions to Southeast Asian Ethnography* No. 4:165–214.

Sellato, Bernard

1987   Note préliminaire sur les sociétés "àmaison" àBornéo. In C. Macdonald and members of l'ECASE (eds) *De la hutte au palais: sociétés "àmaison" en Asie du Sud-Est insulaire*, pp.15–44. Paris: CNRS Press.

Singarimbun, Masri

1975   *Kinship, descent and alliance among the Karo Batak.* Berkeley: University of California Press.

Traube, Elizabeth

1980   Mambai rituals of black and white. In J.J. Fox (ed.) *The flow of life*, pp.290–314. Cambridge: Harvard University Press.

Tryon, Darrell T.

1993   *The comparative Austronesian dictionary.* Berlin: Mouton de Gruyter.

Waterson, Roxana

1986   The ideology and terminology of kinship among the Sa'dan Toraja. *Bijdragen tot de Taal-, Land- en Volkenkunde* 142:87–112.

1990   *The living house: an anthropology of architecture in South-East Asia.* Singapore: Oxford University Press.

Whittier, Herbert L.

1978   The Kenyah. In V.T. King (ed.) *Essays on Borneo societies* (Hull Monographs on Southeast Asia No. 7), pp.92–122. Oxford: Oxford University Press.

Young, Michael W.

1971   *Fighting with food: leadership, values and social control in a Massim society.* Cambridge: Cambridge University Press.

1983   *Magicians of Manumanua: living myth in Kalauna.* Berkeley: University of California Press.

Notes

I would like to thank all of those individuals who offered comment and suggestions in the preparation of this introductory essay. In the first instance, thanks are due to the contributors to this volume, since this paper is written as a result of the careful reading of their contributions. In particular, I would also like to thank Penelope Graham, Charles Grimes, Clifford Sather and S. Supomo.

[1] Care and caution is necessary in attempting to trace the various reflexes of * *lepaw*. Whittier (1978), for example, notes that the Kenyah term for 'village' is *lepo*. This term is not to be confused with the Kenyah term *lepau*, meaning 'field hut'. Some Kenyah populations, such as the Lepo Tau, Lepo Tukang and Lepo Jamuk, use *lepo* as an identification of their specific origins. Cognates of *lepo* meaning 'village' would seem to be widespread. Thus, for example, among the Lamaholot-speaking populations from east Flores to Alor, *lewo* designates 'village', marked by a communal ritual house, which functions as a meeting-house of the clans as well as a temple of the ancestral religion (P. Graham, personal communication). From this perspective, it would appear that the Ma'anyan term *lewu'* for 'village house' (Hudson and Hudson 1978:215), and the Melanau term *lebu* for 'village longhouse' (Morris 1978:41) are cognates of the Kenyah term *lepo* rather than of *lepau*. Alexander, in her paper, provides further strong evidence for this distinction. The Lahanan clearly distinguish between the two terms *levu*, meaning 'longhouse', and *lepau*, meaning 'farmhouse'.

[2] In terms of a comparative sociology of Borneo societies, the *tilung pu'un* of the Lahanan is structurally (as well as metaphorically) similar to the *lamin po'on*, the 'natal household' group described by Whittier (1978:104-106) for the Kenyah, although among the Kenyah there appears to be a lesser tendency toward female lines of continuity.

[3] This kind of ordered succession of places names, which is similar in structure to an ordered succession of ancestral names, is a common feature in many Austronesian societies. Such an ordered succession of place names, analogous to a genealogy, is what I have labeled a 'topogeny' in a paper entitled 'Genealogy and topogeny: toward an ethnography of Rotinese ritual place names' in a forthcoming collection of comparative essays on ideas of 'place' in Austronesian societies — *The poetic power of place* (Fox n.d.b).

Views of a Lahanan longhouse and its communal veranda

Chapter 2. The Lahanan Longhouse

Jennifer Alexander

Longhouses are the archetypical form of Bornean domicile, although this form of dwelling is also found in other parts of the world.[1] Much larger than most visitors expect, longhouses are built on piles and comprise a row of individual domestic units accommodated under one roof. This unusual form of architecture has provoked considerable speculation concerning the reasons for its development and for its persistence in contemporary societies which are otherwise rapidly changing.

A functional explanation for the siting of the longhouse on piles has been sought in the protection it provides from flood and heat in a tropical monsoon climate. It is also ecologically effective in that household waste ends up beneath the longhouse where it is disposed of by foraging pigs and poultry; and economical because a longhouse requires less time and material to construct than separate dwellings (Avé and King 1986:56).

A second and perhaps more compelling argument lies in the defensive and security aspects of the structure. Numerous ethnographers (Kelbling 1983:149; MacDonald 1956:103; Rousseau 1978; Sutlive 1978:183) have pointed to the importance of the length of the longhouse in providing protection against enemy attacks. According to MacDonald,

> the bigger the house the stouter its walls. The more numerous its inmates, the more plentiful its guard. That is the simple explanation of the remarkable size of Bornean residences (1956:103).

Kelbling (1983:149-150), in less declamatory terms, states that head-hunting and incessant clashes between indigenous groups made it 'sensible' to accommodate the village under one roof. He also notes two features of the longhouse, apart from its length and unity, which are designed for security purposes: the removable notched ladder by which people gain access from the compound to the gallery, and the doors of apartments which are raised some 50 centimetres above the floor to restrict entry. Avé and King (1986:56) remark on the defensive effectiveness of houses raised high above the ground on massive posts, as well as other features including hidden trenches, man traps and palisades.

But while all these writers stress the fortress-like nature of the longhouse they also see it as facilitating interpersonal relations and contacts between households (see also Rousseau 1978:80). This final point seems the most convincing argument for the persistence of the longhouse form in contemporary Borneo societies, for all appear to place a very high value on sociability. While they rely on the jungle for their livelihood, many members of these societies regard the longhouse as a domestic haven in a dangerous and hostile environment. The individual apartments afford sufficient privacy for domestic life, but the permeability of the adjoining walls, the close proximity of neighbours and the communal veranda provide the opportunities for highly valued social interaction.

Balui Longhouses

The Lahanan are one of the core groups of the Kajang[2] who regard themselves as the original settlers of the Belaga region in Sarawak's Seventh Division. Their position has been usurped by two main groups of later arrivals. The Kayan, who left the Apau Kayan in Kalimantan more than 200 years ago, pushed all of the Kajang, apart from the Lahanan, downriver to the lower Balui and 'imposed' Kayan wives on Kajang chiefs. The Kenyah also originated from the Apau Kayan and began migrating in waves either prior to or at the same time as the Kayan. One of the earliest Kenyah groups to arrive was the Uma Kelap Kenyah now located immediately downriver from the Lahanan longhouse in the middle Balui, but Kenyah migration has continued until recent times. Both groups have a record of disputes and armed conflict with the Lahanan (Guerreiro 1987).

Interethnic conflicts, head-hunting and war are part and parcel of the early settlement in the Balui region, but the Kayan were largely subdued and their expansion halted by a punitive expedition organized in 1863 by Charles Brooke, the second Rajah of Sarawak (de Martinoir 1974:267). Early this century the Iban started raiding the Balui region, and the Kayan, Kenyah and Kajang joined forces to repel the invader, although the Lahanan at times apparently acted as mediators.[3] The Iban raids continued until the early 1920s — at times restricting farming and trade in jungle produce. In 1924 armed conflict came to an end with a peacemaking ceremony in Kapit (Runciman 1960:238).

Over the past 350 years the Lahanan have established a great many longhouses over a wide area. Settlement patterns have largely been a response to the demands of swidden agriculture, but head-hunting and warfare have also played a part. Early this century Balui Kayan and their Lahanan allies established a group of longhouses near the mouth of the Linau River in response to the Iban attacks. These settlements later dispersed when land suitable for agriculture was exhausted. Demands on land and the establishment of boundaries around longhouse communities and their lands have led to the increasing sedentarization of the Balui ethnic groups, while the introduction of fertilizers, weedicides and cash crops have enabled them to cope with restrictions on expansion into new territory.

In the Belaga district, the Kayan, Kenyah and Kajang peoples all build substantial dwellings of ironwood. The Balui longhouse is frequently, but not universally, conterminous with the village. Most Kayan and Kajang communities consist of one longhouse, but the Kenyah usually build two or three longhouses within the one village.[4]

The massive nature of these longhouses has been attributed to the hierarchical social structure of the Kayan, Kenyah and Kajang and also, in comparison with the Iban, their less predatory agricultural practices (Avé and King 1985:56). These societies, in contrast to the Iban, were stratified into four ranks or hereditary strata. The *laja/maren*, commonly glossed as 'aristocrats', belong to the ruling family's apartment. The *hipui* are 'minor aristrocrats' with kinship relations to the *laja*. The *panyin* or 'commoners' form the bulk of the longhouse community. The fourth rank were 'slaves' (*lippen/dipen*) commonly captives of war. The substantial nature of the longhouse structure has been linked to the aristocrats' vested interest in maintaining control. Not only is the apartment of the *laja* much larger than others but, under traditional *adat*, *panyin* could not secede from their natal longhouse to form a new longhouse unless they were accompanied by a member of the aristocratic group.[5] This, in conjunction with the absence of a preference for farming primary jungle, is seen as inhibiting resettlement and favouring solid, enduring buildings.

The *Levu*

The Lahanan distinguish between a *levu larun*, a longhouse containing a number of individual apartments, and a *levu karep*, a detached dwelling occupied by a single domestic group. But the word *levu* usually refers to the longhouse, and is also the term for the communal veranda or gallery. The veranda side of the longhouse faces the river and the longhouse itself runs parallel to the river or stream on which it is located. Longhouse people orientate themselves in relation to the river. *Naju* refers to 'upriver' and *nava* to 'downriver', and many activities are also viewed in terms of the river and longhouse: one 'goes up' (*baguai*) to the longhouse but 'down to work' (*ba'ai nyadui*); that is, down to the river to paddle the canoe to the fields. Unlike the Iban longhouse described by Sather (this volume), the Lahanan longhouse, as with most other longhouses on the Balui River, is not orientated in terms of the sunrise and sunset.

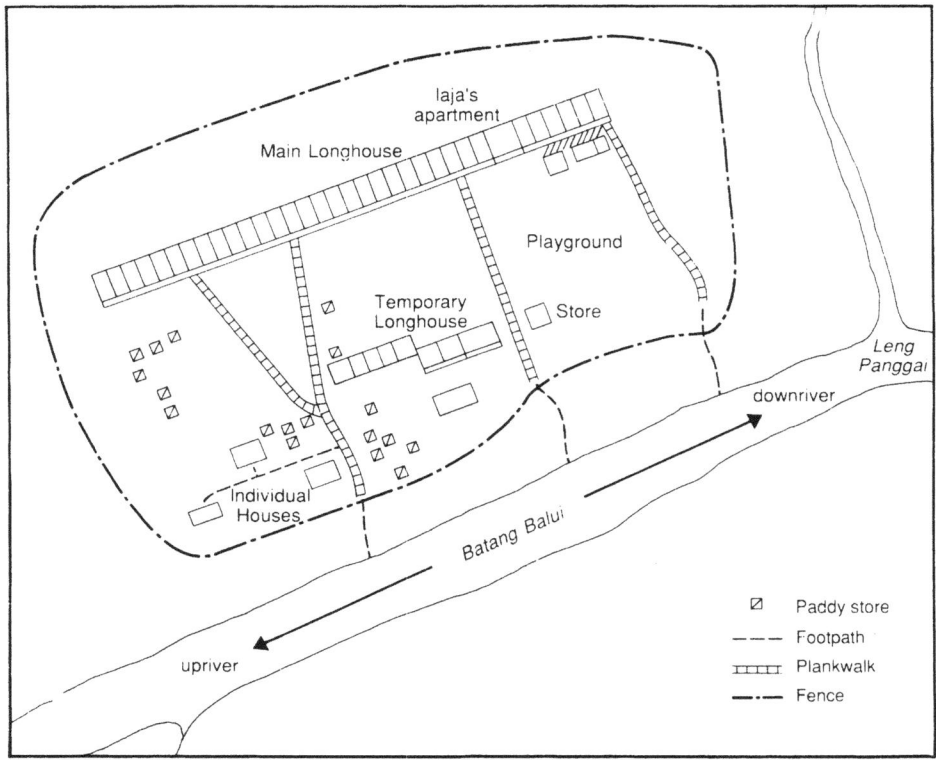

Figure 1. Levu Lahanan, Leng Panggai

The Lahanan *levu* is located on a river bank near the confluence (*leng*) of the main river (*batang*) with a smaller stream (*hungei*). Their current longhouse on the Balui River is about 50 metres from the river up a steep slippery incline, although of course, the river rises and falls dramatically according to the season and weather. It is located just upriver from Leng Panggai hence the name Levu Lahanan, Leng Panggai (see Figure 1).

The Lahanan build massive dwellings of hardwoods — the exceptionally durable *belian* (*Eusideroxylon zwageri*), *meranti* (*Shorea* spp.) and *berangan* (*Castanopsis* spp.) —supported by a number of vertical posts some 3 metres in height. The main posts are sunk 1.5 metres into the ground and pass through the floor to support the roof and rafters above. The structure consists of a front section forming a long gallery extending the entire length of the longhouse and a rear section containing individual household apartments. Each apartment (*tilung*) comprises sleeping quarters, a hearth and living area. Access is through a door (*bah tilung*), literally the mouth of the *tilung*, to the common gallery. The gallery not only provides access to each apartment, but also serves as a playground, workplace and relaxation centre. Each apartment 'owns' and is responsible for the upkeep of the gallery in front of it. The rice mortar (*lesung*), frequently many years older than the longhouse itself, is placed in the front of the apartment on the gallery, and other goods such as paddles, spears and fishing nets are stored in the rafters of the *levu*. Before the introduction of the Bungan cult[6] in the early 1950s, the skulls of victims of head-hunting raids were also hung here.

Each apartment also has a rear entrance reached by a notched log, and, in the past, access to the gallery was gained by means of removable notched logs. It is not uncommon to have open doorways between contiguous *tilung* belonging to close friends and relatives. Neighbouring apartments may also be entered via the drying platform located in the centre of many apartments. Most are blocked off by a low fence, which does not hinder conversation between neighbours working in the area.

In the past the Lahanan sometimes built longhouses of two storeys with sleeping quarters on the second one, but their current longhouse is a single-storeyed dwelling place. *Belian* shingles were the ideal roofing material, but these have now largely been replaced by zinc roofing, which has inferior insulation properties.

Longhouses may also be identified in terms of their *laja* (headman), and the aristocrats (*linau laja*) have been referred to as the 'house-owning' group (Leach 1950:61). Political authority is vested in the *linau laja*, the only longhouse people to trace a direct genealogical link to a founding ancestor. In the case of the Lahanan, a quasi-mythical ancestor called Laké Galo legitimates the *laja*'s authority.

The present headman's (*laja*'s) apartment is considerably bigger than most others, but does not have the raised roof, extended gallery or elaborate paintings decorating the front wall as in many Kayan and Kenyah longhouses, although these may have been present in earlier Lahanan structures. The gallery in front of the headman's apartment is a locus of religious and social activity. During the period of the old religion and also Adat Bungan, the *levu* (veranda) of the *tilung baken* (literally 'big apartment', denoting the headman's living quarters) was the setting for most of the important communal religious ceremonies. The longhouse was formerly split into two for minor ceremonies with downriver apartments following ceremonies at the headman's *tilung* and the upriver apartments at the *dayong*'s (ritual expert). With the introduction of Christianity and the headman's conversion to Catholicism, Sunday services are now conducted on the *levu* of the *tilung baken* and all public Bungan ceremonies take place in front of the *tilung* of the *dayong*. Representatives from each *tilung* attend longhouse meetings to discuss matters of common interest — the building of a new longhouse, the visit of a distinguished guest and communal clean-ups of the longhouse compound — on the *levu* of the *tilung baken*. The headman, deputy headman and the working committee usually dominate proceedings, but also adult men and women make their views known.

When a new longhouse is built the headman's apartment is the first erected and most adults perform corvée work (*mahap*) to construct the dwelling. In the past elaborate rituals were held before the erection of the house posts but there is no evidence to suggest that the Lahanan, like the Kayan, sacrificed a slave at this time (see Avé and King 1986:61). While the headman's *tilung* is twice as large as any other apartment, it has little else to differentiate it other than a wooden fence at either end of the front gallery designed to keep out the hunting dogs which roam around.

Although the Lahanan build durable longhouses, they have moved fairly frequently over the last twenty years, living in two different *levu larun* and two temporary longhouses or *luvung*. This appears to have been a common pattern. Some moves can be attributed to epidemics, bad omens or natural disasters. Flood and fire are not infrequent hazards and the Lahanan have been victims of both. In 1942 their longhouse was swept away by floods, fortunately with no loss of life. More recently an elaborate two-storeyed longhouse consisting of twenty-five apartments, which was located across river from the present site, was destroyed by fire, a mere seven years after it had been built. Many heirlooms and the long ritual drum (*tuvung*) were destroyed in the blaze. At the time most households were living in their field huts (*lepau*) and the Lahanan now cite this fire as a reason for their reluctance to stay in the farmhouses for long periods and for keeping heirlooms in separate storehouses. Gongs and other valuables are now placed on display only during important ritual occasions, such as marriage ceremonies, and the most common form of decorative display is the sunhat (*siung*) decorated with beadwork, embroidery and cloth inserts.

The current community at Leng Panggai consists of two longhouses plus associated detached houses and storage huts sited within a fenced compound. The original longhouse contains twenty-nine apartments. When there was no longer room to expand lengthwise, three semi-attached *tilung* were built onto the front. Four detached houses and a further haphazardly constructed longhouse consisting of eight apartments have recently been built. This longhouse is usually termed a temporary structure (*luvung*) rather than a *levu*, and replaces a similar structure which was dismantled. One of the reasons for the Lahanan's strong desire to build a new longhouse, cited in their application for government assistance to prepare and level a site, is that the people wish to be housed under one roof again. Most longhouse people wish to retain their life-style, with only a few 'dissidents' seeing an attraction in independent dwellings within separate household compounds.[7]

The Kayan, Kenyah and Kajang have a dual mode of residence: most households spend at least some periods residing in their farmhouses (*lepau*). For some households the *lepau*, where they prepare the midday meal and relax, is a simple shelter, but for most it is a small, but solid, dwelling where they may spend up to a month during peaks in the swidden rice-cultivation cycle. People anxious to escape the restrictions of the longhouse actively enjoy the more intimate and relaxed atmosphere of family life in the *lepau*, but others find the isolation in the jungle environment too intimidating and are only too willing to return to the security of the longhouse.

The *Tilung*

Apartments consist of the *tilung* proper, which is located at the front and is where people sit and entertain, and the *baleh* (kitchen), usually linked by a *sepatah* (drying platform). The barest apartments contain merely some form of covering for the wooden flooring — a traditional rattan mat (*layang guai*) and/or cheap plastic. Most households have at least one wardrobe and this is usually placed in the *tilung*. More elaborate *tilung* contain a table and chairs as well as cupboards. Separate cramped sleeping quarters (*siluk*) are usually constructed at the front or side of the the main room, but the *siluk* may consist of a curtained-off, raised platform. The *tilung* is used as a sleeping area in more crowded apartments and guests commonly sleep in the *tilung* on rattan mats provided by the hosts. Further sleeping quarters are sometimes located at the rear of the kitchen (see Figure 2).

The *baleh* is usually separated from the *tilung* by a washing and drying platform (*sepatah*). Piped water runs from one end of the main longhouse to the other and each household has one tap. A latrine is located on the platform or in some cases at the rear of the apartment. The kitchens themselves are simple and consist of a raised fireplace (*benun*) boarded up with planks and filled with clay. Wood fuel is stored both below the fireplace and above it on drying racks. Other furniture includes cupboards for food storage and a dish rack, as well as a table — all recent innovations. The *baleh* are dark and gloomy with only narrow openings high on the walls allowing a little light to filter through. People often seek the light and fresh air of the gallery to work in.

New *tilung* are built on a reciprocal labour basis, each household supplying one-person day per *tilung*. Apartments vary slightly in size and construction as wealthier persons build roomier and more elaborate dwellings. The adjoining walls are flimsy and afford little privacy. Numerous slits and holes provide opportunities to observe whatever is happening in a neighbour's household and this curiosity is in no way restrained. Access to *tilung* is also relatively unrestrained and people move freely in and out of the apartments of others, but it is regarded as impolite to enter the sleeping quarters, or the kitchen when a household is having a meal.

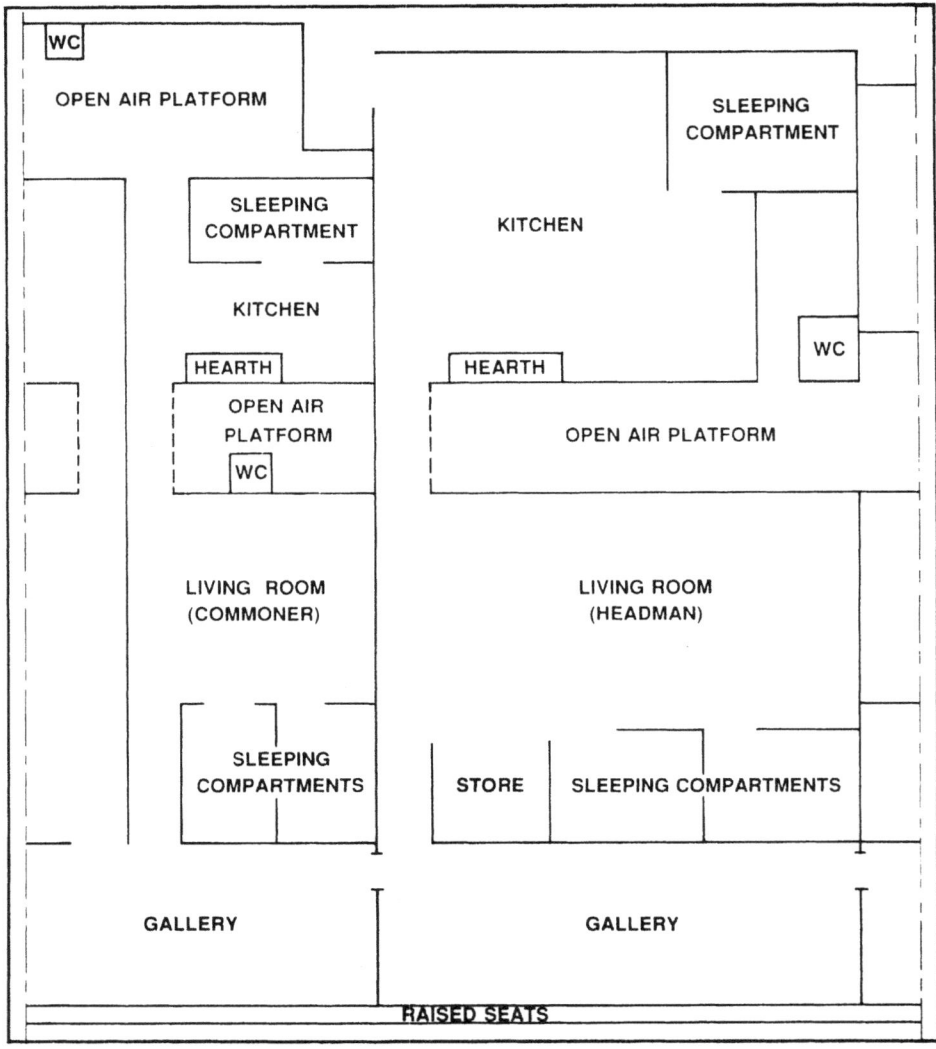

Figure 2. Floor plan of longhouse

The *tilung* is the crucial unit for the organization of labour. The women of each *tilung* are responsible for the maintenance of vegetable and tobacco gardens where they work on their own (*nyadui karep*). But much agricultural work, including swidden rice and cash-crop cultivation, is organized on the basis of exchange labour (*pelado*). *Pelado* is calculated in terms of the exchange of work days between *tilung*. Membership of the work team is usually based on the proximity of swiddens or gardens, but workers are also recruited on the basis of friendship, kinship and/or residential proximity. Each individual or, if they are unavailable, another member of the *tilung* provides one day's labour for each team member who works on their land.

While exchange labour is not regarded as essential for the cultivation of either hill rice or cash crops such as cocoa or pepper, almost everyone, but the young in particular, prefer working in a group to working on their own. Despite the admission that there are positive economic benefits in cultivating pepper and cocoa using household labour alone, exchange labour persists because of the high value placed on sociability. People enjoy working in a group, time appears to pass more quickly, and they enjoy a communal meal. Even women who are working alone in their tobacco and vegetable gardens try to ensure that there are female companions nearby so that they can gather together for snacks and a communal meal.

Tilung Composition

Each apartment contains either a nuclear, a stem or an extended family, although it is desirable and prestigious to maintain as large a *tilung* as possible. However, limitations of space and the splitting off of domestic groups create cyclic fluctuations in *tilung* size.

Most apartments contain a single household — the consumption and production unit; for those which have split into two households will normally establish a new apartment (*tilung karep*, literally 'own separate apartment') when circumstances permit. Of the forty-one occupied apartments at Levu Lahanan, thirty-two (78 per cent) form a single production and consumption unit, but nine (22 per cent) are split into 'two cooking pots' (*legua buyun*). This implies not only separate cooking arrangements but also separate production and consumption units. All nine of these apartments house more than the average of six members, ranging from seven to sixteen members with the majority containing nine or ten persons.

The most common form of *tilung* organization is a stem family with parents and unmarried children, plus a married daughter, her husband and their children. Twenty apartments (49 per cent) contain stem families. Extended households usually contain more than one married child — usually two married daughters — but this is always a transitory form as the expectation is that all but one married daughter will eventually establish their own apartments. Extended households number six (14 per cent). Only fifteen households (37 per cent) consist of a single nuclear family, in two cases a surviving spouse and child. Eight of these nuclear families have established their own *tilung* within the last five years, all of them splitting from the wife's natal apartment. The remaining five nuclear families are the surviving members of a *tilung* in which previous members have died or moved to another apartment. Twenty-one apartments have a genealogical depth of three generations and five have a genealogical depth of four.

Continuity of the *Tilung*

In a narrow sense *tilung* refers to the physical longhouse apartment. The occupants of an apartment, who comprise a single unit for routine social, political and religious activities, may also be referred to as a *tilung*, although this social group is more commonly termed *linau tilung* (people of the *tilung*). While the *linau tilung* has a consanguineal core, it also includes affines, adopted and foster children, and any others living in the apartment and taking part in its activities.

Ownership of the dwelling and its contents, heirlooms and rights to land, however, are not vested in the *linau tilung* but in the *tilung pu'un* or *tilung asen* (*tilung* of origin). This is a kinship group comprising all persons with consanguineal links to the *tilung*, irrespective of where they may be living. The *tilung pu'un* is a continuing entity in that at least one child remains in the 'natal apartment', although the apartment may be rebuilt and the longhouse relocated. Childless couples adopt children, commonly from siblings, and parents of a sole surviving son insist on virilocal post-marital residence, to ensure survival of the *tilung pu'un*.

Heirlooms (*laven pusaka*), including beads, gongs and brass jars, provide a symbolic focus for the *tilung pu'un*. Rights to heirlooms are held by all members of the *tilung pu'un*, including those living elsewhere, but custody is entrusted to the senior member of the *linau tilung*. This person also allocates land to members of the *tilung pu'un* returning to live in the longhouse. Despite the custodial role of the senior member of the *linau tilung*, however, all important decisions are based on extensive consultation.

Lahanan, other than the *laja*, have a strong preference for uxorilocal residence after marriage, which is compulsory for the initial period following the marriage ceremony; 90 per cent of currently married couples at Leng Panggai are living in the wife's *tilung* or in an apartment which has split from it. Consequently, *tilung* continuity is usually achieved through female lines, and most custodians of *tilung* property are women. This has important implications for gender relations which are characterized by a strong egalitarian ethic. Lahanan women are prominent in social and political discussion and carry out a large part of the agricultural work.

In some respects it might be claimed that men are peripheral to the *tilung pu'un*. Thirty-five per cent of Leng Panggai married women have husbands from other ethnic groups, mainly Kayan, but also Kenyah and Iban. Conflicts within the longhouse are not infrequently couched in ethnic terms and divorce is more common in inter-ethnic marriages. But despite their initially marginal position, inmarrying men with established families adopt the *levu* and *tilung* affiliation of their spouses and may have a prominent role in longhouse affairs.

The *pu'un* concept is also of considerable significance regarding the continuity of the longhouse as a distinct community. Lahanan retain strong emotional ties to their natal *levu* and its ancestral lands (*daleh Lahanan*); people residing elsewhere return, if they are in a position to do so, at least once a year, particularly during the harvest festival. Even persons who have had an advanced education or have worked in the city for a number of years maintain a strong attachment to their place of origin and enjoy the traditional activities of the longhouse when they return. While the Sarawak government has been responsible for many innovations in longhouse life, the high value Lahanan place on sociability has maintained the longhouse as an enduring form.

References

Alexander, Jennifer

1989   Culture and ethnic identity: the case of the Lahanan of Ulu Belaga. *Sarawak Museum Journal* 40 (Special Issue No. 4, Part I):51–59.

1990   Lahanan social structure: some preliminary considerations. *Sarawak Museum Journal* 41(62):189–212.

Avé, Jan B. and King, Victor T.

1986   *The people of the weeping forest: tradition and change in Borneo.* Leiden: Rijksmuseum voor Volkenkunde.

Freeman, Derek

1970   *Report on the Iban.* London: Athlone.

Guerreiro, Antonio J.

1987   The Lahanan: some notes on the history of a Kajang group. *Sarawak Gazette* 113 (1500):17–28.

Hose, Charles

1926   *Natural man: a record from Borneo.* London: Macmillan.

Hose, Charles and McDougall, William

1912   *The pagan tribes of Borneo* (2 vols). London: Macmillan.

Kelbling, Sebastian

1983   Longhouses at the Baluy River. *Sarawak Museum Journal* 32:133–158.

Leach, E.R.

1950   *Social science research in Sarawak.* London: His Majesty's Stationery Office.

Martinoir, Brian L. de

1974   Notes on the Kajang. *Sarawak Museum Journal* 22(43):267–274.

MacDonald, Malcolm

1956   *Borneo people*. London: Cape.

Metcalf, Peter

1983   Warfare and community size in nineteenth century Borneo. *Borneo Research Bulletin* 15(1):26–30.

Nicolaisen, Ida

1977–78   The dynamics of ethnic classification: a case study of the Punan Bah in Sarawak. *Folk* 19–20:183–200.

Rousseau, Jérôme

1975   Ethnic identity and social relations in Central Borneo. In J.A. Nagata (ed.) *Pluralism in Malaysia: myth and reality*, pp.32–49. Leiden: E.J. Brill.

1978   The Kayan. In Victor T. King (ed.) *Essays on Borneo societies*, pp.78–91. London: Oxford University Press for the University of Hull.

Runciman, Stephen

1960   *The white rajahs: a history of Sarawak from 1841 to 1946*. Cambridge: Cambridge University Press.

Satyawadhna, Cholthira

1991   A comparative study of structure and contradiction of the Austroasiatic system in the Thai-Yunnan periphery. In Gehan Wijeyewardene (ed.) *Ethnic groups across national boundaries in mainland Southeast Asia*, pp. 74–101. Singapore: Institute of Southeast Asian Studies.

Sutlive, Vinson

1978   *The Iban of Sarawak*. Arlington Heights, Illinois: AHM Publishing Corporation.

Whittier, Herbert L.

1978   The Kenyah. In Victor T. King (ed.) *Essays on Borneo societies*, pp.92–122. London: Oxford University Press for the University of Hull.

Notes

This paper was initially written while I participated in the Comparative Austronesian Project at The Australian National University. The final draft was completed at the Netherlands Institute for Advanced Study in the Humanities and Social Sciences, Wassenaar.

[1] The longhouse form is also found among many of the hill tribes of Burma and Assam and the South Sea Islands of the Pacific (Hose 1926:71). See also Satyawadhna on the Lua longhouse (1991).

[2] The core group of the Kajang — the Lahanan, the Kejaman and Sekapan — are regarded as the original settlers of the Belaga region where they have lived for several centuries. Other groups linked with the

Kajang include the Punan Bah, Sihan and Bah Mali, but these links appear to have a political rather than a cultural basis (Alexander 1989; Nicolaisen 1977–78:191–192; Rousseau 1975:39).

[3] The Kajang were frequently victims of the endemic warfare between Iban and Kayan (Guerreiro 1987:22).

[4] According to Hose (1926:74) and Hose and McDougall (1912, 1:54), the Kayan villages consisted of several longhouses, whereas Kenyah villages consisted of only one. In contrast Whittier (1978:99) argues that Kenyah communities commonly have more than one longhouse and Rousseau (1978:80) that the Kayan have only one.

[5] The Lahanan split into two communities five generations — perhaps 125 years — ago when a conflict over the leadership of the longhouse led to the loser and the occupants of two apartments (*tilung*) establishing a new longhouse at Sungei Murum with ten Punan households. By the 1880s they had moved to Sungei Belepeh, a tributary of the Murum, and adopted the name Lahanan Belepeh. Between 1896 and 1904 the Lahanan Belepeh were involved in disputes with the Kenyah Badeng and subsequently the Iban. As a result they changed places of residence several times, but by 1940 they had moved to the lower Balui and their current place of settlement at Long Semuang (Alexander 1990). See also Freeman (1970) and Metcalf (1983) for discussions of the process of longhouse fission and fusion.

[6] The Bungan cult abandoned the burdensome taboos and auguries associated with the old religion in response to religious and economic changes. In the Middle Balui the cult is still active, but declining, with 70 per cent of the population at Levu Lahanan, for example, still belonging to the cult.

[7] This calls to mind Leach's (1950) statement: 'The inference is very strong that the house, as such, is a very strong element of cohesion and that long-house domicile is not abandoned until the traditional social system has already suffered irreparable damage' (p.63). Cf. Metcalf 1983.

Chapter 3. Good Walls Make Bad Neighbours: The Dayak Longhouse as a Community of Voices

Christine Helliwell

Within the anthropology of Borneo, the Dayak longhouses found throughout the island have typically been depicted as each consisting of little more than a line of independent household apartments. It has consistently been argued, within this literature, that any apparent communality suggested by the fact that a number of apartments are joined into a single longhouse structure is an illusion; that each apartment is in fact a highly discrete entity. In this view, the 'independent' character of an apartment reflects a priority of household over community within Dayak social organization. Several ethnographers have taken this so far as to draw a parallel between the structure of a Dayak longhouse — with its 'public' veranda and 'private' walled-off household areas — and that of an English-style street of semi-detached houses (see, for example, Geddes 1957:29; Freeman 1970:7, 1958:20).

For most anthropologists of Borneo, the household is the pre-eminent Dayak social unit (cf. King 1978:12–13). I have argued at length elsewhere that this view is mistaken with respect to at least some Dayak societies — in that there the primary social entity is not necessarily co-residential, and therefore does not properly constitute a 'household' — and that unwarranted stress on the 'household' can lead to serious misunderstandings concerning the character of Dayak social relations (see Helliwell 1990, 1991). My aim in this paper is a related one: to problematize the pervasive view within the Borneo ethnography of the Dayak household as profoundly independent from other households as well as from wider, more encompassing forms of social grouping.[1]

Gerai is a Dayak community of some 700 people, located in the northeast of the *kabupaten* (sub-province) Ketapang in the Indonesian province of Kalimantan Barat (West Borneo).[2] Cultivation of rice in swiddens on the northern sunny slopes of hills is overwhelmingly the most important economic activity of Gerai folk, but most are not content to live at subsistence level and actively seek to create a little cash income. This is achieved through the sale of locally produced or obtained products (rubber, sawn wood, sandalwood), through providing services to the local population (carpentry services to neighbours and kin, translation and domestic services to the missionaries, bearer services to the traders), or through working at one of the nearby timber camps.

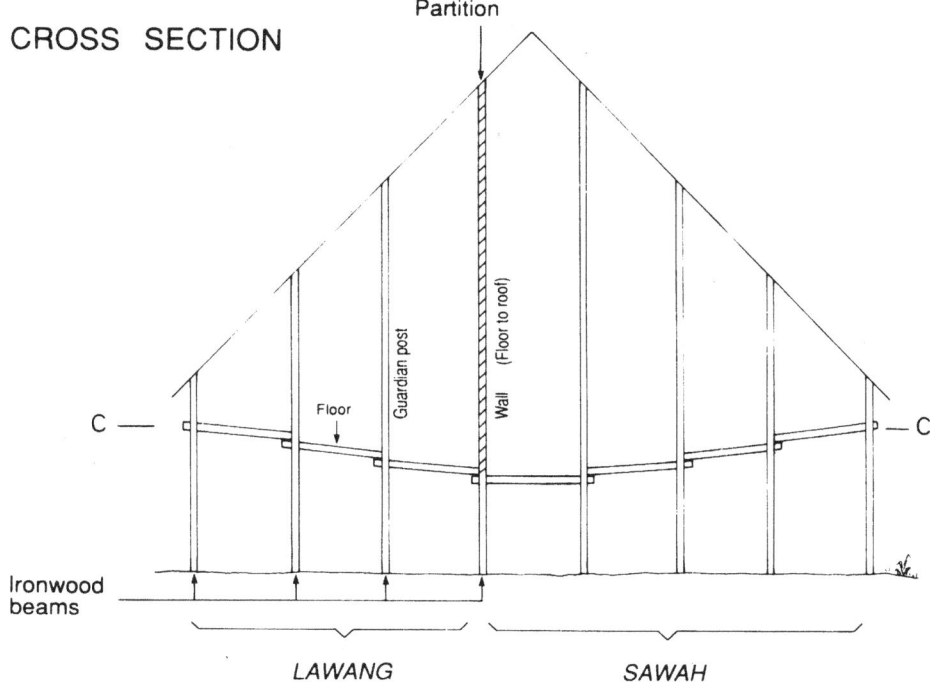

Figure 1. Gerai longhouse apartment in cross section

Twenty-five years ago the Gerai village proper consisted of four longhouses clustered together on the banks of a tiny stream. Of these, only two now remain. In the spaces where the other two once stood, and beyond, a plethora of free-standing dwellings has sprung up; these extend constantly the boundaries of the village. In 1986 the Gerai community contained 121 permanently inhabited dwellings, 106 of which were found in the village and fifteen outside.[4] Only twenty-three of the 106 village dwellings were found in the two longhouses (fourteen apartments in one and nine in the other), the remaining eighty-three consisting of free-standing houses. It needs to be stressed at the outset of this paper then, that what is described here pertains to a traditional type of living space: one that is becoming increasingly irrelevant to Gerai Dayaks, as residence in their own free-standing houses becomes an important goal in the lives of most newly married couples.

The Gerai longhouse is laid out upon seven separate named levels, each of which is differentiated from the others according to what Gerai people term its *guno nar* (true, essential function). Although any level may be used for a variety of purposes at different times, it is the 'true function' of each which Gerai informants will supply and emphasize in any description of a longhouse apartment. The arrangement of these levels, and the essential function associated with each, is set out in Figure 1. As can be seen from the cross-section view the entire structure is covered by a soaring thatched or shingled roof: leaving no uncovered platform as exists, for instance, in both the Iban and Bidayuh Land Dayak longhouses. Within each apartment a wall stretches from floor to roof, dividing the apartment into an 'inner' household cooking, eating, and sleeping area which is partitioned off from the equivalent areas of those apartments on either side, and an 'outer' gallery area which is not partitioned. Into this separating wall of solid sawn planks a door is set, providing access from one section of the apartment to the other. The name for the inner section is *lawang* (door), although it is at least as frequently referred to as *lem rumah* (inside of the apartment). The outer section is termed *ruang* (platform, space), or more simply (and more usually) *sawah* (outside).

This basic division between an enclosed 'inner' area and an open 'outer' area is one that occurs in Dayak longhouses throughout Borneo. It has usually been portrayed as representing a separation between a 'private' household area and a 'public' community area. At first sight a description of the Gerai *sawah* and *lawang* as a 'public' and a 'private' space respectively, would seem to be borne out by Gerai Dayaks' own account of the differences between the two. If pressed, Gerai people will describe the *sawah* (outer area) as *ramo*, and the *lawang* (inner area) as *yeng diret*. *Ramo* means literally 'freely available to anyone', and refers to the fact that the *sawah* is an area where anybody from within the longhouse or the wider community may stroll, sit, weave, carve or whatever, without requiring permission from the actual owners of the apartment. *Yeng diret* translates literally as 'that which pertains to the self', and so appears to indicate that the *lawang* is an area that is not free to be used by anyone at any time. In fact its use by anyone other than members of the household to which it belongs is governed by strict rules of etiquette. If, for instance, the *lawang* is empty, or if the only inhabitants are sleeping, it may not be entered. Such a distinction between *lawang* and *sawah* does in fact seem very similar to the distinction made in Western society between the open 'public' street and the closed 'private' houses which it links together.

Yet, for the Gerai longhouse at least, such an understanding of this spatial division would constitute a serious distortion of both relations between the household and the wider longhouse community, and the role of the inner *lawang* space in the creation and reaffirmation of those relations. There is no doubt that the Gerai *sawah* corresponds to the social 'public' area found in other Borneo longhouses: like Dayaks elsewhere the Dayaks of Gerai come to this covered open space in the late afternoon and evening to share gossip, tobacco, betel-nut, or simply to stroll in the breeze. However, the implied view of the *lawang* that accompanies this — as a 'private' area reserved for the more exclusive use of the household — is much more difficult to sustain. As we shall see, forms of sociability take a different, less visible, form in the inner *lawang* area, which has led to their being ignored in the literature in favour of the more obvious conviviality of the outer *sawah*. In Gerai, *lawang* and *sawah* represent not an opposition between 'private' and 'public', but between 'inside' and 'outside' (as the very terms *lem rumah* ('inside of the apartment') and *sawah* ('outside') indicate). Implicit in this inside/outside opposition, I would suggest, is an opposition between not 'we, the household' (*lawang*) and 'they, the rest of the community' (*sawah*) but rather between 'we, the longhouse community' (*lawang*) and 'that, the world out there', of which we may also at times be a part, (*sawah*). In other words, the spatial separation parallels a division not *within* the longhouse community but between that community and those without it: between 'we' and 'other'.

This understanding is supported by the Gerai description, already noted, of the difference between these two spaces: of the outer *sawah* as *ramo* (freely available to anyone) and the inner *lawang* as *yeng diret* (that which pertains to the self). For in Gerai the meaning of the word *diret* extends beyond the basic sense of 'self' to mean also 'we/us including the person spoken to'. That the term should encompass these two meanings in English is no accident, for Gerai people tend not to distinguish between oneself and those with whom one is carrying out any particular activity at a particular moment.[5] Describing the *lawang* as a space that is *yeng diret*, then, designates it as pertaining to 'we' (a group of selves engaged together in some particular activity), without excluding the conception of that space as one over which household members are able to exercise particular rights vis-à-vis the community at large. The term *yeng diret* not merely encompasses but, indeed, implies both meanings. The activity which binds us together through our shared engagement in it is our longhouse residence, and the very particular mode of social interaction in which this residence necessarily implicates us.

This portrayal of the nature of *lawang* space fits most comfortably with the clear identification, among Gerai Dayaks, of the *sawah* space as that of strangers and outsiders. Thus, although it most often functions as an area of easy community sociability, the *guno nar* (true, essential functions) of two of its four levels are to do with Malay guests to the longhouse. Gerai informants specify (as seen in the floor plan, Figure 2) that the 'true' uses of the *sadau sawah* and the *paléper sawah* ('outside' equivalents of the *sadau* and the *paléper*, which are both found in the *lawang*) are as a sleeping place and a cooking place respectively for Malay visitors to the longhouse. The Dayaks of Gerai, like many other Dayak groups, tend to define themselves ethnically in opposition to Malays.[6] So deep is this opposition that Gerai folk will often use the term *reng Melayu* (Malay) to mean simply non-Dayak.[7] The association of the outer *sawah* with Malays is thus a clear expression of its status as an area for 'others', as opposed to the inner *lawang* which is 'our' space.

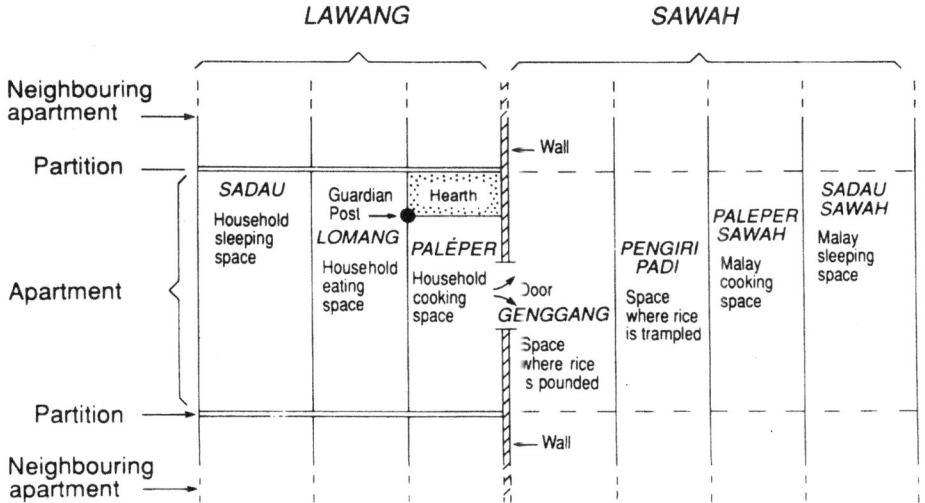

Figure 2. Gerai longhouse apartment floor plan

In past times, Gerai Dayaks were under the control of the Malay *raja* based in Sukadana, some 80 kilometres away on the coast. Although its location far from a river deep enough to be used for transport meant that Gerai had only very rarely received visits from the *raja*'s emissaries, in 1986 Gerai myth and oral history remained full of references to them, and to the *raja* himself. Unlike Dayaks from other longhouses or villages who, during the days of Malay control, had arrived at the longhouse as either friends or enemies (and so could be treated accordingly), Malays had come as neither. Their loyalty and service to the *raja* demanded that they be treated with care and respect in order to avoid the *raja*'s wrath, but the nature of Gerai relations dictated then as now that they be seen as a different order of being, one which refuses pork and rice wine (both prized by Gerai people) and engages in an incomprehensible and highly amusing set of practices with respect to its deities. It is partly because of these taboos that Gerai Dayaks deem it most sensible to banish Malays as guests to the outer *sawah* levels, where they are least likely to be affected by Dayak customs.

But the practice reflects a more deeply held conception of the *lawang* as 'our space' and the *sawah* as 'the space of others' than is accounted for simply through reference to Dayak wishes not to offend. Thus informants told me that in the past a Malay was not permitted, on pain of death, to enter a *lawang*, although Dayak strangers were generally invited to do so. The degree to which this outer area is regarded as a Muslim (that is, Malay) eating and sleeping area was revealed in a statement made to me during my early days in the longhouse, in response to my suggestion that I might build myself living quarters on the *sawah* area of one of the apartments. Longhouse residents were disapproving: 'Only people who don't eat pork should eat and sleep out on the *sawah*. You are one of us — it wouldn't feel right to have you living out there'.

This not only points up the conception of the *sawah* as a Malay area but also demonstrates the degree to which Gerai Dayaks conceive of the world as divided essentially between 'us' and 'those who don't eat pork' (that is, Malays). Another response made to the same suggestion emphasizes the gleeful Dayak joke which is involved in the banishment of their erstwhile masters to the outer veranda space. In order to dissuade me once and for all from building on the longhouse *sawah*, it was pointed out that each household's pigs are kept immediately beneath this section. As living quarters such an area would therefore be noisy and foul-smelling. How much more so for Malays, to whom pigs are so unclean that contact with them of any kind is strenuously avoided!

It is not my intention to go into detail about the nature of the *sawah* space and how it is distinguished from the *lawang* of an apartment. It is sufficient for my purposes here to have demonstrated that the *lawang/sawah* division in Gerai constitutes a conceptual opposition between the longhouse community and those outside it, rather than one within that community. For the remainder of this paper I focus on the *lawang*. The nature of this 'inner' space, and of the community interaction that takes place within it, has been seriously neglected in the anthropological literature on Dayak societies. Yet examination of these is crucial if one is to gain an understanding of the linkages between household and community in Gerai.

Lawang Construction and *Lawang* Space

In line with the overwhelming emphasis within the Borneo literature on the household as the most important unit of social organization most ethnographers of Dayak societies have been content to describe a longhouse simply by outlining a single apartment. The implicit assumption in this approach has been that the nature of the longhouse as a whole may be grasped by the reader through a simple imaginary aggregation of a number of these units.[8] The danger here is that in conceptualizing any longhouse primarily in terms of discrete constituent components, any relationships that operate *between* apartments — and especially those occurring in the private 'inner' setting — may be overlooked. The Gerai longhouse, for instance, certainly does comprise a number of separate widthwise units each associated with a single household. But it at the same time — and equally as importantly — constitutes a single lengthwise entity in space. To isolate a single apartment and describe the relationships that operate across its spatial levels, tying them together into one unit, would be to neglect the relationships that flow from one apartment to another, tying them together into a community. While these community ties may at first sight appear to be sustained largely through easy interaction between the members of neighbouring apartments in the open *sawah* space, they achieve much greater frequency and intensity within the closed-off *lawang* space, shielded there from the eyes and ears of the larger world.

The private, as opposed to communal, ownership of the materials which go to make up any one longhouse apartment is a feature of Borneo longhouses which has been stressed relentlessly in the literature. In this respect the longhouses at Gerai are no exception. Each individual household owns the nails, planks, strips of bamboo, lengths of rattan, units of thatch and so on, which together comprise its longhouse apartment. Such a pattern has often been taken to indicate a set of property relations similar to those which operate in the West, and to provide further evidence both for the importance of individualism in Dayak culture and for the separation of any one Dayak household from those others surrounding it. However, there is no necessary link between ownership of the materials that together go to make up an apartment, and exclusive rights or control over the finished structure and over the space which it circumscribes. In the Gerai longhouse, while the household has certain rights over its own apartment space, such space is at the same time an inseparable part of a larger community space, and therefore subject also to the rights of neighbours. No Gerai Dayak would ever claim (or indeed wish to claim) that any part of a longhouse apartment is radically isolated from those on either side of it in the way that the proverbial Englishman wishes to claim that his home is his castle. This holds as true for the inner walled-off *lawang* as it does for the outer open *sawah*. To describe any part of a Gerai longhouse apartment in terms of a fixed dichotomy between 'private' and 'public' would thus be to ignore the complex and shifting balance achieved between household rights and community rights with respect to that apartment as a whole.

It has long been recognized by anthropologists and sociologists that the arrangement of domestic space is closely linked to the nature of the domestic and social relationships lived within that space. Therefore the analysis of spatial arrangements is seen as potentially able to provide important clues to the indigenous conceptions of those relationships.[9] Most such analyses have focused on the formal division of space and how this accords with (or perhaps masks) patterns of social organization and/or deeper conceptual schemes. In examining *lawang* space I am concerned to avoid a focus on formal spatial arrangements and to concentrate instead on the way this space is lived and experienced in everyday life.

Closer examination in these terms of the wall separating the *lawang* of one apartment from that next to it is revealing. The character of this wall is crucial for any discussion of the longhouse as a lengthwise entity, for it is this which divides that entity up into its constituent units. It is normally made of flimsy pieces of bark and other materials propped up against each other in such a way as to leave gaps of varying sizes, through which dogs and cats can climb, people can hand things back and forth, and at which neighbours can stand while they chat together. Like everything else in the longhouse this wall is always *owned* by one of the two households whose apartments it delimits (by the household that built its apartment first). But in practical terms it is *shared* by both, and it marks off the space of the second as much as it does the space of the first. The dividing wall includes in itself the notion of the next apartment at the same time as it demarcates the apartment to which it belongs. In physical terms it is highly permeable: through it move a variety of resources in both directions.

But the character of the partitions between neighbouring *lawang* is important not only for the relations that it promotes between an apartment and those on either side of it but also for fostering an uninterrupted sociability from one end of the longhouse to the other. The very permeability of the partitions — their makeshift and ricketty character — allows an almost unimpeded flow of both sound and light between all the apartments that together constitute a longhouse.

This flow of sound and light is crucial, for I argue that the Gerai longhouse community as a whole is defined and encircled more by these two things than by anything else. I recall, while living in the Gerai longhouse, writing letters back to Australia in which I constantly referred to the longhouse as a 'community of voices', for I could think of no more apt way to describe the largely invisible group of which I found myself to be a part. Voices flow in a longhouse in a most extraordinary fashion; moving up and down its length in seeming monologue, they are in fact in continual dialogue with listeners who may be unseen, but are always present. As such they create, more than does any other facet of longhouse life, a sense of community. Through the sounds of their voices neighbours two, three, four or five apartments apart are tied into each other's world, into each other's company, as intimately as if they were in the same room.

During my first two months in the longhouse, sharing the apartment of a Dayak household, I could not understand why my hostess was constantly engaged in talk with no one. She would give long descriptions of things that had happened to her during the day, of work she had to do, of the state of her feelings and so on, all the while standing or working alone in her longhouse apartment. To a Westerner, used to the idea that one's home stops at its walls, and that interaction beyond these involves a projection of the voice or of the self, which makes impossible the continuation of normal domestic chores, her behaviour seemed eccentric, to say the least. It was only much later, on my second field trip, that I came to realize that the woman's apparent monologues always had an audience, and that they were a way of affirming and recreating the ties across apartments that made her a part of the longhouse as a whole rather than a member of an isolated household. In addition, I recognized with time that she was almost certainly responding to questions floating across apartment partitions that I, still bewildered and overwhelmed by the cacophony of sound that characterizes longhouse life, was unable to distinguish.

Eventually I too came to be able to separate out the distant strands that were individual voices, which wove together magically in the air and flowed through the spaces of separate apartments. These were never raised as the dialogue moved through four or even five partitions, but their very muteness reinforced the sense of intimacy, of membership in a private, privileged world. Such conversations were to be taken up at will and put down again according to the demands of work or sleepiness: never forced, never demanding participation, but always gentle, generous in their reminder of a companionship constantly at hand. For me, even in memory they remain utterly compelling: the one aspect of longhouse life that distinguishes it most clearly from the Western world to which I have since returned.

Not only sound but light as well flows from one apartment to another — particularly at night, when the longhouse is demarcated against the surrounding blackness by the tiny lights glowing up and down its length. In explaining why they sow the seeds of a plant bearing red flowers along with their rice seed, Gerai Dayaks told me that once in bloom, the flowers serve as 'lights' or 'fires' for the growing rice: 'Just as human beings in the longhouse at night like to see many lights around them and so know that they have many companions, in the same way the rice sees the flowers at night and does not feel lonely'.[10] At night in the longhouse one is aware of the presence of companions by the glow of their lights and their hearths. If a light is not showing in any apartment, its absence is an immediate source of concern and investigation. On at least three occasions when I developed a fever in the late afternoon, and by evening was too ill to get off my mat and light my lamp, it was the darkness in my apartment that brought people anxiously to my aid. 'Why is your apartment in darkness, Tin?' was always the first query, to be taken up immediately in the conversation flowing to further parts of the longhouse. If there was no reply, within seconds neighbours would be pushing open the door.

While the *lawang* partitions may demarcate space within which particular household rights hold sway then, that space is also a crucial element in a larger community space within and across which sound and light must be able to move. For it is this movement which constantly reaffirms to both the household itself, and to those on either side of it, its status as a part of the longhouse, and thereby of the community of neighbours that is enclosed within it. Gerai people themselves are perfectly well aware of the significance of the flimsiness of this wall for cross-apartment relationships. As a result, my attempts, in the early days of residence in my own apartment, to create for myself more privacy by filling in some of the gaps in my side walls with strategically-placed pieces of cardboard and bark, were viewed with extreme disapproval by my neighbours.

They interpreted such behaviour as an assertion of independence at the expense of community membership. In response they so frequently 'accidentally' knocked askew my assorted pieces of filler that I eventually resigned myself to living with the holes.

While I have concentrated here on the phenomenological aspects of cross-*lawang* relationships in Gerai, the character of a *lawang*, as subject to community rights, is also asserted explicitly within Gerai customary law. I shall elaborate on this with respect to two of the obligations that owners of apartments have to the wider longhouse community. Firstly, a representative of the household must light a fire in the apartment hearth every five or six days. Gerai Dayaks are adamant that not lighting a fire with such regularity is a crime against one's neighbours rather than against the spirit world. For this reason, they say, such a lapse is not punished by the supernatural, but in the past demanded litigation against the head of the household. Such litigation would normally be carried out by those neighbours whose apartments adjoined that of the delinquent, and the largest share of any ensuing fine would be paid to them. Gerai people told me in 1986 that nowadays neighbours are reluctant to sue one another on such grounds, yet I noted that this obligation is still strictly adhered to by longhouse members. The requirement to light a fire in the hearth every few days is quite explicitly to do with the need for the all important *api* (light, fire) in an apartment. A dark unlit apartment creates an uncomfortable fission in the smooth flow of communality from one end of the longhouse to the other. An apartment without light, without fire, is most essentially an apartment without human beings; it is this lack which dismays the members of neighbouring apartments. The dark empty space to right or left detracts from their sense of belonging to a larger community — from their sense of being a part of the 'we in here' as opposed to the 'that out there'. Those households which stay at their farm huts for extended periods, while they prepare their rice fields for planting or weed the growing crop, are spoken of with passion as *jat* (bad, wicked): 'They don't care about their neighbours, they just want to live alone at their rice fields'. Significantly, when a household does decide to move as a whole to live at its farm hut for a time, it asks one of its two neighbouring households, rather than a household related by kinship, to take on the task of lighting a fire in the hearth every six days. Longhouse neighbours, then, assume the crucial responsibility for one another's continuing *de facto* presence in the community during any absence. The necessity to maintain this presence is a central tenet of longhouse life.

Secondly, the members of a household must demonstrate their love and respect for their apartment by taking care of it. In the recent past, if they failed in this undertaking, it was again the neighbouring households which sought compensation for the neglect of the apartment adjoining their own. Still today, any signs that an apartment is not being cared for (such as holes in the roof or floor) are cause for community gossip and for shame on the part of its inhabitants. Gerai people say that an apartment that is *buro'* (meaning literally 'rotten', but in this case 'falling apart, run down') is essentially an apartment without people. Its presence, therefore, constitutes a denial of the rights of neighbours to live next to an apartment that is inhabited.

In summary, the space delimited by the *lawang* construction in Gerai is not 'private' space, radically separated from the similar spaces beyond its partitions in the way that the space within an English semi-detached house would normally be. The Gerai longhouse is built in a style that both asserts the autonomous status of each of the individual households holding formal rights over the separate apartments of which it is composed, and generates the embeddedness of those groups in the broader longhouse community. The very construction of a longhouse apartment, and the way it articulates with those on either side of it, both encodes and, indeed, generates relationships of interdependence between the separate households that together comprise the Gerai longhouse community: '*Biarpun banyak lawang, pokok-e sebetang ja*'. ('Although there are many apartments, basically there is only one trunk').

Lawang Behaviour: Public or Private?

Not merely resources, light and sound are shared across the permeable boundaries between Gerai longhouse apartments. The human gaze also passes through that wall, and thus *lawang* structure both encodes and gives rise to a particular form of social control.[11]

Socially acceptable forms of behaviour may be enforced within any *lawang* in Gerai by means of a sliding scale of sanctions, ranging from community disapproval to the imposition of fines. In particular, each household is ritually linked through its hearth to a 'parental' household known as its *bungkung* (root, origin). The head of a *bungkung* apartment is morally, and in some cases legally, responsible for what takes place in such affiliated apartments. In cases of seriously unacceptable behaviour — such as the maltreatment of a child — he will intervene in the affairs of the household and demand a change in behaviour. If his advice is ignored, he may be compelled to take legal action against the offender(s).

But the monitoring of behaviour which might lead to the application of such sanctions is made possible by the very permeability of the barriers separating apartments. The fact that the *lawang* is so open to the scrutiny of neighbours places those inhabiting it under much greater pressure to conform than would be the case if *lawang* were truly 'private' areas. For example, Gerai values place enormous emphasis on the importance of sharing between households, such that when any household obtains a relative abundance of a resource — and particularly of food resources other than rice — it is expected to share it out among neighbours and close kin. Thus, a longhouse resident who hears her neighbour return from a hunting trip or from checking fish traps, from gathering fruit or collecting vegetables, moves to the partition, and, with a greater or lesser degree of surreptitiousness (depending on the nature of the relationship between herself and her neighbour), examines the booty that has been brought in. Concomitantly, at any time that she herself arrives home with (or without) game, fish, vegetables and so on, she knows that the neighbour's gaze will be upon her.

In the Anglo-American anthropological writings on Dayak societies there is little information on the means by which social norms may be affirmed and social control asserted over deviant individuals, or on the role played by longhouse apartment structure in this process. As a result, Dayaks have sometimes been portrayed in this literature as rather wayward and contrary, specific individuals concurring with social norms only when the whim takes them, and only if it is in their own best interests to do so (see, for example, Geddes 1957:20–26). A consideration of the gaze as a technique ensuring the functioning of social control in Gerai is instructive in this regard, for Gerai Dayaks would appear to be as individualistic and even as 'anarchistic'[12] as any others in the ethnographic region.

Knowledge of the gaze of others among Gerai longhouse members is a powerful force for conformity. In the case of the Gerai person who returns to the longhouse with a plentiful haul of meat, fish, vegetables, or whatever, awareness of being under observation is generally enough to persuade him/her to resist any temptation to miserliness, and instead to share out the goods. In not sharing, such a person would risk the networks by which he/she receives as well as gives, for neighbours will quickly tell others of his/her lack of generosity. Not to share is also to risk general opprobrium and the *jat nar* (very bad, wicked) label: an unpleasant prospect in such a small community.

There are of course households in Gerai — and increasingly more of them today, with the growing importance of a cash economy — which are prepared to take these risks in order to retain a greater portion of whatever resources they may obtain for their own use. However, it is important to note that these people inevitably move out of the longhouse and build independent free-standing dwellings. Due to the very structure of the longhouse with its highly permeable boundaries between separate *lawang*, longhouse living becomes incompatible with a reluctance to share resources.

But the gaze of neighbours is able to focus not only on the ways in which a household is dividing up its resources, but also on the more general actions and behaviours of apartment inhabitants. Just as goods, light and sound flow freely back and forth so, too, do advice, opinions, soothing words. I was once in a friend's apartment several doors down the longhouse from my own, when a heated argument between husband and wife broke out in the apartment next door. My friend immediately moved to the partition, arriving in time (as she told me later) to see the husband, squatting on the floor in the eating section, kick out and strike his wife on the leg. 'What's going on?' my friend enquired, while the wife burst noisily into tears. The husband explained that in the heat of argument his wife had snatched the plate that he was eating from and emptied its contents through the bamboo-slatted floor. He had kicked her in response. My friend, assured that one wrong had balanced another and that no major row was about to break out, returned to sit next to me. Her presence had calmed the situation and prevented any escalation of events.

The behaviour that takes place within any particular Gerai *lawang*, then, is subject to an extraordinary degree of interference by the wider longhouse community. This is mainly through the presence of the gaze, which acts as both a surveillance technique, by means of which information may be gathered, and an enforcer of conformity in its own right through people's awareness of their visibility. Just as the knowledge that others may be watching at any moment makes it almost certain that households will share their resources with one another according to social norms so, too, does it ensure that most of the time the members of any particular *lawang* behave towards one another in ways that are generally considered acceptable. The construction of the *lawang* itself, far from mirroring any household's wish for independence, actively promotes community interference into, and control over, the lives of household members. The wish to escape community pressure was the main reason given to me for their impending move by a number of younger couples, who intended to build free-standing dwellings, and so leave the longhouse. In addition, the two households at the very ends of the longhouse (one at each end) in which I lived in 1985 and 1986 were far more reluctant to share with neighbours and to take part in general forms of sociability than any other groups resident in that longhouse. Because they each adjoined only *one* apartment, their activities were much less open to scrutiny, and hence much less amenable to community pressure than were those of other households.

Yet, it must be stressed that a recognition of the community's ability to enforce certain types of behaviour within any particular *lawang* space does not constitute a denial of the rights over that space held by members of the household themselves. In particular, the household has rights over use of the *lawang* space: in the absence of any household members, only very close and trusted friends or kin may enter that space. Even these people should enter under such circumstances only for a very specific purpose, such as to borrow a utensil. More prolonged visits to an empty *lawang*, or visits by those who are socially more distant, may lead to accusations of intention to steal or, worse, of intention to introduce malevolent spirits into the hearth. Disappearance of household items or illness of a group member following such a visit may well lead to litigation.

In addition, apartment inhabitants who spend a great deal of time examining the goings-on in neighbouring apartments are said themselves to be *jat* (wicked, bad), and a variety of motives may be attributed to their actions in this respect: ranging from the wish to steal goods to the intention of bewitching or poisoning their neighbours. Ironically, it is the constant possibility of surveillance that keeps in check excessive use of such a technique. There is in fact a code of etiquette operating in Gerai, which any person should follow when gazing into a neighbouring apartment. This specifies intention (the reasons why one is looking at that particular moment) and notification (the act of indicating to one's neighbour that he or she is under observation) as the two most important factors in distinguishing 'when and how one should look' from 'when and how one should not look'. One may peer or glance casually for just a moment, as already outlined, but if the gaze is of longer duration, its social approvability will be assessed in accordance with these two factors. One may never stand and stare into an apartment whose inhabitants are sleeping or not present, for instance, since the gaze lacks the element of notification. Similarly, it is said that one should never stand and watch a neighbour's misfortune, such as a household fight or a person's grief, unless one has sincere, good intentions in doing so. Apartment inhabitants have rights to privacy within their own *lawang*, then, even while that space constitutes part of a broader community space.

It is precisely because of the constant affirmation of its status as community space — its very openness to the public voice and gaze — that the *lawang* of an apartment is almost the only place in the village where one may be alone without inviting suspicion and public discussion of one's motives and actions. Gerai people in general dislike being alone, and rarely see a point to it. Thus it is well-nigh impossible to be alone in open parts of the village. A lone person sitting working in the *sawah* section of the longhouse, for instance, will soon attract others to his or her side, whose arrival might well be prefaced with 'You poor thing — sitting there all alone!'. In the same way, someone who needs to carry out a task away from the village will normally seek a companion, and the sight of a lone person in the jungle thus attracts attention and questions. In particular, a married woman headed alone into the jungle, even if she has a perfectly legitimate task to perform such as foraging for bamboo shoots or collecting firewood, automatically invites suspicions about her possible engagement in an adulterous liaison (the jungle being the usual location for such liaisons). If a man is seen in the area, they may both be subject to litigation. In a longhouse apartment *lawang*, on the other hand, it is possible, easily and naturally, to be alone — simply because one is recognized as never being alone.

The relaxed openness of a *lawang* to a neighbour's eyes and ears means that only extraordinary behaviour inside it makes a deep impression on those without. Otherwise the presence of its inhabitants is largely taken for granted: they are part of the background audience which always surrounds one while in a longhouse. Glancing into a *lawang*, unless done for a specific purpose, such as inspecting a newly-arrived load of foodstuffs, involves nothing more than a casual orientating of oneself *vis-à-vis* the members of that other household. As such it does not impinge on the rights of those others over that space. For my own part, I found that my longhouse neighbours were highly sensitive to my own needs for 'privacy', so long as they were able to locate my presence in the apartment from time to time.

It is this recognition of the individual apartment as inevitably a part of the larger community — such that it is impossible to discuss it in terms of the 'public' and 'private' realms found in our own streets of separate houses — which renders problematic any attempt to depict the Gerai longhouse either as an aggregate of separate dwellings or as a unified community. Residence in a longhouse means that one can belong to both household and community at once, or to either at different times. This is why it is possible to be alone in an apartment through the very act of not being alone.[13]

Concluding Remarks

For the Dayaks of Gerai, as for most Dayak groups, household autonomy is a central cultural value, and there is no doubt that in Gerai (as elsewhere) certain features of longhouse structure are linked to this fact. Yet, examination of the spatial arrangements within the Gerai longhouse does not support a view of the Gerai household as an isolated and inward-turning entity. Rather, it indicates its embeddedness in the larger longhouse community of which it is a part. Emphasis on the apartment's orientation widthwise as part of a single longhouse structure should not be taken as a denial of its lengthwise identity as a separate unit within that structure. The apartment is both of these at the same time, just as its member household is both autonomous and yet highly dependent on the longhouse community of neighbours. Freeman's (1970:129) implication that the Iban longhouse must be viewed as either (but not both) a collection of discrete entities or as unified longhouse group assumes a series of conceptual dichotomies — between 'self' and 'other', 'private' and 'public' and so on — which do not fit comfortably with the Gerai notion of the interdependence of person, household and community. Indeed, these conceptual oppositions look dangerously similar to those generated within Western thought by opposition between person and society.

It is at least possible, that the Gerai longhouse is not unique in this respect. It seems likely that the inordinate emphasis on the priority of household within the literature on Dayak societies is the result of an understandable preoccupation among an earlier generation of ethnographers with questions concerning the capacity of Dayak forms of social organization to generate stable and enduring social relations (cf. Appell 1976:4-6). Freeman's inspired demonstration of the role of the Iban household in this respect, established once and for all the credentials of cognatic societies as no less viable than their unilineal counterparts. But at the same time it bequeathed to the anthropology of Dayak societies both an underemphasis on the importance of wider community groupings and a discourse in which jural considerations hold sway at the expense of how institutions are lived and experienced.

The Gerai longhouse division into *lawang* and *sawah*, and the nature of the relationships between separate *lawang* spaces, only becomes comprehensible when viewed in the context of the permeability of the boundaries separating a *lawang* from those on either side. Such interstitial zones are as important to an understanding of the nature of domestic space as is the actual inner arrangement of that space. The American poet Robert Frost implicitly recognized this point when he asserted that in his own American rural community 'good fences make good neighbours'.[14] In this respect many Western domiciliary arrangements contrast sharply with those found in the Gerai longhouse. There it is not the walls which make good neighbours, but the gaps and tears that occur within them. It is these that allow an easy flow of communality along the length of the longhouse. In this flow lies both the threat of community disapproval and sanctions and the promise of resources and companionship but a spoken word away.

References

Appell, G.N.

1976   Introduction. In G.N. Appell (ed.) *The societies of Borneo: explorations in the theory of cognatic social structure*, pp.1–15. Washington: American Anthropological Association.

1978   The Rungus Dusun. In Victor T. King (ed.) *Essays on Borneo society*, pp.143–171. Oxford: Oxford University Press for the University of Hull.

Avé, J.B.

1972   Kalimantan Dayaks — introductory statement. In Frank Lebar (ed.) *Ethnic groups of insular Southeast Asia*, Vol. 1, pp.185–187. New Haven: Human Relations Area Files Press.

Bourdieu, Pierre

1977   *Outline of a theory of practice*. Cambridge: Cambridge University Press.

Freeman, J.D.

1958   The family system of the Iban of Borneo. In Jack Goody (ed.) *The developmental cycle in domestic groups*, pp.15–52. Cambridge: Cambridge University Press for Department of Archæology and Anthropology, Cambridge University.

1970   *Report on the Iban*. London: Athlone Press.

Geddes, W.R.

1957   *Nine Dayak nights*. Melbourne: Oxford University Press.

Harrison, Robert

1976   Hamlet organization and its relationship to productivity in the swidden-rice communities of Ranau, Sabah, Malaysia. In G.N. Appell (ed.) *The societies of Borneo: explorations in the theory of cognatic social structure*, pp.87–109. Washington: American Anthropological Association.

Helliwell, Christine

1990   The ricefield and the hearth. PhD thesis, The Australian National University, Canberra.

1991   Many voices: rhetoric and ethnographic understanding in a Borneo Dayak community. In Andrew Pawley (ed.) *Man and a half: essays in Pacific anthropology and ethnobiology in honour of Ralph Bulmer*, pp.241–248. Auckland: The Polynesian Society.

Hudson, A.B.

1970   A note on Selako: Malayic Dayak and Land Dayak languages in Western Borneo. *Sarawak Museum Journal* 28:301–318.

King, Victor T. (ed.)

1978   Introduction. In Victor T. King (ed.) *Essays on Borneo societies*, pp.1–36. Oxford: Oxford University Press for the University of Hull.

1979   *Ethnic classification and ethnic relations: a Borneo case study*. Hull: Centre for South-East Asian Studies, University of Hull (Occasional Papers No. 2).

Lebar, Frank M. (ed.)

1972   *Ethnic groups of insular Southeast Asia*, Vol. 1. New Haven: Human Relations Area Files Press.

Mauss, Marcel with Henri Beuchat

1979   *Seasonal variations of the Eskimo: a study in social morphology* (translated with forward by James J. Fox). London: Routledge & Kegan Paul.

Miles, Douglas

1976   *Cutlass and crescent moon: a case study of social and political change in Outer Indonesia*. Sydney: Centre for Asian Studies, University of Sydney.

Sather, Clifford

1976   Kinship and contiguity: variation in social alignments among the Semporna Bajau Laut. In G.N. Appell (ed.) *The societies of Borneo: explorations in the theory of cognatic social structure*, pp.40–65. Washington: American Anthropological Association.

1978   The Bajau Laut. In Victor T. King (ed.) *Essays on Borneo society*, pp.172–192. Oxford: Oxford University Press for the University of Hull.

Notes

This paper was originally presented in October 1987 as part of a seminar series on concepts of space in Asia held in the Department of Prehistory and Anthropology at The Australian National University. I wish to register my gratitude to Douglas Miles (who organized that series) for persuading me to participate in it. The written version has been read by many people: thanks to, in particular James J. Fox, Barry Hindess, Douglas Miles, Nicholas Thomas and Michael Young for their careful scrutiny and comments. I also wish to thank Michael Jackson for his initial suggestion of several fruitful lines of enquiry which are taken up here. This paper is also published in *Oceania* 62, 1992 and is reproduced here with permission.

[1] Some accounts of Dayak societies have emphasized the embeddedness of the household in wider social groupings, but they are unusual. See especially Sather (1976, 1978) on the 'household cluster' among the Bajau Laut; Harrison (1976) on the 'hamlet' among the Dusun of Ranau; and Appell (1978) on, particularly, the longhouse among the Rungus Dusun.

[2] Following Hudson (1970), I would classify Gerai Dayaks (who neither distinguish themselves by any ethnic name nor affiliate themselves with any Dayak group) as a 'Malayic Dayak' people, descending from Proto-Malay-speaking ancestors who crossed to Borneo before Islam reached South-East Asia. This categorizes them linguistically with the Iban and other Ibanic-speaking peoples, although many aspects of their social organization and culture are more strongly reminiscent of the 'anarchist' and diffident Land Dayak traditionally thought to have inhabited this entire region (see, for example, Avé (1972:186); also Lebar's (1972) unpaginated map of the ethnic groups of Borneo).

Fieldwork in Kalimantan Barat was carried out between March 1985 and February 1986, and between June 1986 and January 1987. It was funded by a PhD research scholarship from The Australian National University.

[3] Several men in the community now own chainsaws.

[4] Eight households cluster into two tiny extra-village hamlets, while a further seven live in ramshackle huts at their rice fields.

[5] I must make it clear that I am not arguing in favour of a Lévy-Bruhlian (for instance) depiction of 'primitive societies' as lacking individuals: individual consciousness having been swamped by a larger social consciousness completely dictating thought and action. Such a view comes out of a Western dichotomization of individual and community that does not occur in Gerai.

[6] Among anthropologists the problem of distinguishing between the ethnic identities of Dayaks and Malays has often been seen as a very complex one, since Dayak groups which adopt Islam and form separate communities after their conversion generally are known as Malays, even though they may live as part of Dayak communities with pagan Dayaks and share many of their traditions and practices (see Avé (1972: 185); King (1979:28–34); also Miles (1976)). The Dayaks of Gerai do not share the anthropologist's difficulty here: the adoption of Islam, and particularly of the taboos on eating pork and drinking alcohol that accompanies it, means that one has 'become Malay'.

[7] Although, if pressed, they will of course distinguish between Malays, Chinese, Dutch and so on.

[8] Appell is an exception. His 1978 article stresses the linkages existing *along* a longhouse and states that the longhouse is not considered 'merely an aggregate of member families' (1978:160).

[9] Mauss (1979) was perhaps the first to engage in such an analysis with his classic study of Eskimo dwellings. More recently Bourdieu's (1977) scintillating analysis of Kabyle domestic arrangements has

demonstrated the power of such arrangements to mediate between core cultural schema and social practice.

[10] Gerai Dayaks believe that rice shares a descent line with human beings. Because of this it must be treated as if it were human, and so a number of features of the layout of a rice field parallel human life within a longhouse.

[11] Douglas Miles has pointed out that the movement of the gaze is linked to the flow of light already described.

[12] Geddes uses the term 'anarchist' to refer to the Bidayuh Land Dayak (for example, 1957:20, 21).

[13] Geddes (1957) notes that longhouse residence has 'solved a great human problem — how to be independent and yet never be isolated ... In the longhouse it is possible to be an individual and yet lead a cosy life of company' (p.32).

[14] In one of his most well-known poems, entitled 'Mending Wall'.

The *ruai*, or communal area of the Iban longhouse.

Chapter 4. Posts, Hearths and Thresholds: The Iban Longhouse as a Ritual Structure

Clifford Sather

Social and symbolic features of the Iban longhouse have been extensively described (see Freeman 1960, 1970). These descriptions, however, have consistently given priority to the longhouse as a built form. In this paper I begin by taking a very different approach, viewing the Iban longhouse, in the first instance, as a ritually constituted structure.

Ritual is described by the Iban in what are largely dramaturgical terms. Ritual is thus 'enacted' (*nunda*) or 'played' (*main*) upon a stage; it is performed, that is to say, within a symbolically ordered setting. For the Iban, the longhouse is the pre-eminent setting in which the great majority of rituals are performed. In the course of these performances, architectural and spatial features of the longhouse are assigned signification as elements constituting a dramatic idiom that reflects on aspects of both the visible world and alternative, unseen realities. This process not only makes explicit the basic social and cosmological categories that structure Iban experience, but also evokes the interconnections that exist between them.

In this paper, I briefly consider two major forms of ritual. The first of these consists of rites that centre on the longhouse itself. Included here are rites that accompany house construction and those that establish and preserve the longhouse as a ritual community. The second form of rituals marks major transitions in the human life trajectory. Here, I look specifically at rites of birth and death, showing how each is enacted as a 'journey' (*jalai*) through the longhouse, its itinerary mapping the major contours of the Iban social and cosmological world.

Two points emerge from looking at the longhouse through a ritual lens. The first is that the longhouse represents a plurality of symbolic orders, not simply a single order 'fixed' in the physical structure of the house itself. These orders are not only multiple, but are also alterable, even at times reversible, and are constantly created and re-created in the course of rituals. Second, the representation of the longhouse that emerges from ritual is very different from that which is conveyed by the existing ethnographic literature. In the latter, the longhouse and its constituent *bilik*-families are generally represented as independent, essentially autonomous entities. By contrast, ritual locates these groups, as do the Iban themselves, in an ordered series of part— whole relationships. Here, by focusing on ritual, I hope to reveal a more indigenously based perception of the longhouse and correct the pervasive bias favouring physicality that has tended, in the Bornean ethnography, to colour our understanding of longhouse sociality and symbolism.

The Iban Longhouse

The Iban are a vigorous, outwardly expansive people of West-Central Borneo who number some 400000 in the east Malaysian State of Sarawak. Despite increasing urban migration, the great majority live in longhouse settlements along the main rivers and smaller streams of the interior and subcoastal districts. Here most subsist by shifting hill-rice agriculture, supplemented by the cultivation of perennial cash crops, most notably rubber. All speak closely related dialects of a single Ibanic language, part of a larger complex of Bornean Malayic languages (see Adelaar 1985:1–5; Hudson 1970, 1977).[1] The Iban are divided internally into a number of major riverine groupings. Referred to as 'tribes' in the nineteenth century literature, each of these groupings comprises a loose territorial unit made up of longhouse communities arrayed along the same river or tributary system. The organization of Iban society is bilateral. Descent groups are lacking and marriage is preferentially endogamous within widely ramifying kindred networks. These networks characteristically extend throughout the river region and provide the organizational basis for a variety of individually organized, task-oriented groups (see Freeman 1960, 1961).

The present paper specifically deals with the Saribas Iban population that lives along the Paku River and its tributaries, between the Rimbas and upper Layar rivers, in the lower Second Division of Sarawak (Figure 1). Today, of a total Iban population of some 35000 in the Saribas, the Paku Iban number nearly 4000 and are divided between thirty-three longhouses, ranging in size from six to thirty-nine *bilik*-families, the mean number being 16.5 (see Sather 1978, 1985, 1988).

The longhouse (*rumah*) forms the principal local community (see Figure 2). In the Paku all longhouses are located along the banks of the main Paku River and its chief tributaries: the Bangkit, Anyut and Serudit streams. Structurally, each house consists of a series of family apartments arranged side by side. The same term *bilik* refers to both the longhouse apartment and the family group that occupies it. The *bilik*-family typically consists of three generations — grandparents, a son or daughter, his or her spouse and their children — with membership acquired by birth, marriage, incorporation or adoption (Freeman 1957). Fronting the *bilik*s is a covered, unpartitioned gallery called the *ruai*. This runs the entire length of the house and, while divided into family sections (each built and maintained by an individual *bilik* family) the whole is available for communal use. The wall that separates the *bilik*s from the *ruai* thus bisects the structure into two equal halves (Figure 3).

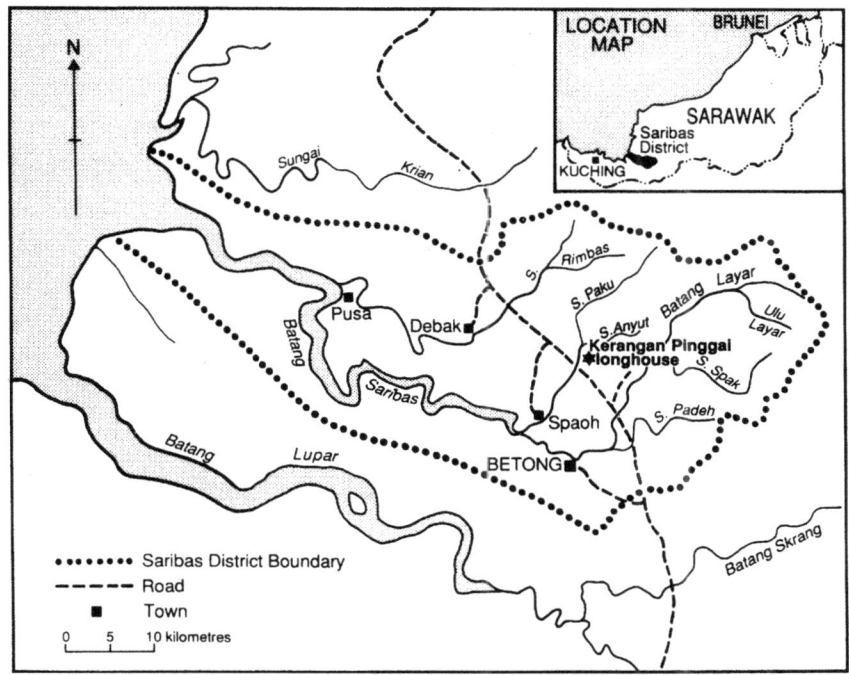

Figure 1. Saribas District

Figure 2. Danau longhouse, Ulu Paku

On one side of this wall, the *bilik* apartments represent each family's domestic space, symbolizing its existence as a discrete corporate group, while the unpartitioned gallery on the other side is a public space, symbolizing the longhouse as a whole and its membership in the larger riverine society that encompasses it.

Sources and Elders

Every Iban longhouse is identified, in the first instance, with a *menoa rumah*, or territorial domain.[2] Here, within this territory, individual *bilik*- families clear their annual farms, grow rice and other food crops, and observe a common body of normative rules (*adat*) and ritual interdictions (*pemali*) which are enforced by the longhouse and express its status as the jural and ritual centre of its domain. The continued existence of the longhouse is thought to depend upon its members behaving as these rules and interdictions require (Heppell 1975:303–304; Sather 1980:xxviii-xxxi). Thus breaches of *adat* and disturbances of the ritual order are said to render a longhouse 'hot' (*angat*), leaving its inhabitants open to infertility, sickness, death and other calamities.

Until the imposition of Brooke rule,[3] beginning in the second half of the nineteenth century, 'elders' (*tuai*) were acknowledged at the level of both the longhouse and the wider river region. Regional leaders, called *tuai menoa*, were drawn mainly from the *raja berani*, literally the 'rich and brave', and were self-made men with a reputation for military prowess, resourcefulness and judgment; they acted primarily as peacekeepers, go-betweens and charismatic war chiefs (*tau' serang* or *tau' kayau*), mobilizing regional followings for raiding and the territorial defence of the river. With Brooke rule, this former pattern of competitive regional leadership was superseded by the creation of formal administrative districts under officially appointed Penghulu, or 'native chiefs', and today the Penghulu act, together with the longhouse headmen, as the principal intermediaries between the local community and the state (see Freeman 1981:15–24; Sather 1980:xiv-xxviii, n.d.).

Responsibility for safeguarding the normative order that, for the Iban, centres in each longhouse domain, rests chiefly with the longhouse headman (*tuai rumah*) and other community elders (*tuai*). The most important of the latter are the *tuai bilik* (family heads). Thus, in matters of *adat*, longhouse and *bilik* elders are said to have 'authority' (*kuasa*) over or 'to speak for' (*jakoka*) other longhouse or apartment residents.

Complementing the role of the *tuai* (elders) in matters of *adat* is the role of the *pun* (sources) in matters of ritual and the custodianship of group sacra. When a longhouse is first built, its 'longhouse source' (*pun rumah*) supervises the rites of house construction. In doing so, he confirms his status as caretaker of its central 'source post' (*tiang pemun*). This post centres the house both ritually and in terms of the internal orientation of its parts. Every longhouse is believed to be susceptible to the intrusion of malevolent spirits and other injurious forces, and to disruptions of its ritual order from within. The task of the *pun rumah* as custodian of the 'source post' and its associated sacra, is to ward off these dangers and, should its ritual well-being be threatened, to perform rites of 'cooling' (*penyelap*) on behalf of the community as a whole, by which the longhouse and its domain are restored to a 'cool' (*chelap*) or benign state.[4]

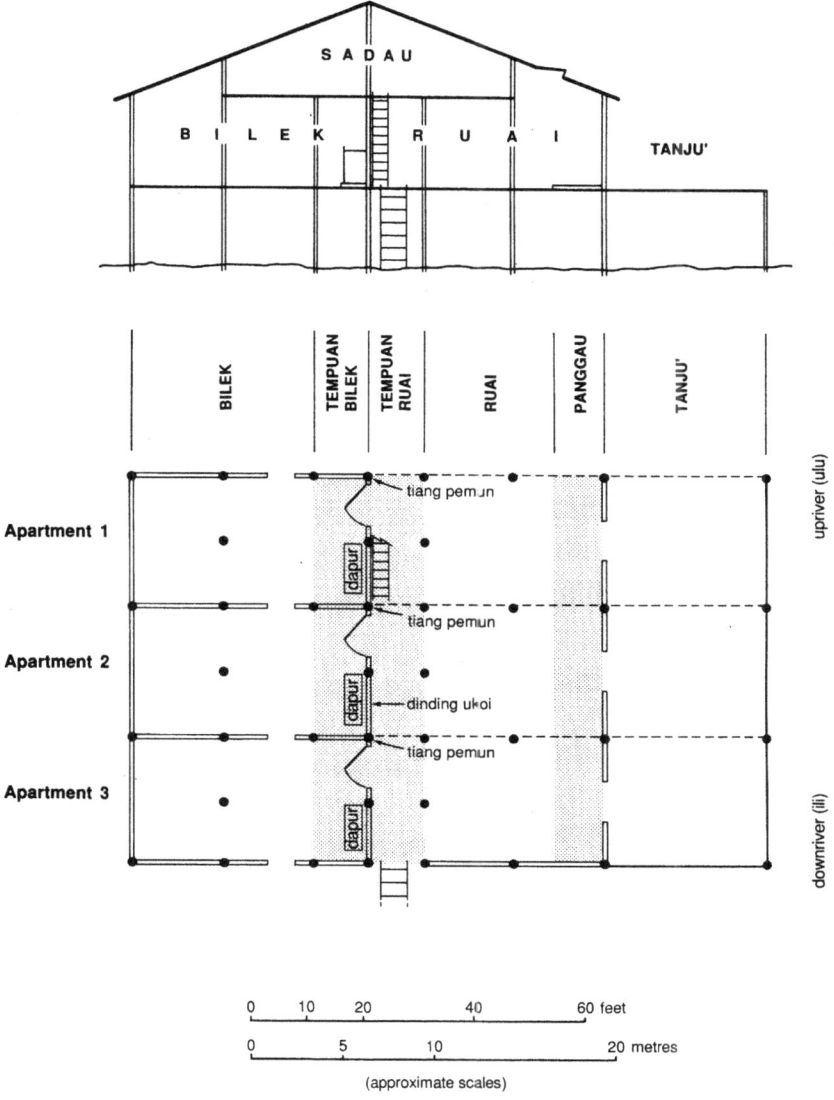

Figure 3. Longhouse section and plan

Each family, too, has a 'source' (*pun bilik*). The *pun bilik*, or family source, is the custodian of the *bilik*'s heritable estate, including ritual sacra that symbolize the continuing life of the family, notably its ritual whetstones (*batu umai*) and sacred strains of rice (*padi pun* and *padi sangking*). The family is ideally an enduring group and the *pun bilik* personifies its continuity (*tampong*). As the senior-most family member and the principal heir through whom family wealth and sacra are transmitted, the *pun bilik* represents the family's living ancestor, the chief link between its present and past generations and the source through whom all family rights devolve.

Hearths and Posts

Every *bilik* apartment contains, at its front upriver corner, a *tiang pemun*, literally a 'source, foundation post' (Figure 3). These posts or pillars are the first to be erected during house construction and, when the longhouse is completed, extend down its central axis to separate the *bilik* apartments from the unpartitioned gallery. Each family's *tiang pemun* is under the care of its *pun bilik* (family source).

However, there is also a central *tiang pemun* which, together with its caretaker, the *pun rumah*, takes ritual priority over all the others. This central *tiang pemun* is the first post to be raised during house construction and is not only the 'source post' of the *pun rumah*'s *bilik*, but represents the primary 'foundation pillar' for the longhouse as a whole. It is through the rites of 'fixing' (*ngentak*) this post that the longhouse is established as the ritual centre of its domain and the *pun rumah* is confirmed as its living 'source'.

As custodian of the central *tiang pemun*, the *pun rumah* is said to 'own' (*empu*) the *adat genselan*, the ritual rules and offerings associated with the post. These rules preserve the longhouse in a state of ritual well-being and include procedures, such as sacrifice and blood lustration (*enselan*) meant to repair disturbances of its ritual harmony, performed particularly at the central *tiang pemun*, but also at other parts of the longhouse, especially at its entry ladders and the *tempuan* passageway. The *pun rumah* is also entitled to collect fines (*tunggu*) from those whose actions break ritual interdictions or in other ways endanger the community's state of ritual well-being. Thus, for example, if a longhouse member dies while outside the house, before his or her body — now a source of 'heat' — can be carried inside, the members of the bereaved family must first sacrifice a pig (or two chickens). This is done under the direction of the *pun rumah* at the base of the longhouse entry ladder (*kaki tangga' rumah*). The *pun rumah* then lustrates the *tiang pemun* with the blood, which is also smeared on the earth at the foot of the house ladder, and on the bottoms of the feet of those who carry the body into the house. In addition, the family must pay a *genselan* fine to the *pun rumah*. Many other acts such as adultery, quarrelling, cursing, threatening others (*nyakat*) or drawing a weapon in anger, when committed inside the longhouse, require sacrifice, offerings and the blood lustration of the central *tiang pemun*. Among the most important of these *genselan* rules, however, are those which sanction the *adat dapur* (family hearth rules). These rules unite the longhouse ritually and preserve its family hearths, in contrast to the *tiang pemuns*, in an antithetical state of 'heatedness' (*angat*).

The ritual priority of the central *tiang pemun* is thus established at the start of house construction. The rites that initiate construction are called *ngentak rumah*, literally 'to fix' or 'drive in the longhouse'.[5] During *ngentak rumah* the main *tiang pemuns* are 'driven into' (*ngentak*) the earth. This is the sole 'work' (*pengawa'*) undertaken during *ngentak rumah* and is performed by a ceremonial work party comprising longhouse men and male guests from neighbouring longhouse. The work is overseen by the *pun rumah* whose central *tiang pemun* is the first post to be 'driven in'. It is also the main focus of the *ngentak* rites.

Ngentak rumah begins with the ritual bathing (*mandi'*) of the central *tiang pemun* by a group of senior women. This act closely parallels the ritual bathing of a new-born infant to mark its entry into the longhouse community (Sather 1988). Bathing is said to 'cool' the post. Later, to mark the completion of house construction, the entire structure is ritually 'bathed' (*mandi' rumah*). After the central *tiang pemun* has been bathed, it is scattered with popped rice, oiled and, beginning at its base, smeared with the blood of a chicken. The gods are then invoked, notably the gods of the earth, Simpulang Gana and Raja Samarugah, and the *antu dapur*, the tutelary hearth spirits. To affirm his ownership of the *adat genselan*, the *pun rumah* sacrifices a pig. Its blood and severed head, together with other ritual objects,[6] are placed in the hole into which the central *tiang pemun* is then driven. After this has been raised, the *tiang pemun* of each of the individual *biliks* is erected in sequential order, moving outward from the central *tiang pemun*, first downriver and then upriver, ending with the final *tiang pemun* at the upriver end of the house. For a small house, the entire ritual may be completed in one day. For a larger house, the first day is generally spent raising the downriver posts; the second day, the upriver posts.

As caretaker of the central *tiang pemun*, the *pun rumah* personifies the living ancestor of the longhouse, just as the *pun bilik* embodies the living ancestor of the *bilik*-family. Ideally the original *pun rumah* and his successors should be able to trace their genealogical connections to the pioneer founders of the community, also known as *pun*, who first cleared its domain of primary forest, through an unbroken line (or lines) of ascent. The *pun rumah*'s genealogy (*tusut*) should thus serve, ideally, as the main line or *batang tusut* ('trunk genealogy') by which other longhouse members trace their connections to the community's ancestors.[7]

While the relationship between the *pun rumah* and *pun bilik* is established through the ritual priority of the central *tiang pemun*, the relationship between the *tuai rumah* and *tuai bilik* is expressed most clearly in the ritual rules that surround the installation and use of the family hearths.

An Iban hearth (*dapur*) consists of an earth-filled firebox (*entilang*), supported in a frame (*para'*) whose posts extend through the house floor directly into the earth below. Above the hearth is a rack for storing and drying firewood and for keeping the family's salt stores (*telak garam*). Traditionally the hearth was constructed immediately behind the front wall of the *bilik*, inside an area of the family apartment called the *tempuan bilik* (Figure 3). (Today most hearths are built at the rear of the *bilik* in a separate cooking area.) Being of earth, the *dapur* is said to belong to Simpulang Gana, the Iban god of the earth. In Paku myths, Simpulang Gana acquired dominion over the earth by inheriting the *dapur* of his father Raja Jembu after the other gods, in his absence, had divided the family's magical sacra among themselves, leaving Simpulang Gana without a share except for the hearth (Harrisson and Sandin 1966:261–262; Sandin 1967a; Sather 1985:34). The hearth is also associated with the *antu dapur*, the tutelary hearth spirits. All of those who make use of the same hearth are said to come under the authority of the *tuai bilik*, including visitors and temporary guests residing in the family apartment. Within the longhouse, the hearths represent the principal link between the *bilik*-family and the longhouse's *menoa*. This link is signified by the earth from which the *dapur* is made and by the hierarchy of authority that extends as a result of its use from *bilik* elders, through the headman, to the god Simpulang Gana, the earth's 'owner'.

This hierarchy of authority is established in respect of the hearths through the rites of house construction. As soon as the new longhouse is completed a ceremonial 'moving in' (*pindah*) takes place. This is followed by the 'bathing of the house' (*mandi' rumah*) and, in the past at least, by a ritual 'striking of posts' (*gawai pangkong tiang*). The latter accompanies the setting in place of the ridge-capping (*perabong*) along the top of the longhouse roof. This capping 'completes' the structure. 'Moving in' precedes the 'striking of posts' and is initiated by a ritual installation of the family hearths. During *pindah* each family carries its possessions into the longhouse in a prescribed order, beginning with mats (*tikai*) and ending with trophy heads (*antu pala'*) and weaving-looms (*tumpoh*) (see Richards 1981:312). The entry of each family is in order of the precedence established during *ngentak rumah* when each family's *tiang pemun* was erected.[8] This order determines, in Iban terms, relative relations of 'who went first' (*orang ke-dulu*). Possessions are carried into the house by both the upriver and downriver entrances, so that ideally they are never carried past the central *tiang pemun* nor past one another in violation of their upriver–downriver order, that is to say, 'across', or 'in front of' (*meraka*) those who 'went first' (*ke-dulu*)[9] in erecting their 'source post'.

Before *pindah* begins, the members of each *bilik*-family collect earth (*tanah*) from the longhouse *menoa* and mix it with earth taken from the family's previous hearth to make the new *dapur*. At the start of *pindah*, the earthen firebox is carried into the longhouse and installed by the *tuai bilik* in the newly constructed hearth frame. After all families have installed their hearths, the first fire is lit by the *tuai rumah*.[10] The other families then take their first fires from the headman's *dapur*, thereby establishing the latter's priority.

The installation of the hearths binds the separate *bilik*-families together into a single ritual and *adat* community. From the time the hearths are installed in the house until the structure is dismantled and replaced by a new one, they must not be allowed to grow 'cold' (*chelap*). A 'cold' hearth signifies an unoccupied apartment, indicating, in turn, the family's withdrawal from the community (*neju' ka rumah*). To prevent the hearth from growing 'cold', a fire must be lit and rice cooked on the *dapur* at least twice each lunar month: at *anak bulan* (new moon) and *bulan pernama* (full moon). A 'standin' (*pengari*) may be employed to cook rice on the hearth not more than once each lunar cycle.[11] Should a family fail to keep its hearth 'warm', the family 'elder' must pay *adat genselan* and make offerings to the central *tiang pemun*. Observance of the hearth rules prevents the permanent dispersal of longhouse families and so keeps them from leaving the community without first paying compensation for the ritual damage their departure causes. Following the installation of its hearth, should a family subsequently break the ritual unity of the community by moving to another, its members must pay both *genselan* and *adat* fines. In addition they must also make offerings to the central *tiang pemun* and perform a ritual 'throwing away of the hearth' (*muai dapur*). This 'throwing away of the hearth' marks their formal withdrawal and restores the ritual solidarity of the remaining community. Only by maintaining a *bilik* hearth may a family exercise membership in the longhouse community and cultivate land within its *menoa*.

As a final ritual act, the community may perform a 'striking of the post' festival. Once house construction is completed, the *tiang pemuns*, as corner posts, are typically enclosed behind *bilik* walls, so that on public occasions their place is usually taken by the exposed pillar at the edge of the *tempuan* passageway between adjacent *biliks* (Figure 3). During the 'striking of the post' ritual, the base of each of these pillars is wrapped in *pua' kumbu'* cloth to form a series of *bilik* altar-places (*pandong*) around which the bards circle as they sing the *gawai* chants. At the pillar representing the central post, a man conceals himself inside the cloth enclosure. Here he speaks the part of the principal *tiang pemun* as the pillar is struck (*pangkong*) by a bamboo tube containing cooked rice, promising wealth and spiritual well-being to the members of the house. The festival thus highlights the ritual significance of the *tiang pemun* in safeguarding community well-being and the relation of precedence that exists between the central longhouse post and the individual source posts of each family.

Upriver, Downriver, Parts and Wholes

As riparian settlements, Iban longhouses are built along rivers and streams with their long axis ideally oriented parallel to the main river course. Consequently, the two ends of a longhouse are normally distinguished as the 'upriver' (*ulu*) and 'downriver' (*ili'*) ends.[12] This orientation, as well as the presence of a centralizing 'source', is basic and is evoked constantly in everyday speech. Thus the location of an individual's apartment is characteristically indicated by its position *vis-à-vis* the upriver or downriver end of the longhouse; that is, as being within its upriver or downriver 'half' (*sapiak*), at the head of one or the other of its entry ladders (*pala' tangga'*), or as so many *bilik*s from its upriver or downriver end.

The distinction between upriver and downriver functions, in particular, with respect to the location of the *pun rumah*'s *bilik*. During house construction, the *pun rumah* is expected to locate the door to his *bilik* apartment on the downriver side of the central *tiang pemun*.[13] Thus, the central *tiang pemun* serves as the corner post between the *pun rumah*'s *bilik* and the next *bilik* upriver. The *pun rumah* locates his *bilik* hearth on the downriver side of his door, while, on the downriver side of his hearth, the *tiang pemun* of his downriver neighbour similarly forms the corner post between his own and the latter's apartment (Figure 3). This orientation of *bilik* posts one to another thus identifies the *bilik*, in the first instance, as a constituent of the longhouse, with the central *tiang pemun* to which each *bilik* post is oriented representing the longhouse as the overriding totality.

The way the longhouse is constructed clearly represents this whole—part relationship between the longhouse and the *bilik*. During *ngentak rumah*, beginning with the raising of the central *tiang pemun*, the order in which the other *tiang pemun*'s representing particular *bilik*s are erected reflects the order of precedence existing among the *bilik*s themselves, moving outward in sequence — first downriver and then upriver — from the house's central post. Each family's *tiang pemun* is thus located at the upriver corner of its apartment, separated by a door and hearth from the *tiang pemun* of its downriver neighbour (Figure 3). Thus the *tiang pemun* is clearly a threshold marker. It is located at the juncture (*antara*) between individual *bilik*s and between the *bilik* and the gallery. The location of individual *bilik*s relative to one another, and by way of their common orientation to the central apartment of the *pun rumah*, clearly identifies the *bilik*, not as a free-standing entity, but as the component member of an encompassing whole.

This encompassment is marked in two other ways as well: firstly, by the side-walls that separate one apartment from another and secondly, by the rules of *adat genselan*. During house construction, only the *pun rumah* erects two side-walls, one on each side of his *bilik* apartment. All other *bilik*s erect only one side-wall, on either the upriver or downriver side of their apartment, depending on the *bilik*'s location relative to that of the *pun rumah*. Similarly, each apartment stands on three rows of posts: one central row and two side rows shared by neighbouring *bilik*s (Figure 3). Only the *pun rumah* erects all three rows; every other *bilik* erects only two, the central row and either an upriver or downriver row, depending, again, on its location relative to that of the *pun rumah*. Thus the longhouse shares a common orientational centre and is perceived as growing outwards laterally, or bilaterally, from each side of the *pun rumah*'s apartment. The lateral addition of *bilik* apartments to the longhouse, both during and after its initial construction, is referred to by the same term, *tampong*, as the generational succession of *bilik* members through time, with the *pun rumah* serving as the primary reference point in the first process of growth, the *pun bilik* in the second.

Finally, the *pun rumah*, by performing sacrifice during *ngentak rumah*, binds the longhouse together as a ritual community so that if a family should subsequently break this unity by withdrawing, its members must ritually remove their hearth, pay *genselan* and present offerings at the central *tiang pemun* in order to restore ritual harmony to the community.

Trunk, Base and Tip

The distinction between upriver and downriver is allied with another between 'base' and 'tip'. Anything that has both a base and a tip (or tips), or forms the main member of a totality composed of parts, is called a *batang* or 'trunk'. Thus both the longhouse and the main river on which it is located are described as *batang*. Like the trunk of a living tree, both rivers and longhouses are seen as extending between a beginning point — a source or 'base' (*pun*); and an end point or points — a destination or 'tip(s)' (*ujong* or *puchok*).[14] At one level the metaphor is botanical and spatial. For a river, its 'base' is downriver at its mouth, and its 'tip' is upriver at its headwaters.[15] But the metaphor is also totalizing. Thus the Paku Iban refer to the entire Paku River region — including both its main river and tributaries (*sungai*) and all of its inhabitants taken together — as *sekayu batang Paku*, literally, 'the whole of the Paku trunk'.

For the Iban, the notion of source or origin is signified by the term *pun*, or by related forms such as *pemun*. Literally, *pun* means source, basis, origin or cause (see Richards 1981:290). 'Its root meaning is that of stem, as of a tree' (Freeman 1981:31). In terms of social actors, *pun* describes a person who initiates or originates an action; one who announces its purpose and enlists others to participate in bringing it about. *Pun*, in this sense, has the meaning of 'founder' or 'initiator'. Most groups formed by *pun* are ephemeral. But some, like the longhouse and the *bilik*-family, endure. Once an enduring group takes form, the *pun* becomes, like the *pun rumah* and *pun bilik*, the 'source' through whom its continuing life is thought to flow from one generation to the next. Thus the notion of *pun* incorporates a sense of both origin and continuity (Sather n.d.). Similarly, 'trunk' represents the entirety of a process, from its initiation to its realization, from beginning to end, from — to follow the botanic metaphor — 'stem' to 'tip'.

Situated between downriver and upriver, the longhouse is also constituted, like the river itself, as a *batang*. Similarly, the ordering of its parts mirrors that of a living tree. The timbers employed in its construction are placed so that their natural 'base' is down or towards the *pun* of the house, and their natural 'tip' is up or towards its *ujong*, reflecting the orientation that the wood originally had in its forest setting. Thus when trees are felled and cut into timbers, the *pun* end of each timber is marked so that its correct orientation can be preserved. Similarly, the central *tiang pemun* represents a centralizing 'base' or 'stem'. It is this central base that 'fixes' the house, that is, determines the order of the other parts, while it is from its lateral 'ends', the upriver and downriver 'tips' of the house, that the longhouse continues to 'grow' or 'extend' (*tampong*), adding new *bilik*s as established households undergo partition or as new families join the community. The imagery of 'origin', 'tip' and 'trunk' is thus not merely classificatory, but essentially processual as well as botanic in nature.

The rituals of house construction not only make these base-tip relationships explicit, but assign them a temporal ordering as well. Thus the central *tiang pemun* is the first pillar to be erected. Ideally, it is located near the centre of the house and is driven into the earth, or 'fixed', base-first, its natural base-end downward and its natural tip upward. The latter, together with the 'tips' of the other *tiang pemun*, support the ridge-capping (*perabong*) at the highest point of the house. In temporal terms, this capping is the last part of the house to be constructed following the erection of the entry ladders at each end. Fixed to the 'tips' of the 'source posts', it ritually marks the structure's completion. When the central post is bathed, oiled and lustrated before being raised, these acts, too, are performed base-first, while the offerings that affirm the post's ritual status are buried in the earth beneath its base and explicitly symbolize this idea of 'rootedness'.[16] Finally, once this centralizing 'base' is located, the secondary *tiang pemun* are erected in order, first extending downriver from the central post and then upriver, establishing in this way a temporal relationship between the 'base' of the house and its lateral 'tips'. At the same time, in moving upriver and downriver, the 'tips' are associated in a mirror-like reversible relationship, extending bidirectionally from a single centralizing 'source'. Symbolizing the 'stem' or origin of the house, this central source takes ritual priority over the tips, 'coming before' them in time (*ke-dulu*), while the latter are essentially co-equal and represent, for the house, points of new or continuing growth.

Finally, while the ordering of the *tiang pemuns* creates an image of the longhouse as an upright tree, with a central 'base' (*pun*) and 'tips' (*ujong*) that grow outward at each of its lateral ends, the longhouse may be also conceived of as a tree lying down, with its 'base' at one end and its 'tip' at the other end. Both images correspond to the natural orientation of the wood used in the house's construction. The contrast between them is shown in Figure 4.[17] Both images apply not to the upstanding *tiang*, but to the second major category of building material, the *ramu*, horizontal elements, specifically in this case, its lengthwise beams. The first image represents the longhouse as originating from a central *pun*, its *ramu* growing outward, bilaterally, towards both a downriver (*ili'*) and an upriver (*ulu*) *ujong* (Figure 4, Type I). This is the characteristic orientation of houses in the upper Paku. In the second image, the longhouse represents a tree trunk lying down with either a downriver *pun* and an upriver *ujong* or alternatively if the direction of the wood is reversed, an upriver *pun* and a downriver *ujong* (Figure 4, Type II).

The direction in which the *pun* points is determined by the arrangement of the mortice-and-tenon joints by which one beam is joined to another as they are slotted through the main support pillars, including the *tiang pemun*. In each joint there is an upper and lower tenon, and these are always arrayed in the same direction throughout the structure. The Iban say that the *pun* 'falls on' (*ninggang*) the *ujong*. Thus the *pun* end of the *ramu* forms the upper tenon and the *ujong* end, the lower tenon, corresponding to a series of trees fallen, end-to-tip, with the base of one 'falling upon' the tip of the next, so that the base of each beam points in the same direction, either upriver (*kulu*) or downriver (*kili'*) (Figure 4). The direction in all cases applies, moreover, not only to the individual beams, but in a totalizing sense to the longhouse as a whole, thus establishing one of its ends as its *pun*, the other as its *ujong*, or, more commonly in the Paku, establishing a central *pun* with a pair of lateral *ujong* (Figure 4). For the Skrang Iban, Uchibori (1978:93) maintains that the *pun* end of the longhouse is always upriver and the *ujong* end always downriver, and that the *pun* end is welcoming and the *ujong* end polluting.[18] In the Paku and Rimbas, however, while some houses have an upriver *pun*, others have a downriver *pun*, while yet others have a central *pun* and both ends are *ujong*. The same symbolism nonetheless applies in all three cases. Thus, for example, if a *bilik*-family withdraws from the longhouse, its hearth, when removed, is always 'thrown away' (*muai*) from the *ujong* end of the structure, whether this is upriver or down. Similarly, the *pun* is also ritually marked so that, for example, when the bards call for the coming of the spirit heroes while singing the *besugi sakit* songs, they hang the swing on which they sit so that it faces towards the *pun ramu*, whether this is centrally oriented or toward one or the other end of the house.

Type I

Pun ramu oriented towards the central *tiang pemun*; thus an image of the longhouse as an upright tree, with a central base and lateral tips.

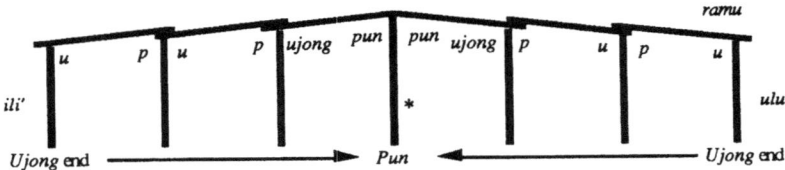

Type II

IIa. *Ninggang kili'*. The *pun ramu* 'falls on' (*ninggang*), or rests upon the *ujong* end, so that the *pun* points towards *ili'* (downriver); that is, presenting an image of the longhouse as a tree lying down with its base downriver and its tip upriver.

Enlargement of the mortice-and-tenon joint by which *ramu* (horizontal timbers) are joined.

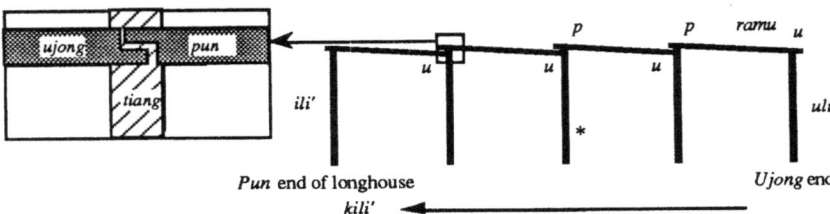

IIb. *Ninggang kulu*. The *pun ramu* 'falls upon' the *ujong* end so that the *pun* points towards *ulu* (upriver); that is, as a tree lying down with its base upriver and its tip downriver.

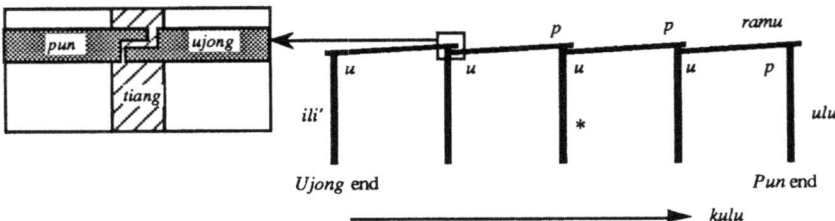

Figure 4. The *pun-ujong* (source-tip) orientation of the longhouse

East and West

Architectural space is temporalized in still another way. A second basic orientation of the longhouse is in terms of the sun's movement through the sky from east to west. In Iban east is called *matahari tumboh*, literally, 'the direction of the growing sun',[19] and west, *matahari padam*, 'the direction of the extinguished sun'.[20] In ritual contexts, east is associated with life, particularly its beginnings,[21] and west with death. So far as the longhouse is concerned, the basic notion is that the east–west course of the sun, as it journeys from horizon to horizon (*tisau langit*), must never coincide with the long axis of the house, such that the sun shines into one or the other end of the structure. Otherwise the community is rendered perpetually 'hot' (*angat*). A house, instead, should mirror the sun's movement within the cosmos. That is, the sun should orbit the house; it should ascend the slope of the roof from the gallery side, reaching its highest point (*rabong hari*, 'zenith'), directly over the central ridge-capping (*perabong*) immediately above the *tiang pemun*, and then descend again as it follows the slope of the roof downward to the horizon, at the back of the family apartments. In other words, the east–west movement of the sun over the longhouse should cross-cut its internal upriver–downriver divisions.

The gallery side of the house should thus ideally face eastward, in the direction of the rising sun. In most houses the gallery side opens onto an unroofed veranda called the *tanju'* (Figure 3). The *tanju'* is strongly associated with the sun and with the daylight phase (*hari*) of the diurnal cycle. In contrast, the interior of the house is associated with night (*malam*) and, in ritual contexts, with its inversion: daylight in the unseen world of the souls, gods and spirits. Thus rituals performed on the *tanju'* characteristically take place during the day, particularly in its early morning hours, while those held inside the house are typically performed in the evening or at night and recreate their inversions, early morning or day in the unseen world.

The Longhouse Bathing Place

The principal point of entry to the longhouse is its *penai'* (river bathing place) (Figure 5).[22] Here canoes are typically tied up, women draw water for household use, and longhouse members bathe. Symbolically, the *penai'* represents the outer threshold of the community. Thus whenever a house is undergoing a 'cooling' ritual, signs are placed at its *penai'* to notify would-be visitors that the longhouse is temporarily taboo to guests. Otherwise, visitors enter the community by way of the bathing place, first bathing at the *penai'* before being welcomed into the house by their hosts. On major ritual occasions, this welcome takes the form of a ceremonial procession. The ritual entry of a newborn infant into the longhouse is marked by a river bathing (*meri' anak mandi'*) similarly structured around a processional welcome to and from the community's *penai'* (Sather 1988). Following death, the soul of the dead retraces this journey, taking leave of 'this world' — the visible world of the living — by way of the same bathing-place through which, as an infant, it made its initial ritual entry.

In so far as *bilik*s are built upriver and downriver, the longhouse itself is construed, like the river to which it is oriented, as a totality produced in time; a unity of parts related by the botanic-morphological metaphor of 'base', 'tips' and 'trunk'. Moreover, just as each *bilik* is part of the longhouse, so each longhouse, too, is part of a larger whole. Each local community is named, and so individuated, by reference to a specific topographic feature[23] which places it within a landscape, the dimensions of which are defined by the configuration of the main river (and tributaries) on which it is built. Thus situated, each longhouse is positioned within a social universe of upriver and downriver neighbours, the ultimate limits of which are defined by the river system itself, its totality metaphorically envisioned as an encompassing *batang* or 'trunk'.

Since most travel was traditionally by river, the location of a longhouse within this system of rivers and streams establishes the basic social identity of its members. Surrounding the longhouse are neighbouring houses bound to one another as 'co-feasters' (*sapemakai*),[24] allies who alternately act as ritual hosts and guests during major bardic rituals (*gawai*). Traditionally, in addition to feasting together, a community's *sapemakai* were its principal allies in warfare and raiding, directing their attacks against enemies living outside their home river system. Thus the horizons of the river also define a further dichotomy distinguishing, very roughly, one's own river, *sapemakai* allies and kindred, from the rest of the world, enemies and strangers.[25]

Within this river-defined social universe, each longhouse's *penai'* serves as the nodal point in a network of river travel, with the river itself defining the horizons within which human undertakings are seen as occurring. For men, reputations derive mainly from ventures undertaken as a result of travel beyond their home river: leading migrations, pioneering new domains, warfare or trading, for example. Rivers in turn are conceptualized in terms of a temporalizing metaphor, as flowing between a 'stem' (source) and outer 'tips' (Figure 5). In death this metaphoric association of life and river travel is symbolically expressed through the soul's journey from this world to the Otherworld of the dead (*menoa sebayan*). Thus, in death, the soul leaves its home longhouse and travels first downriver to the river mouth and then upriver to its headwaters, making a total river circuit from horizon to horizon before entering the Otherworld of the dead, itself conceived of as a river system (Batang Mandai).[26] This journey which is ritually represented in the poem of lamentation sung over the dead precisely replicates the temporal ordering of the longhouse itself, as represented by the order of its 'source posts': first downriver, then upriver and ending, most remotely from its central 'source', at its upriver 'tip'. But in death this journey is reversed and its tips form a mirror-like image so that the final destination of the soul's journey becomes, in the transposed Otherworld of the dead, a new beginning, and its end, a new 'source'.

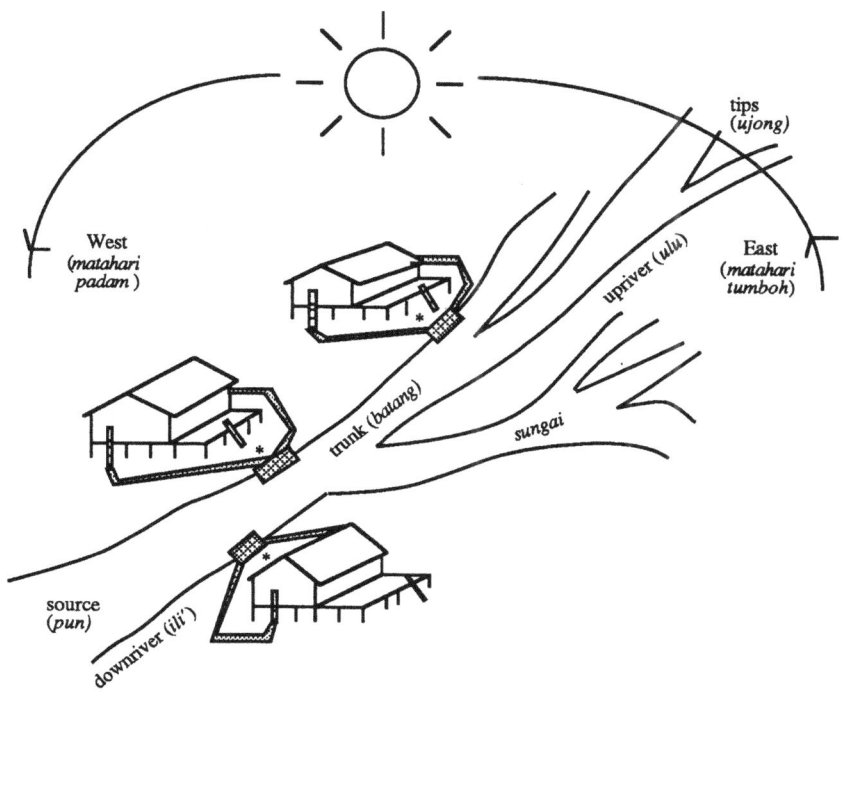

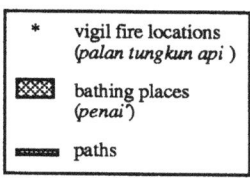

Figure 5. Longhouse orientation

Interior Architecture

The principal internal division of the longhouse is produced by the 'dog wall'.[27] This is attached to the *tiang pemuns* and, extending down the centre of the house, divides the *bilik*s from the *ruai*. Each *bilik* is entered through a door (*pintu*) in this wall from a common passageway, the *tempuan ruai*, that runs from one end of the longhouse to the other (Figure 2). The 'dog wall' itself bisects the intermediating *tempuan* zone into *bilik* and *ruai* sections. From each end of the *tempuan ruai* an entry ladder (*tangga' rumah*) typically descends to the ground. A low side-wall, usually containing an opening through which neighbours may converse or pass objects, separates adjoining *bilik*s. Beyond the *tempuan ruai*, the main gallery extends to the opposite eaves of the house. In contrast to the *bilik* the gallery constitutes the primary setting for public gatherings and rituals and is the centre of longhouse, as opposed to family, sociability. Here visitors are received and entertained, and in the evenings, as families return from their fields, the area becomes a common work place where mats and baskets are woven and tools repaired, and where families exchange news.

The *ruai* contains an 'upper' (*atas*) and 'lower' (*baroh*) zone, each defined by the location of pillars (Figure 3). An identical division applies to the *bilik*.[28] Considered together, the *bilik* is conceptually 'lower' than the *ruai*, while the upper gallery is the 'highest' of these zones and the central *tempuan* the 'lowest'. Thus the arrangement of upper and lower zones cross-cuts the upriver and downriver divisions of the longhouse. Like the house's 'stem' and 'tips', these zones are bilaterally oriented, the inner mid-zone being 'lower' and the opposed outer zones, 'upper'.[29] The uppermost section of the gallery is called the *panggau* (or *pantar*) and is usually covered by a raised platform further emphasizing its elevation (Figure 3). Here male visitors are seated (see photograph on p.64) and at night the area traditionally served as the sleeping place of unmarried men.[30] While the upper gallery represents the 'highest' point within the longhouse interior, the open-air veranda (*tanju'*) is described as being 'above' (*ke-atas*) the upper gallery. It is reached at each family section by a doorway from the gallery-side of the house and in terms of its cardinal orientation, ideally faces eastward.[31] Furthering the botanic imagery of the longhouse, the point at which the gallery and veranda meet is known as the *pugu' tanju'*, the 'rootstock of the veranda'.

The longhouse interior is marked by vertical as well as horizontal gradients. In addition to the conceptual gradients arrayed across the house, the *bilik* itself is divided between an upper and a lower region, the family apartment and a loft (*sadau*) which is built above it and is reached by an entry ladder from the *tempuan* passageway (today more commonly from the interior of the *bilik*) (see Figure 3). Here the family stores its harvested rice in large bark-bin granaries. These granaries are above the family's hearth; thus smoke from the family's *dapur*, filtering through the centre of the loft, is said to warm the rice. While domestic life tends to centre on the *bilik* and public affairs on the *ruai* (see Sutlive 1978:55), the distinction between the apartment and the loft above it is associated with a woman's ordinary domestic tasks and with female prestige and fecundity. Sexual segregation is notably lacking in Iban society and women, like men, compete for status and renown. The loft, in particular, is identified with the activities by which women distinguish themselves; namely, weaving and rice agriculture. Women set up their looms, spin thread, dye and weave cloth in the loft, and here the senior women of the family store the *bilik*'s seed-rice, including the seeds of its sacred *padi pun*. In addition, the loft was traditionally the sleeping place of women of marriageable age. Here, at night, they received suitors and conducted amours.

Finally, the two major zones of the longhouse interior, set apart by the 'dog wall', are associated with different levels of social integration. The *bilik* side marks both the individual *bilik* as an entity and the longhouse as a totality having individual *bilik*s as its constituents; the gallery side marks both the longhouse as a unit and the larger riverine society as a totality having individual longhouses as its constituents. Hence the gallery side of the longhouse is unpartitioned, while the *bilik* side is divided (by secondary walls) into separate, but conjoined apartments. The point of conjunction that joins all of these divisions is formed by the central *tiang pemun* and by the row of secondary *tiang pemuns* that extends bilaterally from it, upriver and downriver.

The Ritual Use of Longhouse Space

Ritual brings into play, at different times, each of the major structural levels represented in the ritual and physical constitution of the longhouse. Thus the Iban divide the greater part of their ritual activity into three major categories: *bedara'*, *gawa'*, and *gawai* (see Masing 1981:34–55; Sandin 1980:40–42; Sather 1988:157–159). The *bedara'* are essentially *bilik*-family rites, small thanksgiving or propitiation rituals held, for example, to nullify ill omens or acknowledge spiritual favours. The Iban distinguish between *bedara' mata'* (unripe *bedara'*), and *bedara' mansau* (ripe *bedara'*). The first are held inside the family apartment, the second on the longhouse gallery. The movement from apartment to gallery marks an increase in the seriousness of the ritual and a shift in its social focus from the family as a separate entity to the family as a part of the longhouse community. The *gawa'* are essentially longhouse rituals of intermediate complexity, while the *gawai* are major bardic rites, witnessed by guests drawn from the larger river region, including the community's *sapemakai* (co-feasting allies). Both are performed on the gallery.

The distinction between these three broad classes of ritual reflects not only social structure but also the processes by which each individual is incorporated into the social and ritual order itself. From birth, Iban children are prepared for participation in ritual activity. Beginning by taking part in small *bedara'* offerings made inside the family apartment, a child's ritual incorporation gradually extends outward to include participation in major longhouse and *gawai* rituals. Only as an adult, however, is a person empowered to act as a ritual sponsor, and maturity marks the beginning, for both men and women, of a life-long quest for recognition of spiritual favour, prestige, power and reputation, pursued largely by ritual means (Sather n.d.).

This process of incorporation and the movement of the individual through the social and ritual order are marked by transformations in the ritual organization of the longhouse itself, the attribution of alternative meanings to its spatial and architectural features. Iban rituals are characteristically structured as journeys (*jalai*) and meanings are conveyed through images arranged linearly, in space and time, to create an itinerary of travel or movement. Thus each person's life trajectory from birth to death is enacted as a series of journeys through the longhouse itself, with significant transitions signalled within this setting by scene changes, the entry and exit of actors, and by ritual processions, inversions and transformations of staging, time and scenery.

Underlying these processes, Iban categories of phenomenal experience posit two parallel realities (see Barrett 1993). The first comprises a wide-awake reality in which each person acts bodily within a social world constituted of other living persons. The second consists of a dream reality in which the soul, ordinarily unseen, interacts with other souls, the spirits, spirit-heroes and gods. The performed reality evoked by ritual reflects on both these parallel realities, creating a mediation in which relations between the two are made explicit, merged, reversed and transformed in ways which, for the Iban, not only 'reflect on' these realities but are instrumental as well, signalling transitions and producing consequences within the phenomenal worlds they evoke.

Rites of Birth

Iban rites of birth clearly illustrate these processes. At birth the mother and infant are confined to the *bilik* apartment. Here, following delivery, the mother is subject to a period of heating called *bekindu'* (literally 'to heat' or 'warm by a fire') which traditionally lasted from a month to forty-one days, its duration formerly reckoned by the use of a string tally (Sather 1988:165–166).[32] During this time the mother heats herself by an open fire kept continuously burning inside the *bilik* and is treated with ginger and other heating agents so that her 'body is made warm' (*ngangat ka tuboh*). At the same time, members of the *bilik*-family observe a series of ritual restrictions (*penti*). These have a disjunctive effect, temporarily setting the family apart from the rest of the community whose members are not subject to the same restrictions. Similarly, heating itself places the mother and infant in a ritual status antithetical to other longhouse members.

For the mother, this status ends when she resumes river bathing at the *penai'*, a 'cooling' act that marks her resumption of normal longhouse life. 'Heating' and 'bathing' are ritually antithetical categories, and before the mother resumes ordinary river bathing, she is first given a steambath (*betangas*) inside a mat enclosure at the *tempuan bilik* in which she is steamed with an infusion of medicinal leaves meant to induce heavy sweating (Sather 1988:166). 'Steaming' in this context can be interpreted as a mediating act between 'heating' and 'bathing'. For the infant, on the other hand, its first bath at the *penai'* is made the focus of a longhouse *gawa'* rite. This rite, the most elaborate of the series surrounding birth, gives social and ritual recognition to the infant's entry into the longhouse community. Following its first bathing, mother and child undergo a secondary bathing rite on the longhouse gallery marking their ritual incorporation. The movement represented is thus from seclusion to incorporation, from heating to cooling.

What is significant here is that this series of rites is enacted as an ordered movement through the longhouse itself: beginning in the relative security of the *bilik* apartment; moving outward to the open-air veranda, the zone of the house most removed from the *bilik*; then journeying in ritual procession from the gallery to the river bathing-place, at the outer threshold of the longhouse, and back again; and ending in a rite of incorporation on the communal gallery. This movement gives cultural construction to the infant's entry into the social and cosmological world — an entry signalled, at its beginning and end, by a fundamental ritual polarity: heating and bathing (or cooling). This polarity recurs at other life transitions as well, including death, and is an integral part of the rites that preserve the longhouse as a ritual entity, symbolized especially by its hearths and posts — the one a source of heat, the other of cooling.

Shortly after birth, as soon as the severed umbilical cord has dropped off, the infant's confinement is temporarily interrupted and it undergoes a secondary birth, this time outside the *bilik*, in a brief rite called *ngetup garam* literally 'to taste salt'. During this rite, the infant is carried from the *bilik* to the open-air veranda. Here it is presented to the sky (*langit*) and to the daylight (*hari*), the latter epitomizing the visible, 'seen' dimensions of bodily reality.[33] It is made to look up into the sky and so 'take cognizance of the day' (*nengkadah hari*). At the same time, a small bit of salt is placed in the infant's mouth to give its body 'taste' (*tabar*). The elder holding the child then pronounces an invocation presenting the infant to the gods (*petara*) and asking them to take the child into their care. Reflecting Iban notions of the dichotomous nature of experience — the contrast between waking reality and the dream world of the soul — the principal gods invoked are Selampandai, the creator-god who, as a blacksmith, forges and shapes the child's visible body (*tuboh*) (and later repairs it should it receive physical injury), and Ini Inda who, as the shaman goddess, is the principal protective deity associated with the soul (*semengat*) and with the invisible plant counterpart (*ayu*) that represents human life in its mortal aspect.

For the Iban, a child's introduction into ritual life is graduated. Thus *ngetup garam* signals the first enlargement of its relational field beyond the *bilik*. Through *ngetup garam* the infant is removed for the first time from the confines of the *bilik* apartment and is introduced to the basic temporal dimensions of the Iban visible world, to daylight and the orbiting sun, and, at the same time, its presence is made known to the gods into whose care it is placed. The principal gods invoked are those responsible for the main constituents of its newly created person: namely, its visible body and its unseen soul. Finally, the journey from the *bilik* to the *tanju'* and back to the *bilik* is seen by the Iban as a movement between areas of minimal and maximal spiritual danger, and back again, within the longhouse.

The main rites of birth conclude with the infant's ritual first bath (*meri' anak mandi'*) at the longhouse bathing place. Ritual bathing gives recognition to the child's social persona within the community, while similarly locating it ritually in a beneficent relation with the spiritual forces believed to be present beyond its threshold. The rite opens at dawn with the preparation of three sets of offerings on the family's section of the longhouse gallery. When prepared, one set of offerings is carried into the *bilik* apartment. There it is presented to the family's guardian spirits (*tua'*). The other two are carried to the river side where, as part of the bathing ritual, one is presented to the spirits of the water (*antu ai'*), the other to the spirits of the forest (*antu babas*).

As soon as these preparations are completed, the bathing party assembles on the gallery and is formed into a procession. After making a complete circuit of the gallery, its pathway strewn with popped rice, the procession, bearing the child, descends the entry ladder and proceeds in file to the river bathing place accompanied by the music of drums and gongs. At the *penai'* the offerings to the water spirits are cast into the river. The chief ritual officiant then wades into the water. Standing in the river, he pronounces a complex invocation (*sampi*) in which he calls on the spirits of the water to form a parallel, unseen procession in the realms beyond the longhouse threshold. The spirits are described in his invocation as arriving at the *penai'* from both upriver and downriver, from the river's headwaters, its many branching streams, and from its mouth at the sea. Like human beings, the spirits, although unseen, inhabit 'this world' (*dunya tu'*). The invocation is characteristically structured as a dialogue in which the officiant becomes a number of different characters, both seen and unseen (Sather 1988:178–180). At first he self-reflexively describes the purpose of the rites and the intent of his own actions. Then, as they assemble, he assumes the identity of the spirits. These include the spirits of turtles, crocodiles and river fish. The spirits, through this dialogue, announce their arrival in processional order. Speaking through the officiant, they describe the magical blessings and charms they have brought to distribute among the bathing party and declare their intention to look after the infant, preserving it particularly from drowning (see Sather 1988:175–180). The guardianship of the river spirits, established at first bathing, is believed to continue throughout an individual's lifetime. In the poem of lamentation following death, the souls of the dead leave the familiar world of the longhouse by way of its bathing place, travel by river to the Otherworld and pass the homes of their former spirit-guardians. As they come to each of these homes in turn, they release the spirits from guardianship and bid them farewell. Later, in rituals that involve the souls' return from the Otherworld, the souls again pass these homes just before they reach the *penai'* of the living.

The spatial imagery thus locates the river spirits within the living world but beyond the boundaries of human society, its outer limits defined in this ritual construction by the *penai'*.

As the infant is bathed, a chicken is sacrificed and its blood is allowed to flow into the river. The final set of offerings is then presented to the spirits of the forest. If the infant is male, these are hung from a spear (*sangkoh*), if female, they are hung from a shed-stick (*leletan*); spears and shed-sticks symbolizing the pre-eminent gender roles of men and women: warfare and weaving (Sather 1988:182). As these offerings are being set out the procession reassembles and, bearing the infant, returns to the longhouse gallery. Here the mother and infant undergo a secondary bathing rite called *betata'*, literally 'to drench' or 'sprinkle with water'. The mother and child are seated together on a gong, covered by a ritual *pua'* cloth, at their family's section of the upper gallery (*ruai atas*). Here they are individually touched with water by other longhouse members and the family's guests from neighbouring communities. *Betata'* thus dramatizes the end of the mother's and child's confinement and their ritual reintegration into the community.

In the series of rites that follows birth, beginning with *bekindu'* and ending with *betata'*, each rite makes use of a different socially demarcated area of the longhouse and its surroundings. As a result, the series as a whole is constituted as an ordered movement through the longhouse community at large. This movement ritually effects the progressive engagement of the newborn infant in an expanding series of social and ritual relationships — moving outward from the *bilik* to the longhouse and beyond to the larger river system that encompasses them both — and from confinement within the spiritually secure *bilik* apartment to location within an all-embracing, but increasingly dangerous cosmological order. Spiritual danger is spatialized and through the ritual organization of the longhouse, this danger is progressively confronted as the infant journeys through the community, becoming in the end a source of efficacy and spiritual protection. Finally, these journeys are always, like the internal ordering of the longhouse itself, bidirectional, returning to the source from which they began. Thus they move from inside to outside the longhouse. to its veranda and river bathing place, then back inside again, first to the *bilik*, then to the communal gallery; hence, not upriver and downriver but along its opposite, life-symbolizing east–west coordinates.

Rites of Death

In death the heating—bathing polarity is reversed. Immediately following death the body is bathed. This takes place, not at the threshold of the longhouse, but at its very centre on the liminal *tempuan* zone within the *bilik*. The floor of the *tempuan bilik* is especially slatted to allow bathing water to flow through it. Aside from containing the hearth, the *tempuan bilik* is also the location of the family's water gourds and it is here, where the water gourds are, or were traditionally, stored that the dead are bathed.[34] After the body is bathed and dressed and three dots of turmeric are painted on its forehead, it is carried from the *bilik* onto the gallery. As it is carried through the *bilik* doorway, family members cast rice grain over it, signifying the separation of the dead from the family's cycle of work, ritual and commensality associated with rice cultivation. The grain represents the dead person's 'share' of the family's rice equivalent to his/her contribution to this cycle. The body is then placed on the lower gallery inside a rectangular enclosure (*sapat*) made of ritual ikat cloth (*pua' kumbu'*). This enclosure is said to shield the rest of the house from the 'heat' of the corpse. The top of the enclosure is similarly covered with a cloth (*dinding langit*) to shield the sky. An external hearth (*bedilang*)[35] is lit and kept burning at the feet of the body on the *tempuan* passageway beside the enclosure.[36] This fire is meant to keep the dead from becoming 'cold' (*chelap*)[37] and is carried by the burial party to the cemetery and extinguished only after the body is buried.

The body remains inside the *sapat* until it is buried. The initial period of mourning vigil, until the conclusion of burial, is called *rabat*. Burial takes place shortly before dawn and, throughout the night that precedes it, a female dirge singer (*tukang sabak*) sits beside the body and sings the poem of lamentation (*sabak*). As she sings, her soul accompanies the soul of the dead on its journey to the Otherworld. The words of her lamentation thus relate the experiences of this soul journey. In these experiences, the route of travel is depicted from this world to the Otherworld of the dead. It begins at the family hearth, with the soul first taking leave of the hearth frame. It then moves through the *bilik* apartment to the *tempuan* passage, and down the passageway to the entry ladder. Thus, its route of travel begins with the familiar landscape of the longhouse interior. In this sense, the lamentation stresses the continuity between this world and the next. The route the soul follows is identical to that later taken by the body as it is removed from the longhouse and carried to the cemetery. But what is significant here is that the words of the lamentation describe the unseen dimensions of this otherwise familiar setting. The soul enters into dialogue with the various features of the longhouse which now appear to the soul in spirit form. Some of these features are transfigured and perceived very differently from their everyday shapes. Thus, for example, the longhouse entry ladder now appears, in some versions of the *sabak*, as a crocodile. In this form, as a guardian of the community's spiritual well-being, it announces its intention to prevent the soul from leaving for the Otherworld. Again, in some versions, the ladder tells the soul that the celestial shamans were invoked by the people of the house and that the ladder was spiritually waved with a fowl in order to prevent longhouse members from departing to the Otherworld, that is from dying (Uchibori 1978:186–187). The soul asks to be allowed to pass, promising that a trophy head will soon be carried into the longhouse by its warriors. And so the ladder relents.[38] Similarly, when the soul reaches the cleared ground at the foot of the ladder (*menalan*), it finds a large tree growing there which it has never seen before. The souls of the dead, who have come to join its journey, tell the soul of the newly deceased that this tree is called Ranyai Padi (see Uchibori 1978:186–187). It is covered with valuable wealth, sacra and magical charms. These the soul collects to give to the living as departing gifts. Later, during the rituals of memorialization (Gawai Antu), the souls of the dead, as they return to the longhouse of the living, again collect valuables from the Ranyai Padi tree which they give to their living descendants. Finally, the soul reaches the longhouse bathing place. Here it bathes in sorrow, knowing that it does so for the last time. Thus, the ritual singing of the poem of lamentation transfigures the longhouse landscape, superimposing an unseen reality on this otherwise familiar setting of everyday social life.

This superimposition of an unseen reality upon the visible features of the longhouse is developed even further by Iban shamans, who manipulate this transformation in order to work upon the social and intrasubjective experiences of their patients. In shamanic rituals of healing (*pelian*), the same journey is frequently depicted, but the course of travel followed by the souls and spirits is even more fully articulated with the physical and symbolic features of the longhouse.

The soul of a patient who is seriously sick may be diagnosed as being absent from the body and journeying on its way to the Otherworld. While in trance, the shaman's soul goes in pursuit, following the same route as the errant soul. As Uchibori writes:

> Usually the shaman claims to have caught the errant *semengat* [soul] at a particular point along the way. He may tell the attendant people that he has caught it, for example, at the foot of a gallery pillar. In the spiritual vision of the shaman, a gallery pillar in the longhouse structure is said to be seen as a *nibong* palm which stands by the path to the Land of the Dead (1978:208).

As in the poem of lamentation, the soul begins its journey at the family hearth. In a complex metaphor, the hearth is described as the *Bukit Lebor Api*, the 'Hill of Raging Fire'.[39] The 'dog wall' separating the *bilik* from the *ruai* appears as a ridge, at the foot of which is a lake called *Danau Alai*. In the everyday landscape of the longhouse this 'lake' is represented by the section of the *tempuan bilik* floor where the dead are bathed. From this 'lake' a 'stream' or 'path' leads to the 'Violently Shutting Rock' (*Batu Tekup Daup*), which continually opens and closes, violently. This 'rock' is represented by the door of the *bilik* apartment. After leaving the *bilik*, the soul enters the main river or pathway running to the Otherworld of the dead. This river or pathway is represented by the *tempuan* passageway. The rice mortars standing along the *tempuan* are seen by the souls as boulders; the main pillars dividing the *tempuan* from the *ruai* as *nibong* palms; and the passageway itself is seen as a broad, well-worn path or as the reaches of the Mandai River of the dead.

The imagery of this superimposed landscape varies in detail between different shamans and dirge singers. According to Uchibori's informants (1978:213), no reputable shaman in the Skrang would pursue a soul past the 'Bridge of Fear' (*Titi Rawan*) most often represented in the longhouse setting by its entry ladder. But in the Paku, shamans regularly travel beyond this point into the Otherworld itself, as well as to Mount Rabong and to the lairs of spirits who have taken the souls of their patients captive.

As in the poem of lamentation sung over the dead, the longhouse becomes a stage, with mundane social space transfigured to represent the reality that the soul experiences in the course of its travels and encounters with other unseen beings. The more serious the patient's illness, the further the shaman's soul must travel into the Otherworld in pursuit. Generally, the middle of the gallery represents the intermediate zone between the world of the living and the world of the dead. The shaman regularly uses props to signify landmarks within this unseen terrain: mortars, for example, as mountains, and a swing hung from the *tempuan* passageway to emulate the flight of his soul from one realm to another. The passageway itself typically represents the Mandai River, while the 'Bridge of Fear', which divides the living from the dead, is represented by a wooden pestle laid across the top of two upturned mortars blocking the end of the *tempuan*. The entry ladder now becomes the Limban Waterfalls (Wong Limban), a prominent landmark in the Otherworld. In this imagery, the Limban River, flowing through a deep chasm, is spanned by the 'Bridge of Fear'.[40]

The clearing at the foot of the entry ladder to the longhouse represents the midway point in the shaman's possible journeys into the Otherworld. At this stage, however, the longhouse of the living now represents the longhouse of the dead. Spatial progression still represents increasing proximity to the dead, but now the direction is reversed. Like the ordering of longhouse *tiang pemun*, this movement is bidirectional. But here the 'tip', represented by the 'tip' of the longhouse (that is, the foot of the entry ladder), is reversed, becoming, not the destination of this movement, but its midpoint in a mirror-inverted journey back to its original starting point. Thus the shaman re-enters the longhouse and his rituals move back toward the *bilik* of his patient, now representing the Otherworld *bilik* in which the errant soul has taken final refuge. The final limit of the shaman's journey is thus marked by his entry into his patient's *bilik* apartment. The starting point of his journey thus becomes, in the inverted Otherworld of the dead, its destination. There inside the *bilik*, where the shaman began his *pelian*, he snatches the straying soul and carries it back to the house of the living. This final journey, from dead 'source' to living 'source', from the centre of the Otherworld to the centre of the living world, is represented by the shaman's physical passage through the apartment doorway, across the liminal *tempuan* passageway, from the *bilik* apartment to the longhouse gallery.[41]

Returning now to the rituals of death, following the singing of the poem of lamentation (*nyabak*), the body of the dead is carried from the longhouse and taken to the cemetery for burial. The route taken follows that of the soul as depicted in the *sabak*. In removing the body, upriver–downriver directions are observed. Thus the body, which is removed headfirst, is never carried past the central *tiang pemun*, but is removed by either the upriver or downriver entry ladder, depending on the location of the deceased's apartment relative to that of the *pun rumah*. In contrast, the body of a shaman is removed by way of the *tanju'*. In the cemetery, the latter is buried with its head upriver, in contrast to the ordinary dead who are buried with the head downriver. The difference reflects the different journey taken by the shaman's soul which, in death, is believed to travel to a separate Otherworld of the dead identified, not with the Mandai River, but with Mount Rabong at the juncture of 'this world' (*dunya tu'*) and the sky (*langit*). Here the souls of former shamans, together with the shaman god, the brother of Ini Inda, and the spirits of celestial shamans, are thought by some to tend the plant images of the living (Sather 1993).

Following burial, during the initial mourning period called *pana*, a small hut (*langkau*) is erected between the river bathing place and the longhouse. Here food offerings are made each evening and in front of the hut a fire (*api*) is kept burning each night of *pana*, in an observance called *tungkun api*. The location of this hut and vigil-fire is called the *paian tungkun api*, 'the *tungkun api* resting-place' (Figure 5). Here the soul of the dead is said to return to eat and warm itself by the fire, its shadowy presence often seen just beyond the edge of firelight. As with birth, heating again signals an important transition. Here it occurs, however, not inside the *bilik* as at birth, but, reflecting the marginal status of the newly dead, outside the longhouse altogether, in the liminal in-between zone between the *penai'* and the foot of the longhouse entry ladder (Sather 1990:29). Its location is said to prevent the dead from re-entering the house of the living, where their presence would pose a danger to the community. At the same time, the *bilik* of the deceased is subject to an inverted temporal order, as an extension of the Otherworld. Thus during the day the apartment windows or skylights are sealed and the interior is kept in total darkness; darkness representing 'daylight' in the Otherworld. No one in the community may work outside the longhouse, and on each night of *pana* an elderly woman, ideally the oldest still alive in the community, eats black rice in the *bilik*. This rice, called *asi pana*, represents white rice in the Otherworld (see Sandin 1980:35). After a final meal of *asi pana*, before the *bilik*'s windows are reopened at dawn to readmit daylight, a chicken is sacrificed and its blood is smeared by the woman on the window frames. Thus, for the duration of initial mourning, the *bilik* is placed in a disjunctive state, with daylight and darkness inverted, mirroring the reversed order of the Otherworld. This state ends with the sacrifice of a chicken and, paralleling the rites of birth, the ritual reintroduction of the *bilik* to daylight.

In addition to a body and soul, every living person is also constituted of a plant image (*ayu*). This image is commonly likened, in appearance, to a bamboo or banana plant, and, like it, is said to grow as a shoot from a common clump made up of the *ayu* of its other *bilik*-family members (see Freeman 1970:21; Gomes 1911:169; Sather 1993). The *ayu* thus grow in family clumps, separate from the body and soul, on, some say, the slopes of Mount Rabong in the shamanic Otherworld.[42] In illness, a person's *ayu* is said 'to wither' (*layu'*), or become overgrown, and in death, 'to die' (*perai*). Thus in healing rituals, shamans often travel to Mount Rabong to 'weed' or 'fence around' a patient's *ayu*, ritually emulating these actions on the longhouse gallery. In death, a person's dead *ayu* must be severed (*serara'*) from his or her family clump in order to safeguard the health and spiritual well-being of the surviving family members. Thus, sometime after *pana* and following *ngetas ulit*, the conclusion of formal mourning, a shaman is usually engaged to cut away the dead *ayu* of the deceased (Sandin 1980:33–38). This is particularly so if family members fall ill or are visited by the dead in dreams. The rite of cutting away the *ayu* is called *beserara' bunga*, literally 'to sever the flowers', and is performed on the longhouse gallery with the shaman's audience seated facing him along the *panggau*. The *ayu* is represented by a bamboo shoot or by the branch of a flowering plant, such as *bunga telasih* or *emperawan*, which is placed at centre stage, in front of the shaman on the patient's *ruai*. Here the shaman carefully cuts away a small piece of the outer sheath of the bamboo or part of the flowering branch. At the conclusion of the rite, the spirit of the dead is believed to appear beneath the *tempuan* passageway. Here the shaman presents it with a sacrifice and special offerings prepared by its bereaved family; these, together with its severed plant image, are then cast beneath the *tempuan* floor. The shaman concludes by placing the longhouse entrance under temporary taboo and by hanging a ritual *pua' kumbu'* cloth over the doorway of the deceased's *bilik* as a ritual barrier (*pelepa'*), thus completing the family's separation from the dead and reconstituting its ritual integrity.

Figure 6. Tomb hut temporarily assembled on the veranda with offerings (below) and *garong* baskets hanging above it (*Gawai Antu*)

The Gawai Antu

The final secondary rites of the dead are the most complex of all. These rites, called the Gawai Antu, constitute major memorialization rituals and are ideally performed by each longhouse roughly once in every generation. Requiring several years of preparation, they memorialize all of the community's dead (*orang ke perai*) whose deaths occurred since the last Gawai was performed by the longhouse. The head of the *bilik* having the oldest dead acts as the 'Gawai elder' (*tuai gawai*). The Gawai Antu feasts the dead and completes their final transformation into spirits (*merantu*). This transformation is effected primarily by erecting, at the conclusion of the Gawai, tomb huts (*sungkup*) over the graves of the dead. These elaborately carved huts are made of ironwood and are equipped with miniature furnishings and *garong* baskets, the latter symbolizing the personal achievements of each individual dead (see Figure 6). In the Otherworld these huts represent full-size longhouses or, in totality, the parts of a single longhouse. The Gawai Antu thus establishes the dead in a longhouse of their own, thereby providing them with the means for a self-sufficient existence independent of the world of the living. For this reason, the Gawai is sometimes described by the bards as a rite of *berumah* (house construction). In this sense, the final rites of death are, significantly, house building rites. But unlike ordinary *berumah*, construction takes place, not in the visible world, but in the Otherworld of the dead, as the *sungkup*, at the conclusion of the Gawai, are reassembled in the cemetery, ritually separated and physically removed from the world of the living.

At its beginning and end, then, the main rites of Gawai Antu are bracketed by major stages of ritual house building. The Gawai opens with the *gawai beban ramu*, the 'ritual fashioning (*ban*) of construction materials (*ramu*)'. This is followed by *ngeretok*, the preparation of the parts of the *sungkup* huts, which are then carried from the forest and assembled by each family for temporary display on its *tanju*'.[43] Finally, immediately following the main Gawai rituals, the *sungkup* are removed from the longhouse and carried to the cemetery where they are reassembled, away from the longhouse, over the graves of the dead.

On the day that precedes *ngeretok* — the preparation of the parts of the *sungkup* — families repair or replace their *panggau* platform and make ready their gallery to receive guests.[44] In the late afternoon, the women begin to soak glutinous rice in the river, while the men construct the bamboo *rugan* altars in which each family feeds its dead. These are attached to the passageway pillar representing the family's *tiang pemun* (see Figure 7). This feeding begins at dusk on the evening prior to *ngeretok* and continues each night until the conclusion of the Gawai. At dusk, the first welcoming of the spirits of the dead (*ngalu antu*) is performed on the longhouse gallery. From now until the end of Gawai Antu, at dusk and at dawn, the spirits are welcomed and seen off, as they arrive in the world of the living and temporarily depart again. The Gawai emphasizes the complementarity of male and female roles, as on the following day when the men perform *ngeretok*, fashioning the *sungkup* huts, and the women plait the ritual *garong* baskets. The work of plaiting is called *nganyam* and is performed by the women inside the *bilik* apartments, while the men work on the upper gallery. Both these tasks are generally completed in a single day. Afterwards, several days of preparation elapse before the main Gawai rites resume.

Figure 7. On the *tempuan* passageway during Gawai Antu: the *rugan* altar on the left; at the top a decorated *garong* basket with a smaller *gadai* (representing a slave attendant); and a woman hanging the furnishing of a newly constructed *bilik* of the dead

Kindred (*kaban*) generally arrive the day before the start of the Gawai proper in order to assist the host families with preparations. They bring with them fowls, eggs, fruit and garden produce. Beginning soon after dawn on the first day of Gawai Antu, guests (*pengabang*) begin to arrive. After bathing at the *penai'*, they are ceremonially welcomed into the house. Among the first to be received are the principal warriors who will later drink the *ai' buloh*, the main ritual rice wine served from the *garong* containers plaited by the women. They are followed by a second group of warriors who will later drink the *ai' timang jalong* wine which is carried by the bards as they sing (*nimang*) the Gawai invocation. The welcoming of guests continues throughout much of the day. The principal guests comprise the house's cofeasting allies (*sapemakai*); they generally arrive and are received in groups, as longhouse communities.[45] At dusk no further guests may be received. Instead, the hosts and guests combine to welcome the gods, spirit-heroes and spirits of the dead. After the latter have been welcomed and feasted with offerings, hosts and guests sit down to the first of a series of feasts consumed in emulation of their spiritual visitors.

During the performance of the Gawai Antu, the total panoply of intersecting social and cosmological categories comes into play and is given formal expression through the ritual organization of the longhouse itself. In everyday life these categories remain largely unmarked. Thus the Gawai makes explicit the basic categories of Iban social life: gender, age, *bilik*-family, longhouse, kindred and so on. The basic order of Gawai seating, for example, gives formal arrangement to gender and age categories. Adult and elderly male guests are seated along the raised *panggau*, while their male hosts sit facing them along the division between the upper and lower gallery. Married women sit either behind them, on the lower gallery, or remain inside the *bilik* where they receive and entertain women guests from other longhouses. While in everyday life these different areas of the house are used by both sexes, and by individuals of all ages, in terms of their ritual signification they are made, in this ritual ordering of space, to constitute these basic social distinctions. Thus the *bilik* is associated with women; the *ruai* with men; the upper sections of the house with men, seniority and age; the lower sections with women, juniority and the young. The transition from domestic to public space thus becomes a transition from women's to men's space, and from the *bilik*-family to the longhouse and its co-feasting allies. When food is served, the same distinctions are made. Young women cook at the hearths inside the *tempuan* section of the family apartment, older women eat in the main *bilik*, while young men carry food in and out of the *bilik*. Older men, both hosts and kindred, eat on the *ruai*, while the most senior male guests are served at the raised *panggau*. Thus, the relationship of domestic space to public space is like that of women to men, lower to upper, family to longhouse, young to old, hosts to guests, and so on. At times, however, in the course of ritual performance, these relationships are altered or inverted. During ritual processions, for example, gender and age distinctions are partially overridden, while other distinctions, such as those between hosts and guests or between ritual officiants and audience, are expressed instead. At other times formal gender arrangements are reversed, with men and women changing places. This occurs, for example, during the Gawai Antu following the invocation of the dead and signifies the state of inversion that distinguishes the Otherworld from the realm of the living.

The ritual organization of longhouse space also underscores distinctions between the living and the dead and between human beings, the gods, spirit-heroes and spirits of the dead. After the human guests have arrived and been welcomed with rice wine at each family's section of the *tempuan*, they are shown to their hosts' *ruai*, where the male guests are eventually 'arranged in order' (*bedigir*) along their hosts' *panggau*. At dusk, the gods (*petara*) and returning spirits of the dead (*antu sebayan*) are invoked by the bards and welcomed to the house by the Gawai hosts and guests through a series of ritual processions (*ngalu antu*) that circle the upper and lower gallery (see Figure 8). But before the bards begin their invocation, the warriors who are to drink the *ai' buloh* wine prepare a pathway for the dead along the gallery floor (*ngerandang jalai*). Dancing along the *ruai* with drawn swords, they cut invisible 'undergrowth' and clear the way of spiritual obstructions (see Figure 9). After this, the warriors who are to drink the *ai' jalong* wine, make the path prepared by the first group of warriors ritually secure by metaphorically 'fencing it with an invisible handrailing' (*ngelalau*). The arrival of the dead is anticipated in other ways as well. While living guests are welcomed into the longhouse by way of its upriver entrance, the dead are believed to come from downriver, retracing the route of their · original departure. Thus, before the spirits arrive, all the mats covering the gallery floor are taken up at the direction of the Gawai elder, reversed, and laid down again, so that their edges now overlap in the opposite downriver-to-upriver direction. This is said to prevent the spirits of the dead from 'tripping' as they walk along the gallery floor, their actions emulated by the processions of human guests.

Figure 8. Maidens in procession 'to welcome the spirits' (*ngalu antu*), Ulu Bayor longhouse, Saribas

The spirits are led in procession by the gods and goddesses of the Otherworld, beginning with Raja Niram and his wife Ini Inan. They bring with them to the living world gifts to exchange with their former family members for food offerings. The bards begin their invocations inside the Gawai elder's *bilik*. They then move, in an important transition, onto the gallery where they sing the main *timang* invocations as they circumambulate the *ruai* floor, going from one end of the house to the other. Their movements at once emulate the journey of the dead and at the same time define the whole of the longhouse as a ritual space. As they sing they carry cupped in the palm of their right hand a bowl of ritual wine called the *ai' jalong*. The invocation they sing recounts the journey of the gods and spirits as they travel from the world of the dead (*menoa orang mati*) to the world of the living (*menoa orang idup*). In this journey, the spirits pass through a series of unseen realms, as in the poem of lamentation, except that now the direction of the journey is reversed. Prominent among these realms, and adjacent to the land of the dead, are the settlements of the spirits of various kinds of birds associated with death, including the Bubut (the coucal or crow pheasant) who watches over the Bridge of Fear dividing life and death. In time, they enter into the longhouse *menoa*. Here they pass ancient house sites and former farmlands, which the spirits of the dead recall from former times when they were still alive. They finally reach the river-landing threshold between this world and the world of the dead. From here they travel by boat. Journeying along the river, they pass the spirit realms of the tortoises, crocodiles, fish and other river spirits who were invoked when the newborn infant received its ritual first bath. After passing these realms, they reach the bathing place of the longhouse holding the Gawai. Here they bathe and are received in a ceremonial procession. They are welcomed with food offerings, and, as they arrive inside the house, the men and women of the longhouse sing songs (*berenong*), in the form of a conversational exchange between the living and the dead, to entertain them. The spirits are also welcomed with a series of cockfights held on the gallery floor. Here cocks belonging to the visitors and hosts are pitted against one another. Those of the visitors represent the cocks of the dead and those of the hosts, the cocks of the living. In these contests, the cocks of the dead always 'lose' to those of the living, no matter what the actual outcome.

Figure 9. *Ngerandang jalai*; a warrior cutting a path for the dead along the *ruai* gallery at the start of Gawai Antu

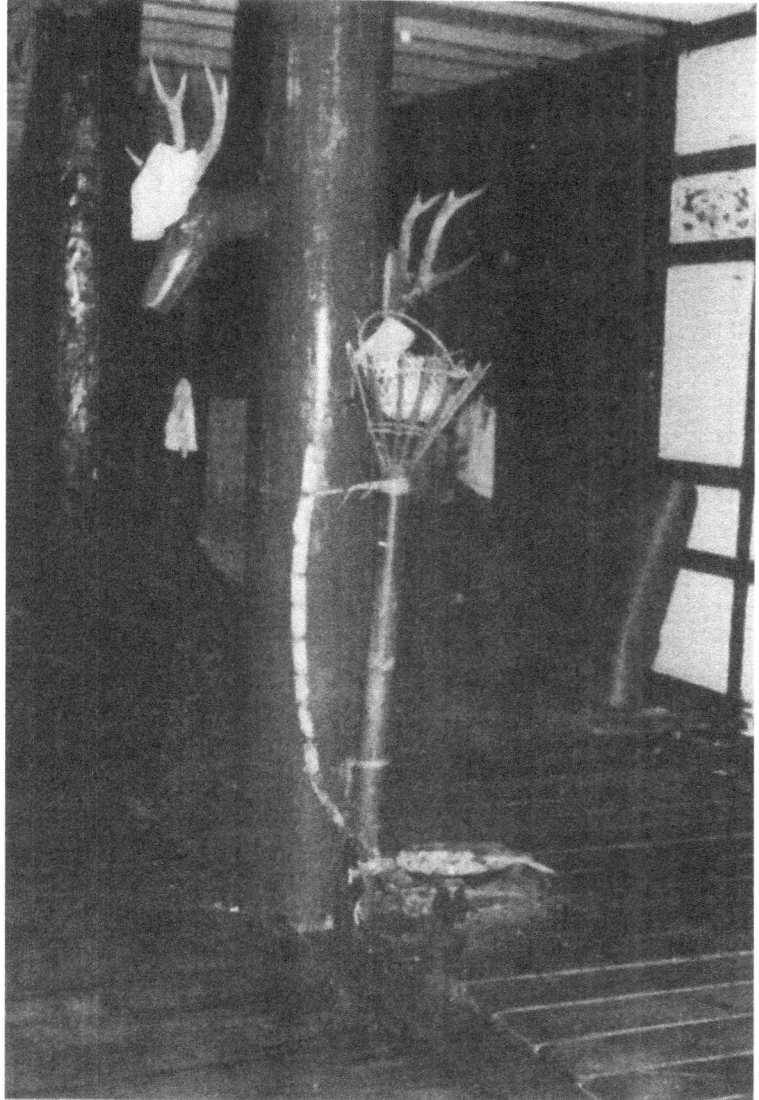

Figure 10. The *rugan* attached to the *tempuan* pillar, with a hearth at its base

From dusk, when they are first invoked, and throughout the night that follows, the gallery itself is believed to be thronged with unseen visitors. In their processions, feasting and drinking, cockfighting, and other actions, the hosts and guests play the part of these visitors: the spirits of the dead, gods, and spirit-heroes and heroines.[46] During the night, older men in the house may sleep on the gallery in order to share the same space with the dead. Yet distinctions between the living and the dead are maintained; the spirits of the family dead are received, not inside the *bilik*, but on the *tempuan* passageway.

Here they are fed in the *rugan* altar, which, together with a stalk of sugarcane, is attached to the *tempuan* pillar representing the *tiang pemun* (see Figure 10). In addition to being given special foods unique to the dead, such as smoked *belau* fish and *keli* eels, the family lights a fire each evening at the base of the *rugan* so that the family's spirits may warm themselves.

As the end of the night approaches, the bards finish their *timang* songs and the second group of warriors who are to drink the *ai' jalong* wine are arranged in a row along the upper gallery with the women who will serve them seated facing them (see Figure 11). A few other guests, as a special honour, are invited to sit beside the warriors. Only men who have received dream instructions or who have killed in war (*bedengah*) may drink these ritual wines. As the men and women are seated, the bards come forward, each carrying a cup of wine. As they approach, they sing praise songs which relate how the Otherworld goddesses Ini Inan and Endu Dara Rambai Geruda are searching for brave warriors to drink the sacred wine. The bards then place a cup in front of each woman, who, representing a goddess, serves it to the warrior facing her. Before he drinks, the warrior first 'clears' the wine with the tip of his sword. Then, after he drinks, he gives a loud war shout. After this, the leader of the first group of warriors who are to drink the *ai' buloh* wine goes from one family's section of the *tempuan* to the next and dismantles the *rugan* altars and cast them under the *tempuan* floor. This is a moment of great poignancy, for it marks the severing for each *bilik* family of its conjunction with its dead for another generation. The next time the Gawai is held some of its current members are likely to be among the newly dead being memorialized.

Figure 11. Women serving the warriors *ai' jalong* during the Gawai Antu; behind them a group of bards with two still holding bowls of wine

Following the 'casting away of the *rugan*' *(muai rugan)*, the climax of the Gawai occurs at dawn when the principal warriors drink the *ai' buloh* (or *ai' garong*) wine from bamboo tubes inserted in the plaited *garong* baskets. One basket is woven for each individual dead, but only those of adults hold wine tubes. They are served by the previous group of warriors in a mock combat. Only men of singular prowess can drink the *ai' buloh*. Many Saribas bards equate this wine with the *ai' limban*, the lymphatic fluids that flow from a decomposing corpse. But in the dichotomous seen/unseen imagery of the Iban, the Limban is also the major river of the Otherworld that separates this world from the next. During the Gawai Antu the Limban River is verbally identified with the *tempuan* passageway, while the Bridge of Fear that spans it — linking the living and dead — is signified by a pestle laying width-wise across it.

Here, then, longhouse space is transformed by Iban rituals of birth and death from the familiar mundane setting of everyday social life to a symbolically organized landscape, displaying basic social distinctions and mirroring a series of superimposed realities, both seen and unseen. Everyday social space is merged with unseen 'spiritual' space and through the ritual organization of the longhouse, the order underlying Iban social experience is given explicit form, while at the same time this order is transformed to conjoin the seen realities of everyday social life with the invisible realities of the soul, spirits and the gods.[47]

Conclusion

In this essay I have examined the ways in which the Iban longhouse is constructed, not so much as a physical form, but as a ritually-constituted reality. In doing so, I have looked in particular at rites which focus on the longhouse itself, its physical construction and persistence as a ritual community, and at those which mark, in a parallel fashion, an individual's passage through the longhouse community from birth to death, as this passage is represented by a series of longhouse journeys. The principal argument I advance here is that the order-making power of ritual correlates spatial and architectural features of the longhouse in a series of meaningful ways. To these features ritual adds 'rules of performance' by which they are combined, in a convincing manner, to form multiple orders of meaning. Working mainly through images of landscape and motion, these 'orders' reveal at once the basic structures of everyday social life and at the same time a series of superimposed realities, positioning the longhouse cosmically as a threshold between the worlds of the living and the dead, the human world and the worlds of the gods, spirits and souls.

Robert Barrett (1993), in a penetrating analysis of Iban shamanism, develops a similar argument. Thus he maintains that

> [t]hrough the processual organization of longhouse space within ritual, the major structures of Iban society are revealed. Gender and age categories become distinct. The relationship between the *bilik*-family and the longhouse community is defined and redefined, first as a discrete group, then opened out and articulated with the longhouse, then circumscribed as a discrete entity again. Within the reality of the *pelian*, the *manang* [shaman] brings into relief the major categories of being within the Iban cosmos — the living, the spirits, the dead and gods — and their various habitats (Barrett 1993:255).

Thus, the organization of longhouse space, through ritual performance, procession and invocation, interrelates its architectural and areal features to display a series of microcosmic images of the Iban social and ritual universe. These images are represented primarily as pathways of biographical transition or as arenas of communication and journeying, in which the welfare of the longhouse, its inhabitants and their domain is continually asserted and preserved, with ritual not only dramatizing but effecting transformations in these relationships and so, in an ongoing way, in the lived experience of its participants.

Today a growing body of ethnographic studies treat the symbolic organization of built forms — the 'house' in particular (Barnes 1974; Bourdieu 1970; Cunningham 1964; Ellen 1986; Forth 1981; Fox 1980; Kana 1980; Waterson 1988, 1990). 'Because', as Ellen (1986) observes, 'so many of our social interactions take place in houses', the house constitutes a 'culturally significant space of the highest order' (p.3). While some studies have sought

> the 'rules governing' the structure of space [itself] ...Most have simply sought to find a symbolic concordance between the house and other collective representations ... not necessarily implying microcosmic status for the house, but merely stressing its fit with more general categories and principles (Ellen 1986:4).

While acknowledging the usefulness of beginning an analysis of local representations with the house, Ellen argues against any assumption that the house enjoys priority in this regard, or that 'house symbolism is a puzzle' to which there is 'one and only [one] solution' (p.4). Basically, Ellen's argument is that the house cannot be isolated from other symbolic domains, or from differing 'levels' of meaning; 'that symbolic worlds', by their nature, 'can only be understood in terms of other symbols' (p.1). Therefore, in analysing the house 'we are dealing with interpenetrating and non-reducible levels of meaning', such that the house, rather than representing a single fixed order located at the centre of an independent symbolic universe, 'depends for its imagery on other symbolic microcosms' (p.5). Without endorsing Ellen's critique of structural studies of the house, the point he derives from this argument is, I think, well taken, namely that

> [w]hat is ... interesting about houses is that they not merely express order, but that the orders [they express] may be of various kinds, understood in different ways [by] different people on different occasions (1986:4).

I would go further and argue that what is more interesting yet, is not simply that the house may express different 'orders', but that these orders are actively created, contested and rendered convincing in the ongoing processes of social life, including, importantly, those of ritual. It is by exploring these processes, I would add, that detailed ethnographic analysis of the house has most to offer.

In this paper I have looked at a few of these ordering processes as they apply to the Iban longhouse. Not only does the ritual organization of longhouse space express multiple 'orders', but, through longhouse and individual life-passage rites, these orders are constantly created and re-created by the participants themselves. As Victor Turner (1967:20) reminds us, rituals and the symbols they employ are 'essentially involved in social process'. Thus rituals help establish and sustain the longhouse as a social community. In doing so, they make explicit the part-whole relationships that exist between its structural elements, expressing these relationships in metaphors of time and process, which not only 'reflect' their existence, but are themselves constitutive of the very social realities they represent.

Ritual, for the Iban, not only 'enacts' but is believed to have actual consequences. Thus, among other things, ritual effects transitions and changes of status, giving cultural construction to what Rosaldo (1980:109) calls the 'articulation of structure and event', the conjunction of social relationships with personal history and experience. Longhouse rituals not only display social categories and relationships, but also mark the entry of individuals into, and their final disengagement from, the community as experienced events in the social life of the longhouse. Consequently the ritual organization of longhouse space supplies coordinates of motion rather than stasis; it forms a terrain, at once social and symbolic, that each person traverses, again and again, in a series of life-journeys, rather than a fixed, physical matrix into which social life itself must be fitted or made to conform. In this regard, the longhouse represents, for the Iban, the setting of biographical events, scenes of vital activity, both seen and unseen, rather than an inert physical structure.

Not only does ritual performance generate multiple 'orders' of meaning, but in doing so, it renders any one of these orders problematic. In this sense, ritual is also involved in the creative work of transforming the lived experiences of its participants. As Barrett (1993) stresses, ritual not so much enacts a 'text' as creates meaning by the interaction of its performers and the structure of their performance itself. Meaning, including the meaning of ritual, is thus open to continual reinterpretation. As Barrett notes, in writing of Iban curing ritual,

> [w]hile it is important to see ritual as a context in which the performance of cultural experts transforms patient and audience, ...it is just as important to see the patient, his suffering and his disturbed social relations, as a social arena within which cultural experts can define and transform the nature of ritual, cosmology, and the basic parameters of lived experience. Through discourse on performance, cultural members articulate ... theories of appearances and their relation to the multiple

realities defined by their culture ... [As a consequence] the relationship between appearances and things is made problematic. Phenomena are demonstrated to be expressions of alternative possible noumena, depending on the reality within which they are defined (Barrett 1993:272)

A final point is that the representation of the longhouse that emerges from ritual differs in important respects from the one most commonly portrayed in the ethnographic literature. For example, the Iban longhouse is described by Freeman (1970:104) as 'a free and conditional association of corporate family groups'. Longhouse membership 'does not deprive a *bilik*-family of its essential autonomy' (p. 129); instead, Freeman maintains,

> [a] long-house consists of a federation of independent families ... [which] must be conceived of, not as a unified group, but rather as a territorial aggregation of discrete units; not as a communal pavilion, but as a street of privately owned, semi-detached houses. Within the long-house all bilek-families are at jural parity ... [A] long-house is without formal hierarchical, or hegemonic organization (1970:129).

Reflecting its federated nature, individual families may freely join any longhouse in which they have kinfolk, their dissociation from one community and acceptance by another being a relatively simple matter.

Such an account, while not inaccurate, presents, nevertheless, only a partial view of the Iban longhouse.[48] While Freeman stresses its individualistic, non-hierachical and competitive elements, ritual clearly reveals another side of longhouse sociality. As Freeman (1981) rightly insists, Iban society is notably lacking in institutions of stratification, hereditary inequality and political hegemony, yet the ritual constitution of the longhouse clearly entails relations of 'hierarchy' in the Dumontian sense of 'encompassment' of opposed categories, or more accurately, of 'precedence' (Fox 1990), which override elements of autonomy and individualism. The basic structural elements of Iban society are located ritually in an ordered series of part-whole relationships, arrayed in turn in a linear, or, more accurately, a bilateral reversible order of precedence, whose relations are defined primarily by orientational notions and by botanic and temporalizing metaphors of 'source' and 'tip'. In maintaining the harmony of the longhouse as a ritual entity, each individual family is subordinated to collective goals, expressed primarily through its hearths and posts, while ritual preserves the relationship between these structural elements, each encompassed by a larger totality: from the *bilik*-family, through the longhouse, to the wider river region. Freeman (1970) has stressed the special status of ritual in this regard and in discussing the 'corporateness' of the longhouse, rightly notes that 'inasmuch as it ... exist[s] it stems from ritual concepts, rather than from collective ownership of land or property' (p. 104). Yet the very notion of 'corporateness', and the proprietary terms in which it is defined, clearly privilege relations of physicality and so, I would stress, present us with only a partial view of the longhouse, at odds, as I have tried to show, with its indigenous representation.

References

Adelaar, K.A.

1985   *Proto-Malayic*. Alblasserdam: Offsetdrukkerij Kanters B.V.

Barrett, Robert

1993   Performance, effectiveness and the Iban Manang. In Robert Winzeler (ed.) *The seen and the unseen: shamanism, mediumship and possession in Borneo* (Borneo Research Council, Monograph Series No. 2), pp.231–275. Williamsburg, Virginia: Borneo Research Council.

Barnes, Robert

1974   *Kedang: a study of the collective thought of an Eastern Indonesian people.* Oxford: Clarendon Press.

Bourdieu, P.

1970   The Berber house or the world reversed. In J. Pouillon and P. Maranda (eds) *Echanges et communications: melanges offerts àClaude Lévi-Strauss àl'occasion de son 60ème anniversaire*, Vol. 2. The Hague: Mouton.

Cunningham, Clark

1964   Order in the Atoni house. *Bijdragen tot de Taal-, Land- en Volkenkunde* 120:34–68.

Ellen, Roy

1986 Microcosm, macrocosm and the Nuaulu house: concerning the reductionist fallacy as applied to metaphorical levels. *Bijdragen tot de Taal-, Land- en Volkenkunde* 142:1–30.

Fox, James J.

1980   Introduction. In James J. Fox (ed.) *The flow of life: essays on Eastern Indonesia*, pp.1–18. Cambridge, Mass.: Harvard University Press.

1990   Hierarchy and Precedence. Canberra: Comparative Austronesian Project (Working paper No. 3), Department of Anthropology, Research School of Pacific Studies, The Australian National University.

Freeman, Derek

1957   The family system of the Iban of Borneo. In Jack Goody (ed.) *The developmental cycle in domestic groups* (Cambridge Papers in Social Anthropology, No. 1), pp.15–52. Cambridge: Cambridge University Press.

1960 The Iban of Western Borneo. In G.P. Murdock (ed.) *Social structure in Southeast Asia*, pp.65–87. Chicago: Quadrangle Books.

1961 On the concept of the kindred. *Journal of the Royal Anthropological Institute* 91:192–220.

1970 *Report on the Iban*. London: The Athlone Press.

1981 *Some reflections on the nature of Iban society*. Canberra: Department of Anthropology, Research School of Pacific Studies, The Australian National University.

Gomes, Edwin

1911 *Seventeen years among the Sea Dyaks of Borneo*. London: Seeley and Company.

Harrisson, Tom and Benedict Sandin

1966 Borneo writing boards. In Tom Harrisson (ed.) *Borneo writing boards and related matters* (Special Monograph No. 1). *Sarawak Museum Journal* 13:32–286.

Helliwell, Christine

1990 The ricefield and the hearth: social relations in a Borneo Dayak community. PhD thesis, The Australian National University, Canberra.

Heppell, Michael

1975 Iban social control: the infant and the adult. PhD thesis, The Australian National University, Canberra.

Hudson, A.B.

1970 A note on Selako: Malayic Dayak and Land Dayak languages in Western Borneo. *Sarawak Museum Journal* 18:301–318.

1977 Linguistic relations among Bornean peoples with special reference to Sarawak. *Studies in Third World Societies* 3:1–44.

Kana, N.L.

1980 The order and significance of the Savunese house. In James J. Fox (ed.) *The flow of life: essays on Eastern Indonesia*, pp.221–230. Cambridge: Harvard University Press.

Masing, James Jemut

1981 The coming of the gods: a study of invocatory chant of the Iban of the Baleh River Region of Sarawak. PhD thesis, The Australian National University, Canberra.

Pringle, Robert

1970 *Rajahs and rebels: the Ibans of Sarawak under Brooke rule, 1841–1941.* London: Macmillan.

Richards, Anthony

1981 *An Iban—English dictionary.* Oxford: Clarendon Press.

Rosaldo, Renato

1980 *Ilongot headhunting, 1883–1974: a study in society and history.* Stanford: Stanford University Press.

Sandin, Benedict

1966 *Tusun Pendiau* (Iban). Kuching: Borneo Literature Bureau.

1967a Simpulang or Pulang Gana: the founder of Dayak agriculture. *Sarawak Museum Journal* 15(30–31):245–406.

1967b *The Sea Dayaks of Borneo before white rajah rule.* London: Macmillan.

1980 *Iban adat and augury.* Penang: Penerbit Universiti Sains Malaysia.

Sather, Clifford

1977a Introduction. In Benedict Sandin *Gawai Burong: the chants and celebrations of the Iban bird festival*, pp.vii-xvi. Penang: Penerbit Universiti Sains Malaysia.

1977b *Nanchang Padi*: symbolism of the Saribas Iban first rites of harvest. *Journal of the Malaysian Branch of the Royal Asiatic Society* 50(2):150–170.

1978 The malevolent *koklir*. Iban concepts of sexual peril and the dangers of childbirth. *Bijdragen tot de Taal-, Land- en Volkenkunde* 134:310–355.

1980 Introduction. In Benedict Sandin *Iban adat and augury*, pp.xi-xlv. Penang: Penerbit Universiti Sains Malaysia.

1985 Iban agricultural augury. *Sarawak Museum Journal* 34:1–35.

1988 *Meri anak mandi'*: the ritual first bathing of Iban infants. *Contributions to Southeast Asian Ethnography* 7:157–187.

1990 Trees and tree tenure in Paku Iban society: the management of secondary forest resources in a long-established Iban community. *Borneo Review* 1:16–40.

1993 Shaman and fool: representations of the shaman in Iban comic fables. In Robert Winzeler (ed.) *The seen and the unseen: shamanism, mediumship and possession in Borneo* (Borneo Research Council Monograph Series No. 2), pp.277–318. Williamsburg, Virginia: Borneo Research Council.

n.d. 'All threads are white': Iban egalitarianism reconsidered. Forthcoming in James J. Fox and Clifford Sather (eds) *Origins, ancestry and alliance.*

Sutlive, Vinson

1978   *The Iban of Sarawak*. Arlington Heights: AHM Publishing Corporation.

Turner, Victor

1967   *The forest of symbols*. Ithaca, N.Y.: Cornell University Press.

Uchibori, Motomitsu

1978   The leaving of this transient world: a study of Iban eschatology and mortuary practices. PhD thesis, The Australian National University, Canberra.

Waterson, Roxana

1988   The house and the world: the symbolism of Sa'dan Toraja house carvings. *RES* 15:35–60.

1990   *The living house: an anthropology of architecture in South-East Asia*. Kuala Lumpur: Oxford University Press.

Notes

The fieldwork on which this paper is based was carried out at Kerangan Pinggai longhouse, Ulu Paku, Saribas, during university holidays, 1976–79, 1981–84, and 1988. The present essay had its beginnings in a paper presented at a session of the American Anthropological Association meetings, sponsored by the Borneo Research Council in 1988, on 'Rites of Passage'. An initial version of the present paper was read at a seminar on 'House and Household' conducted by the Comparative Austronesian Project, Department of Anthropology, Research School of Pacific Studies, The Australian National University in April 1989. I am grateful to those present on both occasions for their comments and criticisms and wish to thank in particular George Appell, Robert Barrett, Aletta Biersack, James Fox, Penelope Graham and Mark Mosko for their critical reading of earlier drafts of this essay.

[1] Besides Iban, the Ibanic group of Malayic Dayak languages includes Mualang, Kantu', Bugau, Desa and Air Tabun (Hudson 1970:302-303).

[2] *Menoa* refers to the territorial domain held and used by any distinct community, not only a longhouse, but also an entire river region. In fact, the term *menoa* may encompass a number of regions; thus the Sarawak Iban describe as their *menoa lama'*, or old domain, the regions of the First and Second Divisions, including the Saribas, that were settled in the course of the first great Iban migrations into Sarawak some 300 to 350 years ago. The *menoa rumah*, or longhouse domain, consists ideally of the 'house, farms, gardens, fruit groves, cemetery, water, and all forest within half a day's journey', the use of which is 'only gained and maintained by much effort and danger and by proper rites to secure and preserve a ritual harmony of all within' (Richards 1981:215). For a discussion of the major features of the longhouse *menoa*, including its forests, fruit groves and immediate longhouse precinct, see Sather (1990).

[3] Members of the Brooke family, the so-called 'White Rajahs', ruled Sarawak for a century (1841–1941) as an independent Raj under British protection (Pringle 1970). Following World War II, Sarawak was administered briefly as a British colony, gaining independence in 1963, as a State within the Federation of Malaysia.

[4] The roles of *tuai* and *pun* may be, and sometimes are, combined. Thus the same person may be both the longhouse headman and the *pun rumah*. In the Paku, however, it is preferred that the two roles be played by different persons, primarily because the disputes and trouble cases that the headman hears

on his family's section of the gallery are thought to jeopardize the central *tiang pemun*, potentially 'heating' it. The role of the *pun rumah* may, in addition, be combined with that of the *tuai burong* (longhouse augur). However, today in the Paku not all houses acknowledge an augur. Like the longhouse *tuai* and *pun*, the *tuai bilik* and *pun bilik* may also be, and much more often are, the same person. In addition, each community, for the duration of its annual farming year, selects at least one *tuai umai* (farming elder) to enforce its *adat umai*, the farming rules that regulate the behaviour of its members while they work their farms outside the longhouse.

[5] These are the major initiating rites. *Ngentak* is preceded, however, by a brief ritual preparation of the site following its selection and confirmation by divination. This is called *ngerembang* (noun form *rembang*), literally, 'to tread down', 'clear a way' or 'make a pathway', and is performed by the owner-to-be of the central *tiang pemun*. During *ngerembang* the longhouse site is measured out, the location of its posts are fixed, and three offerings are made to the principal deities associated with the earth, Simpulang Gana and Raja Samarugah, one each at the middle and two ends of the site. Thus, in the process of reclaiming the site from forest, the basic constitution of the longhouse, as a 'cleared pathway' (*ngerembang jalai*) — with a centre and bilateral ends — is established through offerings and the ritual measuring out or 'treading down' of the site. Significantly, the longhouse is first conceptually realized in the mind of its *pun rumah* and marked out ritually as a 'cleared pathway', before it is actualized in a physical sense through the erection of its 'source posts'.

[6] These objects include fruit of the *apong* palm (*buah tamatu*) representing a spirit repellant; favourable augury sticks (*tambak burong*) collected when the longhouse site was first chosen and the choice submitted to divination; salt (*garam*); skins of the *langgir* fruit used for bathing; a *batu kuai*, a translucent stone for cooling; and a branch of the *mumban* plant. The significance of *mumban* is discussed presently (see n.16).

[7] In Iban oral genealogies (*tusut*) each generation is represented by a married pair (*lakibini*) rather than a single individual. Thus *tusuts* are characteristically recited in the form of 'A takes a husband (or wife) B and begets C; C takes a wife (or husband) D and begets E, etc. (*A belaki diambi' B beranak ka C; C bebini ngambi' D beranak ka E*, etc.). This system of reckoning ascent accords with *bilik* affiliation, which is by marriage as well as by birth, and with the highly ramifying manner in which the Iban trace kindred relationships (Sather n.d.). The Paku River was first settled by the Iban some fourteen to fifteen generations ago, but genealogies of even greater depth are not uncommon (see Sandin 1967b:93-96).

[8] The order of family apartments within the house is negotiated in an open meeting of longhouse members (*aum*) that precedes the start of house construction. Choice is restrained by a number of rules. Thus, for example, it is prohibited (*mali*) for a family to locate its *bilik* between the *biliks* of two siblings. This prohibition is called *mali kepit, kepit* meaning literally 'to squeeze'.

[9] More abstractly, the rule is *enda' tau' meraka' orang ke-dulu*, 'it is prohibited to cross (or pass) in front of those who have gone first'. This rule is observed, for example, by the Iban when they encounter others while walking on footpaths or inside the longhouse. One must not walk, or cut in front of another person without apologizing. When he was small, my son often ran in and out of groups of people walking in file along paths, inviting humorous comments that he was behaving like a puppy (rather than a human being). *Meraka'* (or *peraka'*) also means, more generally, 'to transgress' or 'disobey' (Richards 1981:275). The phrase *orang ke-dulu* is ordinarily used in this connection only for the *pun rumah* and the members of his or her *bilik*, and, in practice, precedence is strictly observed only in regard to 'crossing in front of' the *pun rumah*'s central *tiang pemun*. This accords with the social recognition of precedence, in which only the central *bilik* has ritual priority, being associated with the initiation and ancestry of the house, while the lateral apartments, upriver and downriver, are essentially co-equal and without special ritual status associated with their location within the house.

[10] Significant ritual fines are imposed on families that fail to install their hearths during *pindah* since their failure disturbs this ordered arrangement of precedence between family *dapur*.

[11] Should another member of the longhouse become seriously ill or die, as a result of a *bilik*'s neglect of its hearth, this constitutes a major longhouse offence and the guilty *bilik* is fined according to *adat tungkal dapur* (see Sandin 1980:12). Some say that offences against the *adat dapur* are punished by the *antu dapur* spirits.

[12] Thirty-two of the thirty-three longhouses in the Paku are laid out along an upriver–downriver axis. The one exception, Bangkit Ijok, is built perpendicular to the main course of the Bangkit stream. Here 'downriver' and 'upriver' are replaced, respectively, by 'towards the river' (*baroh*, 'below') and 'away from the river' (*atas*, 'above').

[13] There are occasional exceptions. Thus at Kerangan Pinggai, the upriver–downriver location of the *tiang pemun* is reversed. Nonetheless, the same order of precedence exists between its *biliks*.

[14] The Iban distinguish between *puchok*, the tip of an upstanding object, notably a tree, and *ujong*, the tip of one laying horizontally. Thus, when a living tree is felled, what was its *puchok* (tip) becomes its *ujong*. Only when, as a building timber, it is re-erected as a standing *tiang* does its 'tip' again become *puchok*. This distinction is associated with the major division of construction materials between *tiang*, upstanding elements with *pun* and *puchok*, and *ramu*, horizontal elements with *pun* and *ujong*. While the orientation of the *tiang* has already been discussed, that of the *ramu* is described below and summarized in Figure 4.

[15] Thus Iban reverses the English association of a river's 'source' with its headwaters, associating it instead with its mouth (*nanga*).

[16] Thus, the offerings include a branch of *mumban*, a small shrub (unidentified, possibly *Pleiocarpidia* sp.) that typically grows rooted in rocks in streams or river beds. It is said that *mumban* cannot be uprooted, even by floods and strong currents.

[17] I am grateful to Robert Barrett (personal communication) for reminding me of this alternative *pun–ujong* orientation of the longhouse. Although it is not characteristic of the upper Paku, it appears to be common in other river regions.

[18] Uchibori (1978:63) writes that, following on from the notion that the *ujong* is polluting, corpses are carried out from the *ujong* end (downriver) of the longhouse. This is true of a few houses in the Paku, but not of all. Thus, in Kerangan Pinggai the centralizing notion of *pun* takes priority. As a result, corpses may be removed from both the upriver and downriver ends. The overriding rule is that they not be carried 'in front of' (across) the central *tiang pemun*. Here both the upriver and downriver ends of the longhouse are *ujong* and so, in this sense, equally 'polluting'.

[19] *Tumboh* refers to growth in the specific sense of plant growth. Thus plants, as a general category of living things (*utai idup*), are called *utai tumboh*, literally 'growing things'. *Tumboh* is distinguished from *mesai*, as applied to animals and human beings as well as to plants, meaning to grow in the sense of 'to grow larger'. Figuratively, *tumboh* also means to begin, form or organize.

[20] *Padam*, to go out, be extinguished. Figuratively, to die or death.

[21] Thus, for example, during *manggol* when new farms are cleared, first offerings are made at sunrise facing eastward. Similarly, prior to harvest, rice stalks are bound together near the centre of the family's farm to form a small shrine (*padi tanchang*). This shrine serves both to immobilize the aggregate souls of the rice (*semengat padi*) and to represent the ripened grain as a maiden (*dara*). In constructing it, and while invoking the *padi* souls, the performer similarly faces eastward (Sather 1977b:160–161). Finally, at the conclusion of the harvest rites, before returning home, the performer casts a handful of rice panicles to the west at the boundary of the field for the spirits of diminution and predation (*antu rua* and *antu rangka*) (Sather 1977b:163–164).

[22] Also *pendai'*. From the root *ai'*, water.

[23] Each Iban longhouse has two names. In addition to a topographic name, a house is also known by the name of its current headman. Thus, Kerangan Pinggai is also known as Rumah Renang, after its *tuai rumah* Renang anak Bryon. Kerangan Pinggai refers to a stretch of pebbly river-bed or shingle (*kerangan*) which marks the location of its *penai'*. Many of the pebbles making up this shingle are the size and shape of small plates (*pinggai*), hence the name.

[24] From the root *makai*, 'to eat'.

[25] These relations are complicated by migration. The Paku Iban have close ties with their neighbours in the Rimbas, Krian and Julau river regions, these rivers having been pioneered largely by Paku settlers. Houses, for example, in the far upper Paku form *sapemakai* relations with nearby houses in the upper Rimbas. In addition, the Saribas region was originally pioneered by migrations from the Skrang and in pre-Brooke and early Brooke times the Saribas and Skrang Iban formed a military confederation, mainly against the Balau and Sebuyau Iban, but also for more general coastal raiding (Pringle 1970:46–48). But here the power of rivers to define social boundaries was clearly apparent, overriding even ethnic and religious ties. Thus the Iban in each river region formed warring alliances with the local Malays living downriver, so that the Iban and Malay of one river tended historically to fight against the Iban and Malay of other rivers.

[26] Again, reflecting the dichotomous nature of Iban perceptions, the Batang Mandai also exists as a 'real' river in the visible world, in this case a tributary of the Kapuas in Kalimantan Barat. Similarly, Mount Rabong, mentioned later in connection with shamanism, also exists as a natural landmark in the visible world. Located between the headwaters of the Mandai and Kalis rivers, on the true left bank of the Ketungau, its summit can be seen from many parts of Sarawak, including much of the Saribas (Sather 1993).

[27] The *dinding ukoi*, meant to keep family dogs (*ukoi*) from entering the apartment.

[28] The upper *bilik* (*bilik atas*) contains the family's most valued possessions, including its *tajau* or heirloom jars, while the lower *bilik* (*bilik baroh*) forms the principal sleeping and living area.

[29] While the Iban speak of these different cross-sectional zones of the longhouse interior as 'upper' and 'lower', the house floor is actually level except for the elevated *panggau*. Note that for the Gerai Dayaks, described in this collection by Christine Helliwell, the house floor is actually stepped, in a series of higher and lower sections, so that its *physical* layout is essentially the same as the Iban *conceptual* plan.

[30] From here they could quickly rally to the defence of the community if it were attacked.

[31] The east–west orientation of a house is much more variable than the upriver–downriver orientation. Relatively level sites, sufficiently long to accommodate a longhouse, are scarce. Variation from the ideal orientation is sanctioned during the process of selecting a site by bird divination (*beburong*), which is believed to give direct divine affirmation of a site's auspiciousness whether it is ideally oriented or not (see Sather 1980:xxxi-xliv).

[32] Today most women in the Paku omit *bekindu'* or observe only a few days of heating.

[33] In ritual language, 'this world' (*dunya tu*) is paired with the sky and is most often described in prayer and invocatory chant as 'under the sky' (*baroh langit*) or 'covered by the sky' (*bap langit*).

[34] Today gourds are no longer used and water is generally carried from the river in plastic pails.

[35] These hearths are ordinarily placed on the *ruai* beneath the trophy heads which are suspended above them (for warmth) on special ring-frames. Thus the longhouse has two sets of hearths: the family *dapur* and the external *bedilang*. The latter are placed at the thresholds (*antara*) between adjoining family sections of the *ruai*. Instead of earth, the *bedilang* are made of stone and, like the *dapur*, are of major ritual importance. The position of the *bedilang* in warming the trophy heads (*antu pala*) is analogous to that of the *dapur* in warming the rice, the one located on the communal gallery, positioned between family sections of the *ruai*, the other inside the family apartment beneath its rice storage-bins and between adjacent *biliks*.

[36] The head of the body inside the *sapat* is towards the east or *panggau*.

[37] Some bards deny this, pointing out that the body is already 'hot', and claim that the fire is instead a source of light that guides the dead on its journey to the cemetery.

[38] In the poem of lamentation, the role of the entry ladder in preserving the souls of the living is stressed. Thus the spirit of the ladder is made to account for its inattentiveness in allowing the deceased to die, that is, for permitting his/her soul to leave the longhouse and journey to the Otherworld. Various other parts of the longhouse are not only attributed spirit form, but in this manifestation are similarly thought to safeguard the souls of the living members of the community.

[39] An important motif of both shamanic rituals and weaving.

[40] As we shall see in a moment, *limban* also refers to lymphatic fluid associated with bodily decomposition.

[41] A passage also, note, from west (death) to east (life).

[42] Not all Iban locate the *ayu* there, although this is, in the Paku, the most common shamanic view. Some Iban, in fact, identify the plant image with the hearthframe. This view is consistent with a commonly held notion that the longhouse not only *represents* the unseen cosmos, but, in actuality, *is* this cosmos, including the Otherworld of the dead. Thus, some Iban say that the souls of the dead never really leave the longhouse, but are present, living in an inverted world, most often thought to be located beneath the longhouse floor. Offerings to the dead are regularly dropped through the floor slates, usually under the *tempuan*. Here also, beneath the *tempuan*, the 'severed flowers' and the *rugan* altars are thrown in rites which mark the separation of the living and the dead. This view, equating the longhouse and the Otherworld is, of course, consistent with the reversed nature of the soul's journey and the shaman's representation of this journey in his *pelian*. For another context in which the longhouse interior is perceived as an unseen cosmos see Sather (1978:319–326).

[43] Again, the pieces of the *sungkup* can be carried into the longhouse and assembled on the veranda only after a sacrifice has been made at the foot of the entry ladder and the *tiang pemun* lustrated with blood, together with the *ramu* of the Gawai elder. These lustrations (*genselan*), again, preserve the house from 'heat'.

[44] A house must be in good repair to withstand the press of visitors. During one Gawai Antu I attended at Ulu Bayor, Rimbas, the number of guests was so great that, by the end of three nights, the pillars of the house had sunk more than a foot into the earth under their weight.

[45] Today, in modern Gawai Antu they may carry a banner bearing the name of the longhouse they represent.

[46] Traditionally the night following the Gawai Antu (*malam ngayap maia gawai*) was one of licensed courtship, in which married men and women temporarily resumed bachelor and maiden status and were free to engage in courting in honor of the still lingering spirit-heroes and heroines (Sather 1977a:xiii-xiv).

[47] It is significant to note that the way in which the longhouse may appear to the unseen spirits and souls may also vary, in a parallel manner, just as the house may assume different 'spiritual' forms in the seen world. Thus, for example, if the *ensing*, or common kingfisher, flies into the longhouse and down the *tempuan* passageway past the doors of its *bilik*s, it is regarded as a disastrous omen called *burong rajang ruas*. It signifies that the longhouse now appears to the spirits as a *ruas*, a bamboo cooking tube in which meat and other food is stewed. As an omen, it indicates that the longhouse will catch on fire and some of its members burn to death. Until it can be neutralized, and the 'spiritual' appearance of the structure repaired, all families must temporarily evacuate the house (*bubus rumah*). Ideally, in an inverted way, the longhouse of the living should be invisible to the spirits, just as their lairs are ordinarily invisible to human beings.

[48] Helliwell argues persuasively in this collection, and at greater length elsewhere (1990) against a view of the longhouse as composed of highly independent 'household' units, its social life shaped, in an ontologically-prior sense, by the physical division of the house into walled apartments. Although developed in different terms, this argument and the one I pursued here are, I think, mutually supportive.

A thirty-post traditional Minangkabau house in Nagari Koto nan Gadang, Lima Puluh Kota

Chapter 5. Raising the House Post and Feeding the Husband-Givers: The spatial categories of social reproduction among the Minangkabau

Cecilia Ng

Introduction

The Minangkabau

The Minangkabau are among the largest of the ethnic groups in Indonesia. Besides being known for their matrilineal organization, the Minangkabau are also noted as energetic Muslim traders who have migrated far beyond their homeland in the province of West Sumatra.[1] According to the 1980 census, the population of West Sumatra was approximately 3.4 million, of whom an estimated 3 million were Minangkabau. The majority of the Minangkabau population lives in the fertile upland plains where irrigated rice cultivation is their mainstay.

Minangkabau Social Organization

In this paper I am concerned with the principles of domestic spatial organization in Minangkabau society. The use of space in everyday and ceremonial contexts reveals perceptible patterns relating to the nature of Minangkabau social organization and shows the key definitions of male and female identity. Before proceeding to the discussion on the use of space, I deal briefly with four salient aspects of Minangkabau social organization, which are necessary to understand their divisions of space.[2] I should perhaps remark that my interpretation of Minangkabau social organization differs to some extent from that of other scholars.

First, the population of a Minangkabau village is divided into a number of matrilineal clans (*suku*), which are further segmented into lineages (*sa-payuang*). The lineages are represented by *panghulu* (lineage headmen) and have been characterized by scholars as corporate groups. Most scholars researching Minangkabau society have tended to focus their attention on Minangkabau jural structures. There are, however, other informal patterns of social relations which are significant in the everyday lives of the villagers. One important category of social relations which cannot be viewed as a jural structure is the *sa-kampuang*. The *sa-kampuang* refers to the members with the same *suku* name (but who are not necessarily from the same clan) and who live in the same neighbourhood.

Although the *sa-kampuang* has kinship and territorial connotations, it is not represented by a *panghulu* and is not a jural structure. The *sa-kampuang* is an informal and flexible category whose members come together most visibly on ceremonial occasions. In everyday life the relationships which are defined as *sa-kampuang* are of primary importance, especially to women who, in contrast to men, spend a large proportion of their time in the neighbourhood. Thus, I stress that it is essential to look at the informal though no less significant structures, if we are to understand Minangkabau social order.

My second point is that the emphasis placed on jural structures in the village gives unwarranted significance to the authority of men as mothers' brothers/*panghulu*. In my view, the Minangkabau are not only matrilineal but are also a matrifocal society. It is frequently reported by scholars on Minangkabau society that the mothers' brothers/*panghulu* are the key authority figures, representing their lineages in transactions with other lineages. This emphasis has led to the following statements:

> the structurally most important relationship in the Minangkabau matrilineal system is one between *mamak* and *kemenakan*.

> The *mamak* is the guardian of the *kemenakan* and is responsible for the well-being of the *kemenakan*, who are to continue their lineage ... *The essence of Minangkabau matriliny is above all concentrated in the two generation relation of mamak and kemenakan* (Kato 1977:57-58; emphasis added).

In contrast to men's command in the public domain, women are generally seen as having authority only within the minimal family unit and the matrilineally extended family, that is, within the domestic domain. This dichotomy of women:domestic::men:public is, in light of my findings, inaccurate and misleading. In Nagari Koto nan Gadang, women are vital actors: they negotiate and mediate interlineage relationships and act as representatives of their lineages in the fields of affinal relations and ritual obligations. To understand Minangkabau social organization it is necessary to begin from the perspective of the women, since kin relationships are conceptualized as categories which are based on the difference between groups of women.

Third, affinal categories constitute one of the most significant ways of ordering social relationships in Minangkabau society. These categories I gloss as husband-givers and husband-takers: this usage necessarily implies that men, and not women, are exchanged. One of the reasons for this unorthodox interpretation is that in the wedding ceremony the groom (who is 'rented' or 'bought') is 'handed-over' to the bride's lineage.

A final point concerns the Minangkabau residence pattern. Domestic residence for a boy changes as he grows up. Young boys before they are circumcised (usually at the age of eight to ten), sleep in their mothers' household. After circumcision, boys sleep in the mosque till they marry. There they receive *adat* [3] and Islamic instruction from the senior men of the village. If boys who have reached puberty were to sleep in the same house as their married sisters, it would, according to villagers, create an embarrassing situation for the married couple. Post-marital residence is uxorilocal and even when a new house is built for a married couple the land on which the house is built belongs to the wife's lineage. One of the most important ramifications of this residence rule is that women are spatially grouped together and in day-to-day life women form the core group within the village. This is especially so, too, because Minangkabau men tend to migrate (*merantau*)[4] to urban centres to find a livelihood.

Spatial Organization in the House

There are two types of houses in the village, the traditional Minangkabau house, *rumah gadang* (big house), and the modern house, *rumah gedung* (brick house). Few traditional houses are built these days, as the cost is far greater than that of modern houses. In Balai Cacang,[5] ninetyseven of 135 houses are modern and thirty-eight traditional (see also Table 1). The modern house, which is modelled on the traditional house plan, is usually built within the compound of the lineage's traditional house. Assuming that relations between the households are good, the traditional house is usually used as the venue for any large ceremony sponsored by the household living in the modern house. Investitures of *panghulu* can only be held in the largest type of traditional house, that with thirty posts, and sponsors of the ceremony may 'borrow' (*maminjam*) a house from another villager for the purpose.

Both the modern and traditional houses are based on a rectangular plan. The traditional house is made of wood and the roof may be thatch (from the fibre of the *enau* palm) or, more frequently, of corrugated iron. In Nagari Koto nan Gadang there are three sizes of traditional houses (see Figure 1). The largest is the thirty-post house, and the two smaller ones are the twenty-post and the twelve-post houses. House plans are the same for all three sizes and the traditional house is built raised 1–2 metres off the ground.

At the left end of the house is an annex (*anjuang*) which is slightly elevated from the floor level of the house (see Figure 2). The annex is also qualified as the *anjuang nan tinggi* (the high annex), a reference to both its elevation from the floor level and to its symbolic significance as the pinnacle of the house. Sleeping quarters (*biliak*) are adjacent and are in the rear of the twenty-post and thirty-post houses. Curtained doorways of the *biliak* open out onto the hall (*ruang*). In the thirty-post house, the hall is divided into three zones: the *ruang ateh* (elevated hall) which is immediately in front of the sleeping quarters; the *ruang tongah* (central hall); and the *ruang topi* (side hall) by the windows at the front of the house. There are only two zones in the halls of the twenty-post house, the *ruang tongah* and the *ruang topi*. In the twelve-post house, there are no *biliak* and the hall is not differentiated into zones. The inner recess of the hall is, however, used as sleeping quarters if necessary.

Table 1. Composition of households

category	description of composition	house type	no.	%	category total	%
Single	Single women who are divorced or whose husbands are deceased	modern*	8	5.9	8	6
		traditional	-	-		
Elementary	Woman + children	modern	6	4.4		
		traditional	3	2.2		
	Woman + husband + children	modern	35	25.9		
		traditional	9	6.7		
	Man + children	modern	1	0.7		
		traditional	-	-	54	40
Compound	Woman + Z +/or MZD + (B +/or MZS)† + (spouse +/or ZH/MZ) + children	modern	6	4.4		
		traditional	4	3.0		
	Man + (W) + children	modern	-	-		
		traditional	-	-		
	Woman + (H) + (M +/or F) + her children +/or ZD/ZS + children's H +/or ZDH + children's children +/or ZD's children	modern	15	11.1		
		traditional	10	7.4		
	Woman + SS	modern	-	-		
		traditional	1	0.7		
	Woman + (H) + children + MMB	modern	1	0.7		
		traditional	-	-		
	Woman + (H) + D + (DH) + ZD + (ZDH) + Z + (ZH) + S	modern	22	16.3		
		traditional	11	8.1		
	Woman + S + (SW) + S's children + DS + DSW + DS's children	modern	1	0.7		
		traditional	-	-		
	Woman + D + DH + D's children	modern	1	0.7		
		traditional	-	-		
	Woman + H + D + S + HZD	modern	1	0.7		
		traditional	-	-	73	54
TOTAL					135	100

* Modern houses are brick and concrete buildings.
† Brackets show that these relatives are not part of all households within the described type.

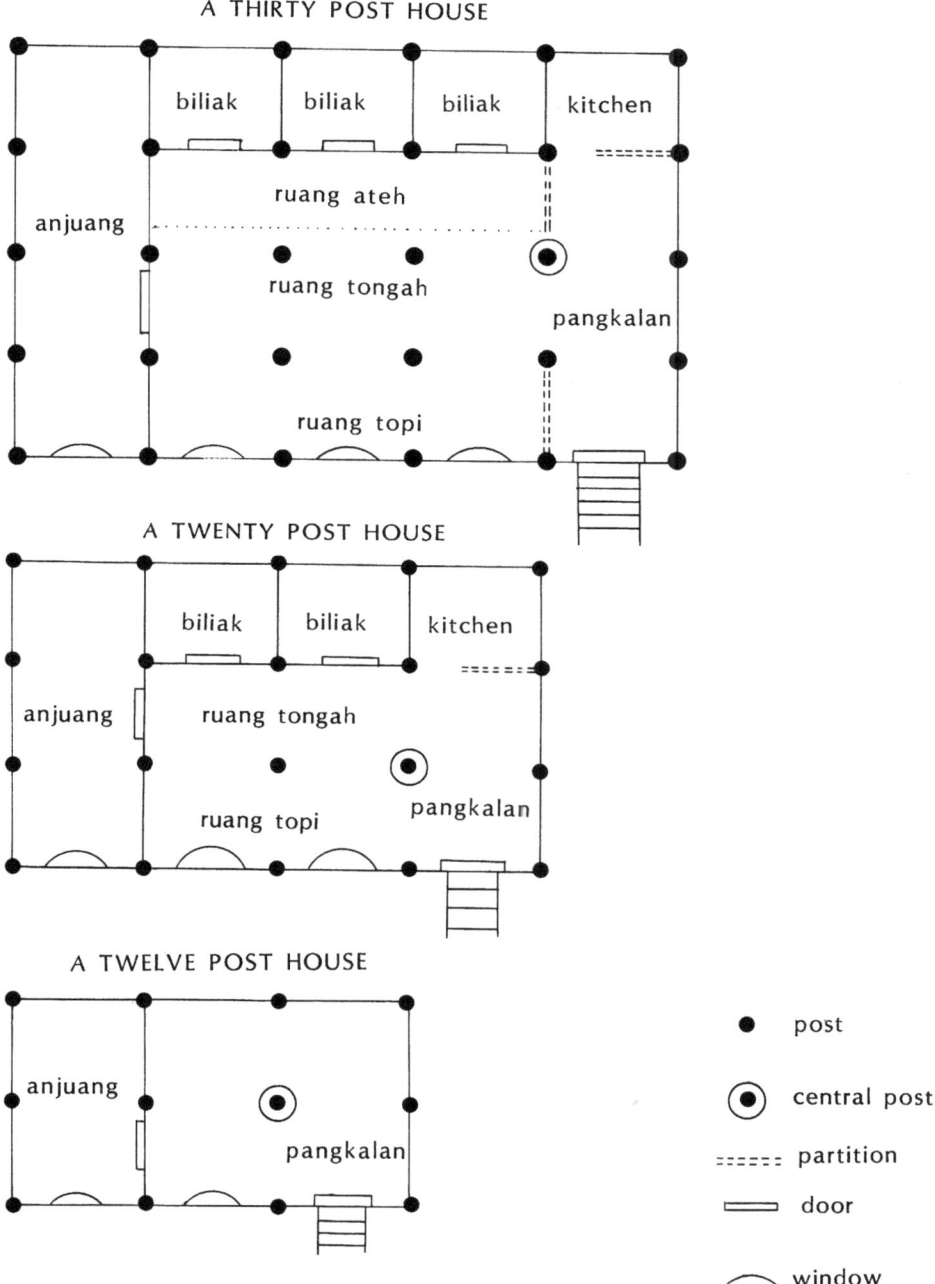

Figure 1. The *rumah gadang*

At the right rear end of the house is the kitchen (*dapur*), which is lower than the floor level of the hall. In some houses, the kitchen is built on ground level and a flight of steps leads down to the kitchen from inside the house. At the right end, in the front of the house, a flight of steps of uneven numbers (usually three, five or seven) leads up to the main door of the house which opens into the *pangkalan* (from *pangkal*: 'base', 'foundation', 'beginning', 'origin'). This space is usually on a lower level than the hall. The windows (two in a twelve-post house, three in a twenty-post house and four in a thirty-post one) are on the front of the house and face the courtyard (*halaman*).

Under the house (*rumah dalam*, inside house), wooden slats or filigree wooden walls enclose the space. Here the looms are set up, the weaver sitting directly below the annex. Chicken coops, firewood and coconuts are kept in the rear of the *rumah dalam* below the kitchen area. If there is more than one household living in the traditional house, another hearth may be built directly below the *pangkalan* or the kitchen.

In everyday life, the house is very much the domain of women and houses are said to be built for them. No self-respecting man would spend too much time during the day either in his wife's or his mother's house. In the daytime, men work in their offices, shops, the market, the fields and wet-rice lands or spend their time in the coffee house (*warung*), a place where men congregate to exchange gossip and news. They return to their wives' houses only after sundown for their evening meal and to sleep.

Women, in contrast, spend much of their time in or around the house, weaving in the *rumah dalam*, drying yarn, padi or rice cakes in the courtyard, pounding rice in the mortar in the courtyard, drawing water, preparing food in the kitchen and spinning or sewing in the *pangkalan*, visible to all the passers-by. A woman should be diligent and be seen or be heard (as in the case of the rhythmic beating of the weaving comb) to be diligent. One is a socially acceptable being only if one's actions are open to public witness. Windows and doors are thrown open in the early morning and are only shut when there is no one in the house and at night. Visitors announce their presence by shouting out from the courtyard and often women in the house can be seen standing by their windows, having conversations with passers-by in the courtyard.

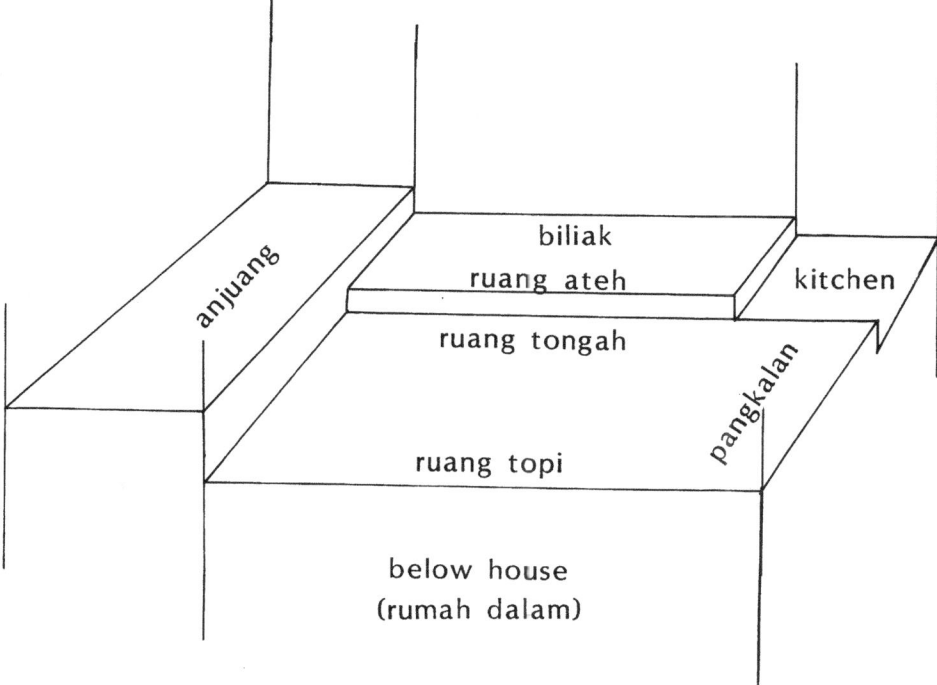

Figure 2. Levels in the *rumah gadang*

Within the house, the hall is a semi-private space. It is converted into a public space by laying mats on the floor. Guests sit on the *ruang topi* by the windows while the household members sit facing the guests on the *ruang tongah*. Most ritual activities are held in the hall and in the courtyard. In a few houses there may be chairs in the hall, but usually there is no furniture, except for a cupboard placed in the *ruang tongah* next to the annex. The valuables of the household, ceremonial cloths, heirloom bowls and jars, are kept locked in this cupboard and the eldest woman of the house holds the key. Daily meals are also eaten on the *ruang tongah* in privacy. Should a visitor call at such an inopportune moment, the meal is cleared away quickly, or if there is insufficient time, the visitor is invited to join in the meal, but the invitation is not meant to be taken seriously. The embarrassment is felt by both the household members and by the visitor for having intruded.

At night, the windows and doors are shut and the house becomes a private space. Generally villagers do not visit each other after nightfall, except on invitation or when there is a ceremony held in the house. This is especially so when there is a recently married couple sleeping in the house.

Sleeping arrangements in the traditional house follow a specific order (see Figure 3). The most recently married girl and her husband sleep in the *anjuang* (annex).⁶ This room is regarded as hers and is kept vacant for her, even if she and her husband are on a protracted *merantau*. On the marriage of a younger girl (either sister or mother's sister's daughter) in the house, she vacates the annex and moves to the bedroom adjacent to the annex. The occupants of the *biliak* move one room down towards the kitchen. Since marriage follows birth order, ideally and generally in practice, the oldest woman sleeps in the *biliak* next to the kitchen. However, if there were insufficient *biliak*, she would sleep in the *pangkalan*. When there is a spare *biliak*, the one adjacent to the annex is kept vacant to ensure the newly married couple has more privacy. Unmarried girls share the *biliak* of their mother if her husband no longer visits her. Alternatively, the unmarried girls sleep on the *ruang ateh* or the *ruang tongah* near the central post (*tonggak tuo*) of the house.

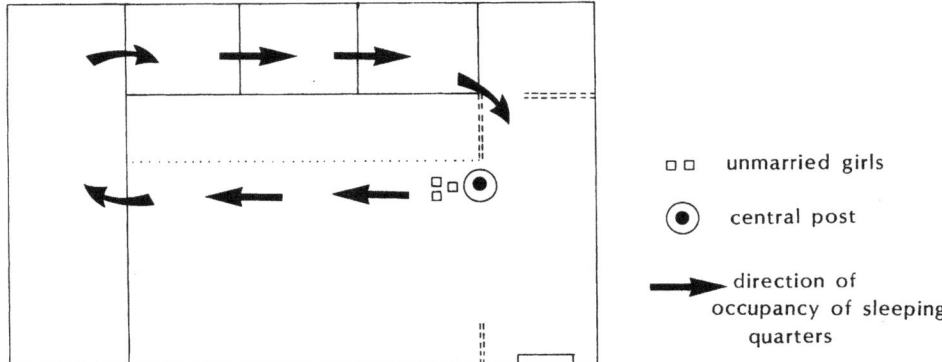

Figure 3. Sleeping order in the traditional house

Beds are the main furniture in the *biliak* and the annex. A sofa and a dressing table are also standard furniture in the annex. The annex and the *biliak* are private spaces and personal possessions, for example, clothes, are kept in the *biliak*. Except on ceremonial occasions and on the invitation of the occupant, female guests do not enter the annex or the *biliak*. The only men who may enter these rooms are the husbands and the unmarried sons of the occupants.

The kitchen is also a private space. Unless one is a close matrilineal relative or a friend, to enter the kitchen during non-ceremonial occasions, or without invitation, is considered as prying since what one consumes as part of daily fare is simple and as a subject of discussion is considered embarrassing (*malu*). During ceremonies, women of the sponsor's *sa-kampuang* may enter the kitchen to assist but guests may not. When ostentatious cooking is done, as for the large ceremonial feasts, a simple shack is erected to serve as the cooking space in the compound, partly because more space is needed and partly to be in public view.

In front of the kitchen is the *pangkalan*. This is a public space which everyone entering the house must necessarily pass through. Guests may sometimes sit in the *pangkalan* instead of the hall. Here, too, older women at the end of their reproductive cycle sleep.

In the traditional house, there are levels of connected meanings. First, there is a division of space where procreativity takes place, and the space for social interactions. The spaces where procreativity (the annex and the *biliak*) takes place are private, while the space where social discourse and interactions are conducted (the *ruang*) is public. There is a gradation of public to private space in the *ruang* itself (see Figure 4); the *ruang tepi* is a semi-public space where the guests sit, and more public than the *ruang tongah* on which the household members sit facing and entertaining their guests. As we proceed to the rear of the house, open space becomes enclosed as the *biliak*, and these rooms are private.

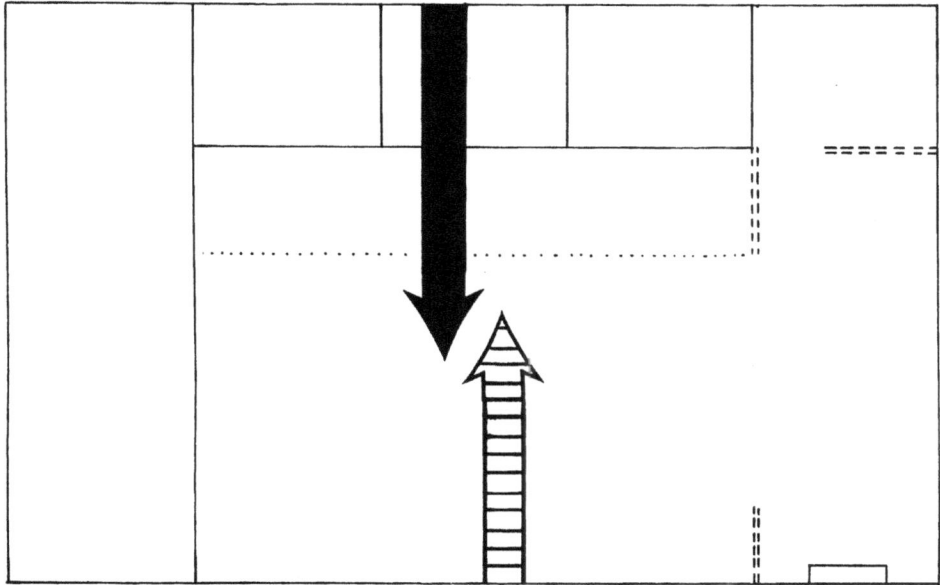

Figure 4. Public and private space

The annex is a private space where a young girl begins her reproductive cycle and here, a groom's agency is transformed into children for the continuity of the lineage. In opposition to the annex, the kitchen area (that is, the kitchen and the *pangkalan*) is where women at the end of their reproductive cycle sleep.

Here too the corpse is bathed before she/he is laid in state in the middle of the *ruang topi* and *ruang tongah*.

The kitchen is where a transformation of another kind, raw food into cooked food, takes place. Food is the means for enhancing and affirming social relationships (see Figure 5). The kitchen is in the rear of the house and connects, in a circular route, the areas of biological reproduction and the public areas (the *ruang* and the *pangkalan*) where social interactions take place and where new elements from the external community, men, are introduced to perpetuate the lineage.

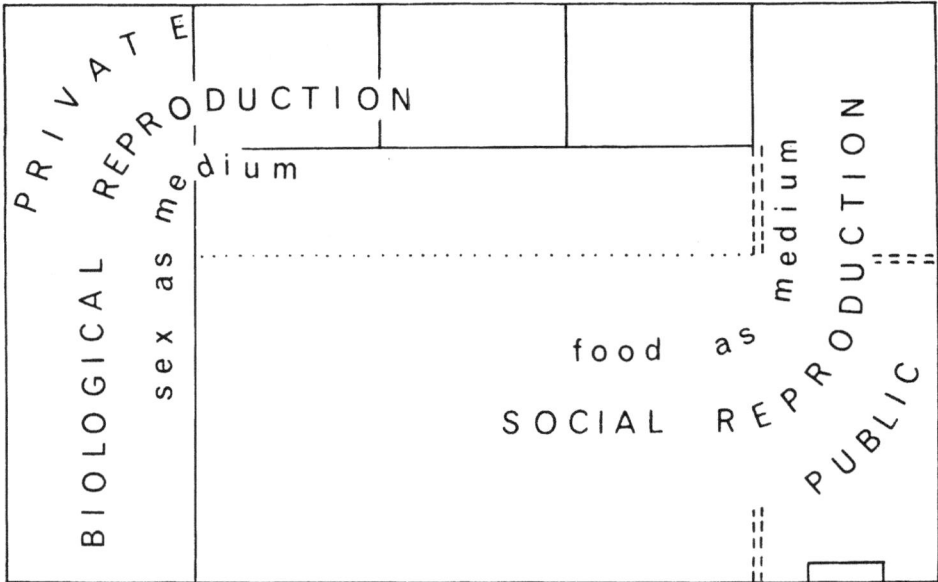

Figure 5. Meanings in the traditional house

We then have a set of oppositions in the meanings underlying the use of space which can be presented as shown in Figure 6.

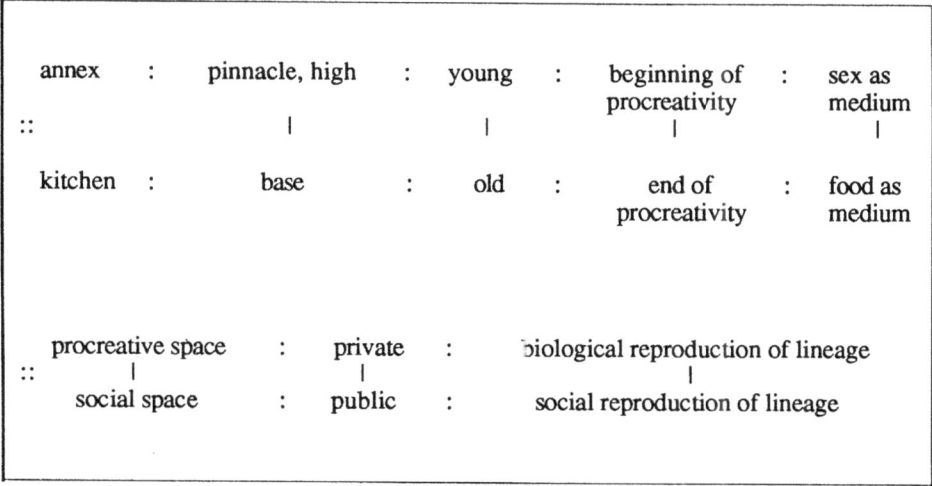

Figure 6. Underlying meanings in the use of space

Implicit in the use of space is the dimension of time; that is, the life cycle of the woman (see Figure 7). When unmarried, a woman sleeps near the central post. She proceeds to the annex as she enters her reproductive phase and then moves down the *biliak* towards the kitchen. At the end of her period of procreativity, she moves into the *pangkalan*. The young girls sleeping near the central post can be interpreted as symbolic of the fact that they are the progeny through whom the lineage will continue. This is indicated in the house-building ceremony (*mandirikan rumah*, literally 'raising the house') where, as the climax of the occasion, unmarried girls of the lineage, for whom the house is said to be built, symbolically pull the central post (*tonggak tuo*) erect. The sexual symbolism is blatant enough, but another meaning is that the young girls form the continuity of the lineage. Further evidence that the central post of the house is closely associated with the continuity of the lineage is the practice of burying the placenta and the umbilical cord of a newborn member of the lineage at the foot of the post.

Use of Space in Ceremonies

So far I have discussed Minangkabau organization of domestic space. In this section I turn to the use of space on *adat* ceremonial occasions. Before proceeding to describe the general principles in the use of space on ceremonial occasions and presenting an account of a specific ceremony, a part of a wedding, it is necessary here to state briefly the sociology of *adat* ceremonies.

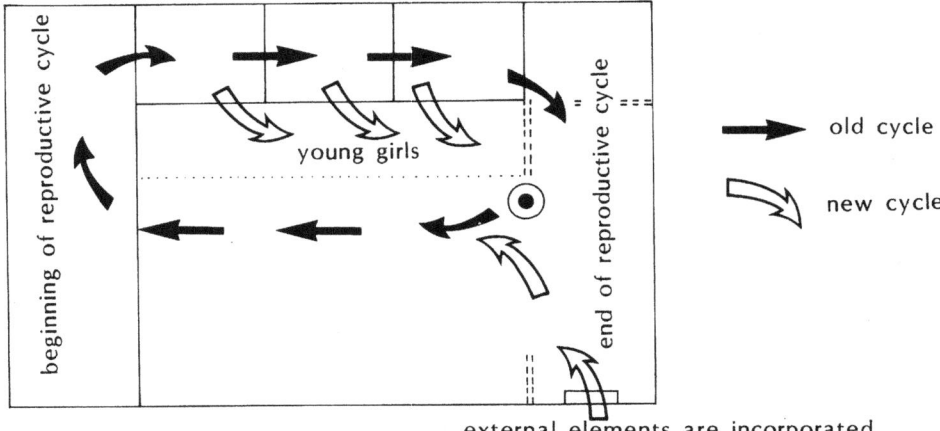

Figure 7. Life cycle in the traditional house

Sociology of Adat Ceremonies

Women are the principal figures in *adat* ceremonies either as organizers or as participants. While women are present in all *adat* ceremonies, including those in which men play central roles, men do not attend those ceremonies where they do not have central roles to perform. This is partly because *adat* ceremonies are always held in the sponsor's house and since the house is mainly women's domain, women's presence is indispensible. This differential participation of men and women reflects their positions in Minangkabau society. Women form the core groups of lineages and are mediators between affinal categories. Since *adat* ceremonies concern kin networks, women's presence is essential on these occasions. In contrast, men who are interstitial to Minangkabau social organization, are not required to participate in all *adat* ceremonies.

In most *adat* ceremonies, the female participants can be divided into the following categories (see Figure 8):

1. Women of the sponsoring lineage and women from the sponsoring lineage's *sa-kampuang*.
2. Women of the sponsor's husband-giving lineages and the women of the husband-givers' *sa-kampuang*.
3. Women of the sponsors' husband-taking lineages and the women of the husband-takers' *sa-kampuang*.

Men participate only in major *adat* ceremonies and in the following capacities:

1. Men of the sponsoring lineage and their *sa-kampuang* men.
2. In-married men (*orang sumando*) of the sponsoring lineage and men of the in-married men's *sa-kampuang*.

3. *Panghulu* of the sponsoring lineage and the *panghulu* of the *sa-kampuang* of the sponsoring lineage.
4. *Panghulu* of the guest lineage and the guest lineage's *sa-kampuang* (the guest lineage would be either the bride's or the groom's in wedding ceremonies).

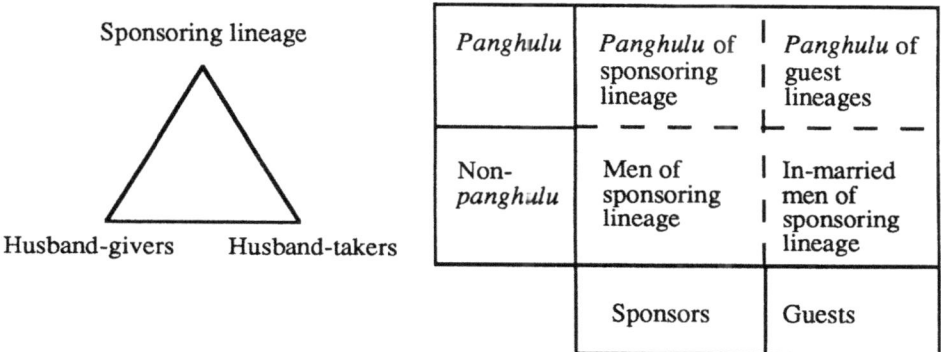

Figure 8. Participants in *adat* ceremonies

General Patterns

This section summarizes the pattern of spatial organization in ceremonial context. The interpretation is based on observation of a wide range of ceremonies (birth, death, weddings), which cannot be elaborated here.

The use of space in ceremonies follows a specific pattern (see Figure 9). Women of the sponsor's husband-giving lineages sit on the *ruang tongah* or in the section of the *ruang ateh* near the annex. The women of the sponsor's husband-taking lineages are allocated the *ruang topi* or the area of the *ruang ateh* nearer the kitchen. In my interpretation this pattern is significant. Husband-givers contribute to the reproduction of the sponsor's lineage and are seated in the areas closer to the space for procreation. In contrast, husband-takers, who do not contribute to the biological reproduction of the sponsor's lineage, are seated further away from the space of procreativity.

When only women participate in the ceremony:

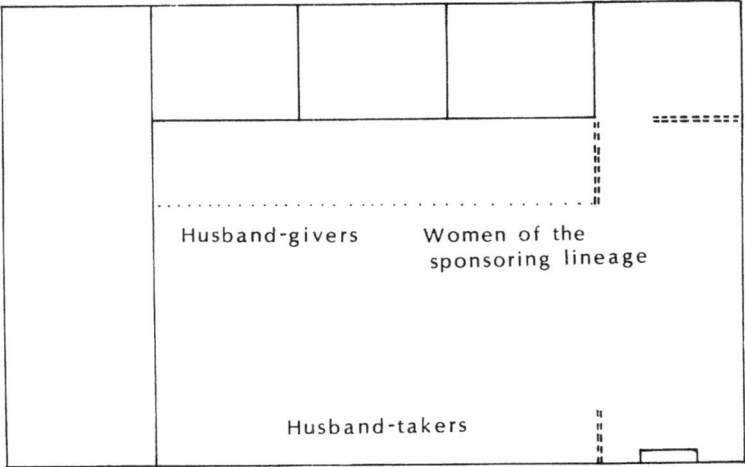

When men and women participate in the ceremony:

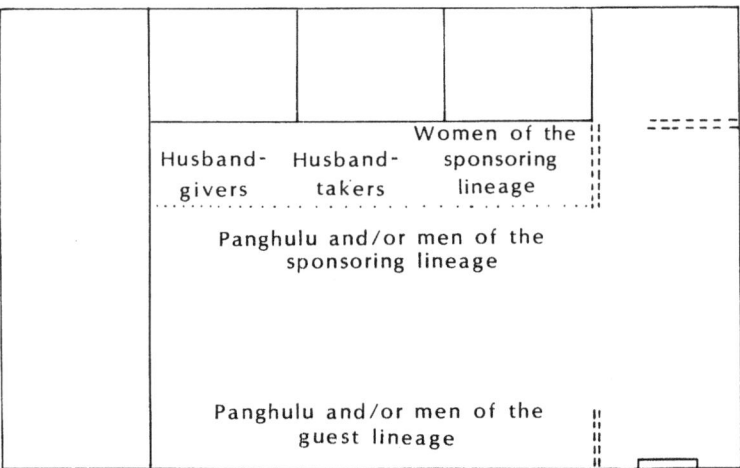

Figure 9. Spatial organization in *adat* ceremonies

For men, when there are only two groups of men present in the ceremony, those who are from the sponsor's lineage sit in the *ruang tongah*, while guests sit in the *ruang topi*, the more public space. When *panghulu* are involved in the ritual as well, those of the sponsor's lineage sit in the *ruang tongah* nearer the annex, while guest *panghulu* sit in the *ruang topi*. The men of the sponsor's lineage sit on the *ruang tongah* near the kitchen end, while the in-married men sit in the *ruang topi* near the door.

A Wedding Ceremony

The following are my fieldwork notes about a specific wedding ceremony, the *malam basampek* ('night of chance [of escape]').[7] This ceremony is held in the house of the bride who sits in full ceremonial costume throughout the ceremony. Acting as sponsors are the women and young men of the bride's lineage and *sa-kampuang*. The ceremony is held in the evening and marks the groom's first night in his wife's lineage house. The use of space in this ceremony is of especial interest, as it shows the incorporation of the groom into his wife's lineage.

The Malam Basampek

At Endy's (the groom's) house, the young boys of his lineage and *sa-kampuang* gather to await the arrival of two boys from Ery's (the bride's) lineage, who will present a betel-nut box to invite the groom to his bride's house on this night. Endy's mother and her sister pack a bundle of his personal possessions (shoes, clothes, sarong, cigarettes) amidst comments from the *sa-kampuang* women, who have begun to gather in the house, that his mother never need wash Endy's clothes again.

After the two boys from Ery's lineage arrive, at about nine in the evening, the women of Endy's lineage and *sa-kampuang* leave with the bundle of his possessions ostentatiously carried on a tray. Unmarried girls also accompany the women. The unmarried boys and Endy form the rear party.

At the bride's house the groom is met at the doorway by two elderly women from her lineage. Ery is seated on the nuptial seat in the *ruang topi*. The unmarried boys of her lineage are seated on the *ruang tongah* and plates of cakes and betel-nut are laid out on the mats. Endy and his boys sit in the *ruang topi*, while the women from the groom's party are shown to the *ruang ateh* and the annex.

Shortly after the guests' arrival, rhetorical exchange between speakers (men) representing the groom's and bride's sections begins. The speaker of the bride's side requests that the groom sit with the bride. The speaker of the groom's side demurs. After much procrastination, the speaker representing the groom's lineage finally agrees to the groom sitting with the bride. Two elderly women from Ery's *sa-kampuang* present a betel-nut box to the speaker of the groom's side as an invitation to the groom to sit with the bride. The women then lead the groom to his seat next to Ery. During this break in the oration, the boys have their refreshments and Endy returns to the *ruang topi*. A second round of rhetorical exchange soon begins with the speaker of the groom's lineage asking to take leave, but the bride's speaker tries to detain the groom's entourage. The groom's group finally manages to depart by one o'clock in the morning. However, there are cases when the oratory continues until three or four in the morning.

When the oratory is over, the boys from the groom's party leave and Endy tries to leave with them. The boys from the bride's side physically restrain him from leaving while the boys of the groom's party pull at him to leave with them. This is acted out playfully, but, as reported by my informants, there have been occasions when fights have broken out between the two parties. When the groom is led back to the house, the senior women of the bride's lineage serve him his meal in the *ruang ateh*. Endy spends the night in the annex with his bride.

Interpretation

The rite of passage of the newly married couple is marked by changes in the use of space. The annex, the room where a girl enters the realm of procreativity, now becomes Ery's personal space. From being a product of the lineage, sleeping near the central post, the symbol of continuity, she becomes a reproducer for her lineage, generating further continuity.

In the groom's case, his change of residence demonstrates that he becomes the agent through whom reproduction of Ery's lineage is made possible. His personal possessions are ceremonially carried to the bride's house by the women of his lineage and solemnly handed over to the women of Ery's lineage. On the first evening that the groom spends in his bride's house, he moves from the *ruang topi*, the most public social space in the house, to the *ruang ateh* where he is fed, a progression towards the private space of procreativity before finally retiring to the annex, the point of entry into the reproductive cycle.

Food

Food is exchanged among female affines in *adat* ceremonies as well as on non-ritual occasions. A generalized hierarchy of food appears in Table 2.

In everyday domestic life, the obtaining, preparation and serving of food are principally women's work. Men contribute towards the food expenses of their wives' households and some men also contribute to their mothers' or sisters' households. Often, however, a man's contribution is minimal, sufficient to meet only the cost of his own consumption needs. On the whole, women are mainly responsible for meeting the major portion of their households' daily food expenses, either from their earned income or by their efforts expended in collecting vegetables in the village or from the gardens, fishing in fresh-water ponds and in attending to wet-rice fields. Daughters from the age of twelve are taught to cook and take on responsibility for shopping, preparing and serving meals. Men do not assist in the preparation of food in the domestic sphere. But they usually cook the main meat dishes for ostentatious *adat* ceremonies and are often cooks in urban Minangkabau restaurants.

Table 2. Hierarchy of food and labour

CONTEXT	LABOUR	FOOD	COST
Ostentatious, highly public occasions such as investitures and large-scale weddings	*Sa-kampuang* men cook the main meat dish or a cook (male or female) is hired; *sa-kampuang* women prepare other dishes and ingredients	Buffalo meat or beef cooked in a variety of spices and in coconut milk	Expensive
Modest weddings, birth and death ceremonies	*Sa-kampuang* women prepare and cook the meal or a cook is hired	Goat meat, chicken and large whole fish	
Meal for *sa-kampuang* helpers	Women and girls of the sponsoring lineage prepare and cook the meal	Vegetables such as jack-fruit and taro stems, small fish	
Everyday, domestic situation	Women and girls of the household prepare and cook the meal	Leafy vegetables, soybean, eggs; less variety of spices and usually no coconut milk used	Cheaper

For feasts in birth and death ceremonies, fish and chicken are served. Wedding feasts must include at least some dishes of goat curry (*gulai kambing*).[8] The more well-to-do villagers serve beef curry as the main dish in their wedding feasts. For investitures, water-buffalo meat is an essential part of the ceremonial feast. Vegetables, except in the form of potato cakes (*perkedel*),[9] a non-indigenous dish, are not served in ceremonial meals, but may be included in the meat dishes. A ceremonial meal usually includes several other side-dishes, like noodles, fried chicken and whole fish. The latter two dishes are often placed on high plates for show, and are not meant to be eaten by guests.

The preparations of refreshments and food for *adat* ceremonies are labour-intensive and mainly women's tasks. Women of the sponsoring lineage and their *sa-kampuang* women are responsible for making various kinds of cakes, grating coconuts, preparing ingredients and cooking the dishes required for modest ceremonial meals. An expert female cook may be hired to cook the goat curry; if not, it is the work of the women of the sponsoring lineage and their *sa-kampuang*. In return for their assistance, the *sa-kampuang* women are served a midday meal by the sponsors. This meal usually comprises rice, a vegetable curry (jack-fruit curry or a taro stem curry) and small fried fish. Butchering of goats, cows and water-buffaloes is done by men of the sponsoring lineage and their *sa-kampuang*. These men (or a male cook who may be hired) cook the beef or water-buffalo meat curries for the high *adat* ceremonies. However, obtaining and preparing the ingredients (chopping onions, grating chillies, ginger, coconuts, etc.) still remain the work of women.

Men's labour is used at highly public and ostentatious ceremonies, while women's labour is employed in the less public, modest occasions and in preparing the ingredients and cooking the rice, potato cakes and noodles for the lavish meals.[10] This pattern in the division of labour with regard to food also occurs in the organization of ceremonies; while women negotiate and implement decisions, men legitimate and validate these negotiations through their oratory.

Exchange of Food

While sex is the means by which a lineage is biologically reproduced, food is the medium for affirming the lineage's social relations, particularly affinal relations. In turn, good social relations make possible further biological reproduction of the lineage. Earlier, in the section on the use of space in traditional Minangkabau houses, I related food to sex. The annex is where virgins are transformed into reproducers of their lineage and where men's agency is transformed into children of their wives' lineages. In the kitchen raw food is transformed into cooked food, a medium for affirming social relations and, therefore, social reproduction. The connection of meanings is not so far-fetched. In Indonesian, *makan* (to eat) is a metaphor for sexual intercourse. That food and sex are connected is also demonstrated in the pattern of food exchange in ceremonial contexts. The items of food exchanged can be classified as: (1) cooked food (often served as a meal), (2) uncooked food (rice, meat, fish, etc.), and (3) cakes and fruit.

Cakes and fruit are a category of food apart from meat, fish, vegetables and rice. Unlike these latter items, cakes and fruit are not considered substantial foods and a meal is not defined by their presence. Cakes, a labour-intensive food, form a high proportion of exchanges between guests and sponsors. Sponsors always serve food, either in the form of a meal or as elaborate cakes, to their guests. On occasions when a meal is served, guests (both husband-takers and husband-givers) give hulled uncooked rice to help, according to my informants, the sponsors with the economic burden. Figure 10 shows details of exchanges between the affines on weddings.

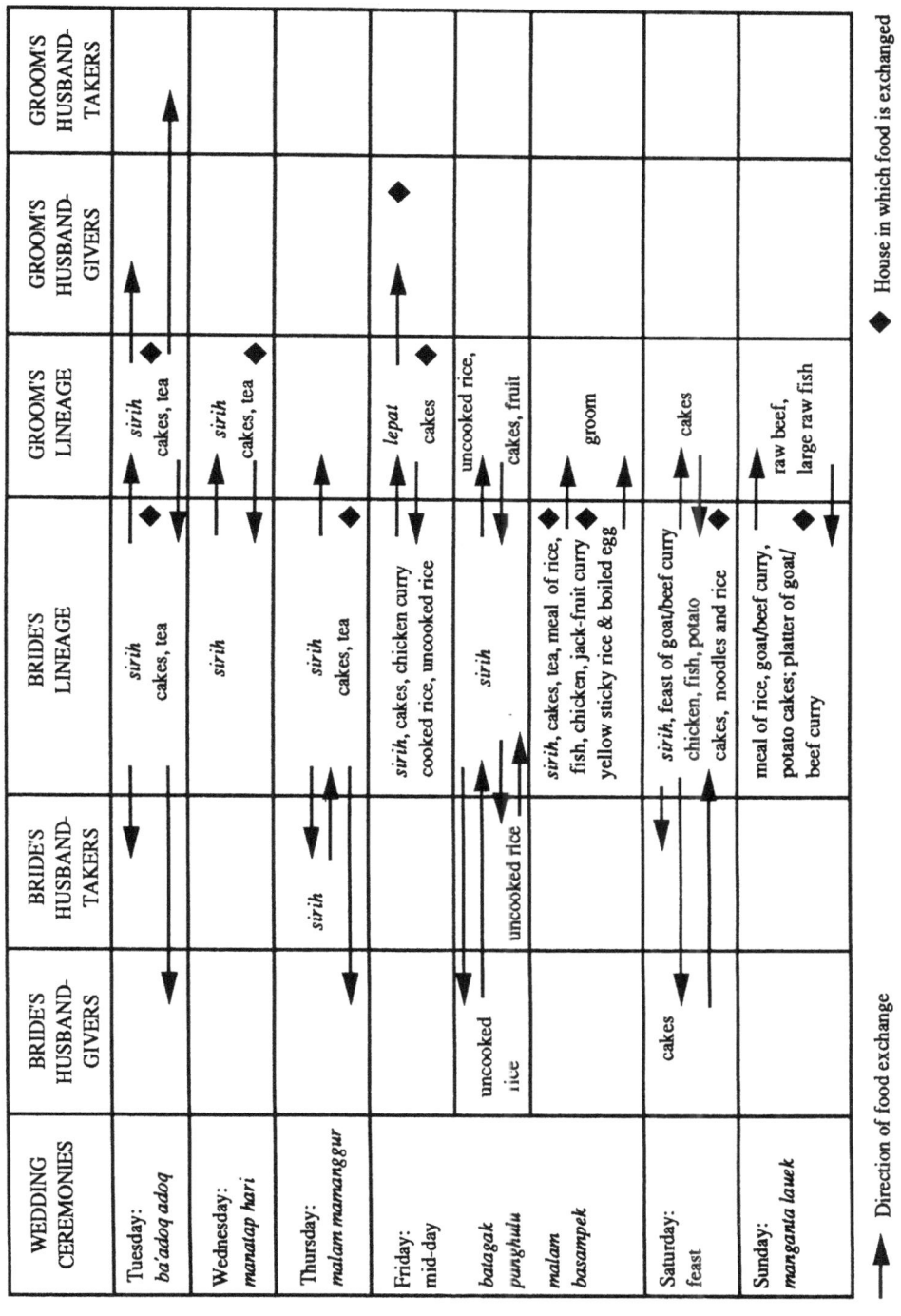

Figure 10. Exchange of food in the wedding ceremony

Leaving out exchanges of cakes and fruit, a noticeable pattern in the exchange of substantial foods is that husband-takers tend to give cooked food to their husband-givers, and the items they receive from their husband-givers are raw food. This pattern of exchange is most explicit in the exchanges between the women of the groom's lineage and those of the bride's lineage. On the day of the main wedding ritual, the bride's lineage women present chicken curry, rice and cakes to the women of the groom's lineage. Further, on the Sunday after the main wedding ritual, the groom's lineage women give raw beef and raw fish to the mother of the bride. In return they receive, besides a meal, a platter of goat curry.

This pattern of exchange, where husband-givers give raw food and in return receive cooked food from their husband-takers, is also shown in the exchanges during the Fasting Month. A common scene during the Fasting Month is women carrying trays of cooked food (meat curries, fried fish, rice, cakes and fruit) to their mothers-in-law. The mothers-in-law give their daughters-in-law coconuts and cash. The pattern of food exchange, that is, husband-givers : raw :: husband-takers : cooked, is but a resonance of a more important one: the exchange of men. The husband-givers, the suppliers of men who are the agents for continuity in their husband-taking lineages, are the givers of raw food. Put in another way, the husband-giving lineages are the givers of raw materials which in their husband-taking lineages become transformed into further life-giving substances. The exchange of food is not only an act of reciprocity but the nature of items exchanged (raw or cooked) explicates the nature of relations between the affinal dyads, the husband-givers and the husband-takers.

Conclusion

Embodied in the spatial organization and the exchange of food are key definitions of male and female identity and of the principles of social order.

Key Definitions

Procreative status is the central source of women's identity. The transitions from one phase in the life cycle to the next (for example, unmarried to married, recently married to married with children, to old with grandchildren — this is evidently marked in ceremonial costumes) are objectified in the use of domestic space, particularly in the organization of sleeping space. As a young girl, a woman sleeps near the main pillar (at the base of which the placenta and umbilical cords of all offspring of the house are buried), then she moves to the annex at the beginning of her procreativity. During her procreative cycle she moves through a series of rooms till she reaches the kitchen area at the end of her procreative cycle.

Women are thus centrally identified with the continuity of their matrilineal group. The woman, the house and the continuity of the matrilineal group are all closely linked. The house is still an important symbol of lineage identity. Even in contemporary times when non-traditional houses are common, lineage members identify themselves with the traditional house where they come from. The house is thus primarily the women's domain, and houses are said to be built for women. Encapsulated in the use of domestic space is the model of lineage continuity. The passage of a woman's life is marked by a circular movement in the house. As she approaches the end of her reproductive life, her daughters would be beginning their cycle of reproductivity and movement around the house. From the womb, then, perpetual cycles of continuity issue. Women's orientation is inwards, fixed within the house and the lineage.

While women are defined as the source of continuity, men are essential to the cycle of continuity. They are the agents who are brought in from the outside or who are sent out to create children, the future reproducers of the women's lineages. The crucial principle in the exchange of food is that husband-givers give raw food, while husband-takers give cooked food, thus identifying the givers of men as the givers of raw material which is transformed into further life-giving substances.

Men's orientation is outwards. A man's life is marked by a series of outward movements: from the house to the mosque at puberty, from there to another neighbourhood (his wife's), and usually to another region outside the Minangkabau heartland to find a better living.

The crucial basis of social order is the circulation of men as agents of continuity for the lineages. This is best demonstrated in the exchange of food. In addition, the use of space during ceremonies also marks the basis on which groups of women are distinguished. In the use of space (and even more so in ceremonial costumes), women are explicitly classified in triadic categories, as women of their own matrilineal group, husband-givers and husband-takers. Husband-givers who contribute directly to the reproduction of the sponsor's lineage are seated near or in the procreative space, while husband-takers, who make no direct contribution to the reproduction of the sponsor's lineage, are allotted space further from the areas identified with procreative activities.

The transitions the Minangkabau make around the house, the allocation of specific space to specific social categories are then a template of the key definitions of male and female identity and underline the divisions in the society.

References

Dobbin, Christine

1983   *Islamic revivalism in a changing peasant economy: Central Sumatra, 1784–1847* (Scandinavian Institute of Asian Studies Monograph Series No. 47). London and Malmo: Curzon Press.

Kato, Tsuyoshi

1977 Social change in a centrifugal society: the Minangkabau of West Sumatra. Unpublished PhD thesis. Cornell University, Ithaca, N.Y.

1982 *Matriliny and migration: evolving Minangkabau traditions in Indonesia.* Ithaca: Cornell University Press.

Naim, Mochtar

1974 Merantau: Minangkabau voluntary migration. Unpublished PhD thesis. University of Singapore.

Ng, Cecilia S.H.

1987 The weaving of prestige: village women's representations of the social categories of Minangkabau society. Unpublished PhD thesis. The Australian National University, Canberra.

Notes

Field research on which this paper is based was carried out between 1980 and 1981, in the village of Nagari Koto nan Gadang in the district of Lima Puluh Kota in West Sumatra.

[1] Islam was introduced in the late sixteenth century through trading connections with Muslim traders from the Middle East (Dobbin 1983:119).

[2] The discussion on Minangkabau social organization is necessarily brief and simplified here. I have elsewhere discussed Minangkabau social organization at greater length (see Ng 1987).

[3] *Adat* is a term which covers a variety of meanings, from legalistic rules, custom and tradition to the right and proper way of living. The term is often translated as customary law. Although *adat* as used in particular contexts can refer to explicit rules (about inheritance, descent group membership, dispute settlements), *adat* in its general sense refers to the Minangkabau heritage, that is those orientations which make for the specific identity of Minangkabau villagers.

[4] *Merantau* (voluntary migration) is from the root word *rantau* (coastal/riverine areas), meaning to go to the *rantau*. Initially, *merantau* was undertaken in groups to extend the Minangkabau territory and for trade. However, *merantau* has become an institutionalized practice where individuals go beyond their natal villages or the Minangkabau heartland, usually to urban centres, to seek their livelihood. *Merantau* can also be regarded as a rite of passage to adulthood for young men. The commonly cited effects of *merantau* are the relief of pressure on subsistence lands in the highlands, and the low ratio of adult men in the villages of the heartland. Up till the nineteenth century, *merantau* was undertaken by men, but currently women may also accompany their husbands to the *rantau*. See Naim (1974) and Kato (1982) for recent studies on the Minangkabau institution of *merantau*.

[5] Balai Cacang is a hamlet within the village Nagari Koto nan Gadang.

[6] In the days before slavery was abolished, a newly married slave girl did not have the privilege of using the annex. Instead she was given a room constructed in the kitchen area where she could receive her husband.

[7] This is only one ceremony of a wedding. A Minangkabau wedding comprises a series of ceremonies over a period of two weeks. See Ng (1987) for a detailed description of the Minangkabau wedding.

[8] A spicy stew of goat meat cooked in coconut milk. Jack-fruit and potatoes may be added for bulk.

[9] Similar to 'bubble and squeak' but spiced with onions and chillies.

[10] This is another typical Austronesian pattern in rituals, where men cook the main meat dish, while women cook rice and vegetables.

A Rotinese head of household on his sitting platform

Chapter 6. Memories of Ridge-Poles and Cross-Beams: The categorical foundations of a Rotinese cultural design

James J. Fox

Introduction

In the classical art of memory from Roman times to the Renaissance, the house was made to serve as a structure for remembering. An imagined construction — with a succession of entry ways, passages, courtyards and rooms, all appropriately furnished — was used to fix the memory of specific objects. To recall these objects, one had only to journey through this familiar mnemonic space and to 'recollect' the memory of the objects that one had purposely stored in a particular place within the house. Images posed in ordered locations within a familiar architecture formed the basis of a complex mnemonic artifice known popularly as a 'memory palace' (Yates 1966).[1]

The structure of many Austronesian houses suggests features similar to those of a memory palace. Austronesian houses are ordered structures that minimally distinguish the categories of 'inside' and 'outside' and more generally establish a progression of designations within a defined internal space. Different parts of the house are identified with specific objects and specific activities.

Often the house itself is conceived as part of a wider-oriented space, which may be grounded in an ordered cosmology. This preoccupation with orientation may require that the proper placement of objects, the location of persons and the performance of cultural activities all occur in reference to the symbolic coordinates expressed in the house. As such, the house becomes more than an architectural design for the 'indwelling' of cultural traditions. It becomes in effect the prime structure for the performance of what are deemed to be those traditions. More than just a 'memory palace', an Austronesian house can be the theatre of a specific culture, the temple of its ritual activities. As in the West, a 'memory palace' of this kind may be regarded as a cosmological forum, a 'theatre of the world.'[2]

On the island of Roti, the traditional house can be considered as such a memory palace. It is not, however, simply an abstract template for the storage of selected memories but rather a physical structure for the detailed preservation of specific elements of cultural knowledge. The house's posts, beams, spars, and even the spaces between these spars, as well as all of the house's levels, partitions, subdivisions and internal demarcations are specifically named; and each location is assigned a symbolic image. The house on Roti thus preserves the same relationship between image, object and location in a fixed physical form as an artfully contrived memory palace.

The Rotinese house is also the place for the performance of rituals or, equally important, the reference point for those rituals performed 'outside the house'. Here the house functions as a fundamental 'intermediate' structure: in relation to the person, it is itself a 'body' and serves as a macrocosm (a replicate body) for ritual performance; in relation to a wider symbolic universe, the house is itself a microcosm that replicates the order of the world. Performances within the house thus function at two levels simultaneously referring to both the person and the cosmos.

Critically important to the house as the locus of ritual performance is an insistence on 'remembering'. Thus one of the most frequent refrains in Rotinese ritual performances is the exhortation to remember: 'Do continue to remember and always bear in mind'.

This refrain is generally stated as a preface to a longer ritual statement and often occurs among the first lines that open a ritual speech. In the language of mortuary rituals, however, this refrain can be used to carry even greater significance. It may be chanted as the direct speech of the deceased instructing his descendants. In the rituals for welcoming a bride into her new house, this same exhortation to remember can become so densely linked to metaphors of the house that specific structures within the house become the physical memento of the event itself.

These excerpts from an address to the bride's group hint at the density of this imagery:

Sadi mafandendelek	Do continue to remember
Ma sadi masanenedak ...	And always bear in mind ...
Hu ndia de lole faik ia dalen	Because on this good day
Ma lada ledok ia tein	And at this fine time
Nde bena emi uma di madadi	Your house posts begin
Ma emi eda ai matola ...	And your tree ladder appears ...
Lakameni tutui	The *lakameni* tree tells its leaves
De ana tui ta sala don	It tells its leaves but lacks no leaves
De don nai uma-lai	For its leaves are in the upper house
Ma nggaemeni o'olu	And the *nggaemeni* sheds its bark

De olu ta sala tean It sheds its bark but lacks no hard core
De tean nai la'o-dale. For its hard core is near the fireplace.
De kae mai uma-lai Climb up into the upper house
Ma hene mai la'o-dale And mount to the fireplace
Te tean nai uma-lai For the hard core is in the upper house
Ma don nai la'o-dale. And the leaves are near the fireplace.

The reply, in ritual language, of the bride's group extends this imagery which transforms the house into a remembrance of the event.

Nde bena lole faik ia dalen Thus on this good day
Ma lada ledok ia tein-na, And at this fine time,
Ke-fetok-ka, ana lali The girl-child, she moves
Ma tai-inak-ka, ana keko And the female-child, she stoops
Nde bena ana keko mai uma-di Stooping she comes to the house posts
Ma ana lali mai eda-ai ... Moving she comes to the tree ladder ...
Nde bena ana molo tunga lelete Thus she steps along a bridge
Ma ana tabu tunga fifino ... And she sets foot along a path ...
Fo ela leo bena So let it be
Ke-fetok-ka, ana molo That the girl-child, she steps
Ma tai-inak-ka, ana tabu And the female-child, she sets foot
Fo ela bena eda-ai natetu That the tree ladder be erect
Ma uma-di nakatema. And the house posts be set.
Fo daeng-nga ela Let the meaning be
Ana dadi neu koni-keak That it become a remembrance
Ma ana moli neu hate-haik And it grow as a memento
Nduku do-na For all times
Ma losa nete'en-na neu. And for all ages.

Here the idea of remembering, based on the verbal pair *neda//ndele*, implies a reflection that focuses on the house. The order and solidarity of the house is an assurance of the strength of the marriage. The transformation of an object into a remembrance (*koni-keak//hate-haik*) points to Rotinese ideas of knowing. The house is architecturally, if not archetypically, a significant locus for two forms of knowledge.

Two Forms of Knowledge: *Ndolu and Lelak*

The Rotinese distinguish between two kinds of knowledge. The first is strategic or technical knowledge which is known as *ndolu*. Such 'expert' knowledge is required in planning, construction and fabrication. As an architectural structure of considerable complexity, the traditional house is a prime exemplification of *ndolu*. The construction of the traditional house is based on a specialized knowledge of measurements and proportions: multiples of so many armspans or fingerwidths, so many spars of an even number to so many beams of an odd number. The craft of construction is much like the art of weaving which requires a minute knowledge of the arrangement of threads and their interrelations. That these crafts are analogous is recognized on Roti. A woman may not tie, dye or weave a cloth while a house is under construction.

There is also a second form of knowledge that involves a deep understanding of cultural matters, of ritual and of tradition. This knowledge is known as *lelak*. As a cultural creation with elaborate symbolic meaning, the traditional house is also a prime embodiment of this *lelak*. What makes a house into a repository of cultural memory, rather than just a skilful arrangement of posts and beams, is *lelak*. To 'know' the house in this sense is to comprehend the basis of Rotinese culture. A portion of the knowledge about the house is vested in a critically important narrative that is intended to explain the origin of the house. Other knowledge of the house is linked to the life cycle rituals, whose performance is associated with appropriate locations within the house.

In Rotinese terms, the house is not simply the coincidence of two forms of knowledge — the expert knowledge of technical construction and the ritual knowledge of cultural design — but rather their combination and fusion. As it is expressed in ritual language, cultural design requires *lelak* as construction requires *ndolu*. In parallel language, these two terms are paired to form a single dyadic set. *Lelak* is supposed to provide the conceptual framework for *ndolu*.

To acquire the expert knowledge of the construction of a house, one may apprentice oneself to a master builder (*ndolu ina*); to acquire ritual comprehension of the house, one must begin by understanding the narrative chant of the 'origin' of the house as revealed by a ritual expert or man of knowledge (*hataholi malelak*). To this must be added the knowledge (and interpretation) of the particular uses of the different parts of the house. In comparison with this particular knowledge, which varies from domain to domain, the knowledge of construction is of a more general nature. Thus it was once a common practice to invite a master builder from one part of Roti to build a house in another. However, the majority of rituals performed in relation to this construction and the naming of the parts of the house after construction followed the traditions of the local domain.

My purpose in this paper is to provide an initial understanding of the house. Specifically, I am concerned with traditions of the house of the domain of Termanu as they are revealed in its narrative of 'origin' and in the ceremonies that are performed within it. My focus is more on cultural design than on physical construction — more on the ritual understanding of the house than on its architectural structure — and thus, specifically, on the nexus between image, object and location.

Since I cannot provide, in this paper, a detailed description of all parts of the house, I concentrate on an outline of some of its main features. In particular, I consider the fundamental orientation of the house and the location of key structures within this oriented space. My reason for this focus is to provide a comparative perspective. I want to identify some of the essential features of the Rotinese house that may relate to similar features of other traditional houses in eastern Indonesia and possibly more widely within the Austronesian-speaking world. I would argue that a notable characteristic of the eastern Indonesian house (and possibly that of most Austronesian houses) is its 'oriented structure'. Although this orientation may differ from society to society or even from locality to locality, features of this system of orientation bear family resemblances. These resemblances may pertain both to construction and to cultural design. The issue of the 'oriented house' thus relates to the wider issue of the transformation of symbolic coordinates and their various uses as ritual referents not just in eastern Indonesia but among Austronesian-speakers in general.

The Origin of the Rotinese House: Textual Foundations

The 'origin' of the first house is recounted in the most important of all Rotinese origin ritual chants. It can only be told guardedly with special hedges and intentional distortions because it reveals the primal sacrifice on which the initial construction of the house was based. This revelation explains the hidden design of the house and the relationship between the different parts of the house. This chant is supposed to be recited at the consecration — the 'making whole or full' (*nakatema*) — of a new house.

In Termanu, this canonic chant is identified with the chant characters Patola Bulan and Mandeti Ledo, the sons of the Sun and Moon. The various versions of this and other related chants suggest that all these narratives may have formed part of a long epic, now told only in assorted parts, that recounted the relations of the Sun and Moon (Ledo do Bulan) and their children with the Lords of the Sea and Ocean (Liun do Sain) and other creatures of the sea depths. In these narratives, the earth provides the middle ground for the interaction between these two complementary worlds and thus men become the beneficiaries of this relationship.

In the chant, the construction of the first house occurs only at the end of a long narrative (see Fox 1975:102–110 for a longer textual analysis of versions of this chant). Briefly summarized, the chant recounts the initial encounter of the sons of the Sun and Moon, Patola Bulan and Mandeti Ledo, with the 'Chief Hunter of the Ocean' and the 'Great Lord of the Sea', Danga Lena Liun and Mane Tua Sain, who, in Rotinese exegesis, are identified as Shark and Crocodile. These paired personages join together to hunt pig and civet cat and, when eventually they catch their prey, they decide to descend into the sea to perform the required sacrifice. There the sons of the Sun and Moon discover a new world of fire, cooked food, decorated houses, numerous essential tools and other cultural objects.

De ala tunu hai bei masu	They roast on a smoking fire
Ma ala nasu oek bei lume	And they cook in boiling water
Nai lo heu hai ikon	In a house roofed with rayfish tails
Ma nai uma sini kea louk.	And in a home decked with turtle shell.

The sons of the Sun and Moon hide a portion of this cooked food and bring it back with them to the Heavens for the Sun and Moon, Bula Kai and Ledo Holo, to taste. In one version of the chant, the Sun and Moon propose to make war on the Lords of the Sea to obtain their wealth but this is discounted as impossible. Marriage is proposed instead as more appropriate so that the Sun and Moon may obtain what they desire as bridewealth from the Sea. In all versions of the chant, there occurs a long and remarkably similar formulaic recitation of the objects that make up this bridewealth. These objects include water-buffalo with crocodile markings and gold chains with snakes' heads, mortar and pestle for pounding rice and millet, tinder-box and fire-drill for making fire and also the tools for the construction of the house. The passage in the chant in which the Lords of the Sea give these objects follows:

Te ala bei doko-doe	But still they continue to demand
Ma ala bei tai-boni.	And still they continue to claim.
Besak-ka ala fe bo pa'a bela	Now they give the bore and flat chisel
Ma ala fe taka-tala la.	And they give the axe and adze.
Ala fe sipa aba-do	They give the plumb-line marker
Ma ala fe funu ma-leo.	And they give the turning drill.

When these bridewealth negotiations are concluded, the chant shifts focus.

Besak-ka lenin neu poin	Now they carry everything to the Heights
Ma lenin neu lain.	And they carry everything to the Heavens.
De besak-ka lakandolu Ledo lon	Now they construct the Sun's house
Ma la-lela Bulan uman.	And they design the Moon's home.

The work of construction, however, does not go well. Various trees are required for different parts of the house — the *keka* (*Ficus* spp.), the *fuliha'a*

(*Vitex* spp.) and the lontar (*Borassus sundaicus*) — but they cannot be erected to stay in proper alignment.

Boe ma ala lo'o	Then they hew
Keka lasi do duak kala	The two-leafed *keka* tree
Ma ala huma	And they chop
Fuliha'a do teluk kala	The three-leafed *fuliha'a* tree
Tao neu sema teluk	To make into the two ridge-poles
Ma tao neu to'a duak	To make into the three cross-beams
Tao neu lo ai	To make into the beams of the home
Ma tao neu uma di.	And to make into the posts of the house.
Te lakandolu nai lain	But they construct it on high
Na ana kekeak leo dae mai.	Yet it tilts toward the ground.
Ma lakandolu nai dulu	And they construct it on the east
Na lai leo muli neu.	Yet it leans to the west.
Boe ma ala le'a la tua tele	Then they draw the lontar palm bent-over
Ma ala lo'o la ai nalo	And they hew the wood straight
De ala lo'o na langa nalo	They hew looking upward
Ma ala tati na laka tele	And they cut bending downward
Ala tao neu sema teluk	They make them into the three cross-beams
Ma ala tao neu to'a duak.	And they make them into the two ridge-poles.
Ala tao neu uma di	They make them into the house posts
Ma ala tao neu eda ai.	And they make them into the tree ladder.
Te laole nai lain,	But when arranged on high
Na ana kekeak leo dae mai	The house tilts toward the ground
Te lakandolu nai muli,	When constructed on the west,
Na soko leo dulu.	It slants to the east.
Boe ma ala dodo neu dalen	So they think to themselves
Ma ndanda neu tein	And they ponder within
Te keka lasi do duak ko	The two-leafed *keka* tree
Ta dadi to'a duak	Will not become the two ridge-poles
Ma fuliha'a do teluk ko	And the three-leafed *fuliha'a* tree
Ta dadi sema teluk.	Will not become the three cross-beams.
Boe te ala boe dodo	Thus they continue to think
Ma ala boe ndanda.	And they continue to ponder.

At this point in the chant, the telling falters and intentional distortions and omissions generally occur. Both chanters and commentators agree that it is dangerous to utter the next sequence. One version, however, reveals what other versions obscure. Without a model, the house cannot be constructed. For this reason, the Lords of the Sea, Shark and Crocodile, are summoned and sacrificed. Their skeletal structure is transformed into the house with the aid of a Heavenly Stick-Insect and Spider, Didi Bulan and Bolau Ledo.

Touk Danga Lena Liun	The man, Chief Hunter of the Ocean
Ma ta'ek Man' Tua Sain	And the boy, Great Lord of the Sea
Ala taon neu uma di	They make him into the house posts
Ma ala taon neu eda ai.	And they make him into the tree ladder.
Besak-ka kalu kapa ledo ha'an	Now his sun-heated buffalo sinews
Ma dui manu au te'e na	And his dew-moistened chicken bones
Ala tao(n) neu sema teluk	They make them into the two cross-beams
Ma taon neu to'a duak.	And make them into the three ridge-poles.
Besak-ka Didi Bulan mai	Now Moon Stick-Insect arrives
Ma Bolau Ledo mai.	And Sun Spider arrives.
De lae: 'Deta ape.	Then they say: 'Dip spittle.
De deta ape neu be	Where the spittle is dipped
Ma lolo neu ndia'.	There lay the planks [legs]'.
Boe te Bolau lolo ape neu be	So where Spider lays spittle
Na ala solu limak neu ndia	There they rest the arms
Ma Didi deta ape neu be	And where Stick-Insect dips spittle
Na ala fua lolo neu ndia.	There they rest the legs.
Besak-ka sema teluk kala dadi	Now the three cross-beams are made
Ma to'a duak kala tola.	And the two ridge-poles arise.
Besak-ka ala soe saiki ikon	Now they incise a tail design
Ma tati solo-bana langan.	And they cut a head pattern.
Besak-ka lae: 'To'a duak'	Now they say: 'Two ridge-poles'
Ma lae: 'sema teluk'	And they say: 'Three cross-beams'
Losa faik ia boe	To this day
Ma losa ledon ina boe.	And until this time.

The revelations of this origin chant provide an initial but only partial indication of the design knowledge (*lela*) that informs the knowledge of construction (*ndolu*).

Orientation and Exegesis

The text of this chant — here based mainly on one of several recorded versions, that by the chantress, L. Adulilo — provides only the barest indications of the structure of the house. The chant contains references to ridge-poles and cross-beams, house posts and a tree ladder. References to a 'head' and 'tail' for the house indicate an orientation to the structure of the house. None of this, however, is sufficient to provide an architectural plan of the house or its layout.

Knowledge of the house is built upon this chant and begins with the exegesis that accompanies it. The chant is a composition in ritual language and the conventions of ritual language require the pairing of terms. These pairs are the starting point of an exegesis. As is often the case, the terms that make up various dyadic sets in the chant are drawn from different dialects of Rotinese (Fox 1974:80–83). Exegesis must begin with a 'translation' of terms into the dialect of Termanu and an explication of their meaning detached from the conventions of ritual language. Thus in the case of the set *to'a*//*sema*, *to'a(k)*, the term for ridge-pole, occurs in ordinary speech in Termanu but *sema* is a term in western Rotinese dialect for what is called the *papau(k)*, beam(s) in Termanu. The categories of two//three that are used to refer to these key structural features of the house (two ridge-poles//three cross-beams) are conventional numbers and are not to be taken literally. A house should have a single ridge-pole and four cross-beams but the numbers one//four do not form an acceptable dyadic set in ritual language. Yet because the origin chant emphatically refers to 'two *to'ak*', ritual commentators provide an esoteric interpretation that identifies this second *to'ak* — in opposition to the *to'ak* at the top of the house — as a special beam beneath the planks of the house. Moreover, because the first *to'ak* is conceived of as 'male', the second *to'ak* is said to be 'female'. The wood chosen for each of these *to'ak* is supposed to be of the appropriate gender category. Probably more than any other example, this esoteric interpretation illustrates the way in which cultural design knowledge (*lela*) informs the knowledge of construction (*ndolu*).

Following a similar dual mode set by the conventions of ritual language, no creature can be named on its own. Hence in this origin chant, pig is paired with civet cat; crocodile with shark. In commenting on this chant, Rotinese insist that it was a pig that was hunted and sacrificed and that it was the crocodile, rather than the shark, whose body was used to create the house. There is, however, a further complexity in the association of the crocodile and the house. In the chant (and in other tales as well), the crocodile gives water-buffalo as bridewealth from the sea. The first water-buffalo from the sea, who are the progenitors of all water-buffalo, possess distinctive pied markings. These animals are described in Rotinese as 'buffalo with crocodile-body markings' (*kapa ma-ao foek*). There is thus an explicit association made between the body of the water-buffalo and the body of the crocodile, and the water-buffalo may be a sacrificial substitute for the crocodile. Hence the model for the structure of the house may be said to be that of a water-buffalo as well as a crocodile. Describing the house in this way disguises the nature of the original sacrificial act. Since, however, the crocodile takes on a human appearance in his excursions upon the land, the complete symbolic equation for the house links man to crocodile to water-buffalo.

The crucial feature of the first house, emphatically reiterated in the initial attempts at construction, is its oriented structure. The basic spatial coordinates of this orientation are those that are supposed to define all houses: east (*dulu*)//west (*muli*); right/south (*kona*)//left/north (*ki*); and above (*lai*)//below (*dae*). These coordinates are also the coordinates of the island itself and, as complementary pairs, are given conscious asymmetric valuation. Rotinese do this by citing a series of symbolic syllogisms. Thus, for example, the east//west coordinates represent the path of the sun. In one common syllogism, the sun is said to come from the east, hence the east is to be regarded as greater than the west. In another syllogism, north, which is the term for left, and south, which is the term for right, are equated but 'power' is said to come from the south, hence the south is given 'greater' categorical weighting than the north (Fox 1973:356-358;1989:46). A similar logic is applied to the categories of above//below. These categories are linked to the east and west directionals. On Roti, to go east is to go 'upward' and to go west is to go 'downward'.

In rituals, there exists a less explicitly articulated but nonetheless pervasive association of colours and qualities with the different directions. East is white (*fulak*) and associated with life; west is black (*nggeo*) and associated with death. The west is associated with the spirits of the dead and with the fertility they provide. There is thus a close association between death and decay and the sprouting of new life. The invariant life-giving qualities of the sun are associated with the east and the waxing and waning of the moon are associated with the west. The sun is identified as 'male' and is referred to as 'father' while the moon is 'female' and referred to as 'mother'. Their complementary relation is as a couple. Continuing this logic of multiple oppositions, the south is red (*pilas*) and associated with power and control while north is a blue-green-yellow (*modo/momodo*) and associated with sorcery and deception but also with curing. These associations are most clearly expressed in mortuary rituals and in an elaborate set of directional prescriptions for the orientation of the corpse and coffin (Fox 1973).

Yet another set of coordinates that are crucial to this system of orientation are the oppositional terms that link time and space. The term *ulu* means 'prior, earlier, former' in time and as a noun, *uluk*, refers to the 'first-born child'. By contrast, *muli*, which is the same term as 'west', means 'younger, later, subsequent in time' and as a noun, *mulik*, refers to the 'last-born child'. In

Rotinese tales, it is the youngest child who is favoured by the spirits and it is the last-born male child that inherits the house.

The result of all this is an orientation system with auspicious directions, power points, and deep associations with special qualities, with time and with the human person. South and east are both auspicious male directions and, in a system of four quarters, the south-east represents the most auspicious of power points. The land of the dead is located to the west but it is also the direction of the spirits whence fertility derives. The north is the direction of sorcery but also of marvellous contrivance. During the colonial period the Dutch were identified with this direction.

In the chant of the origin of the house, a further coordinate is announced only when the construction of the house is achieved. This is the distinction between head (*langa*) and tail (*iko*), which can only be spoken of after the sacrifice of the crocodile. On Roti, this distinction is superimposed on the east—west coordinate and, in cultural terms, this distinction provides the 'setting' for the proper orientation of all houses. Every house has a 'head' which should look to the east and a 'tail' which should be turned toward the west (see Figure 1). The ridge-pole (*to'a*) of the house, when properly erected, follows this alignment. Houses, however, are man-made structures and can be put up in any order. Any house with its head turned in the wrong direction courts misfortune.

The same categories apply to the island of Roti as a whole. The island is spoken of as having its 'head' in the east and its 'tail' in the west. One goes upward toward the 'head' of the island and downward toward its 'tail'. Right and south are therefore synonymous as are left and north. The implication of these categories is that Roti itself is an immense crocodile floating with its head raised toward the east. The directional coordinates transcend as well as encompass the order of the house.

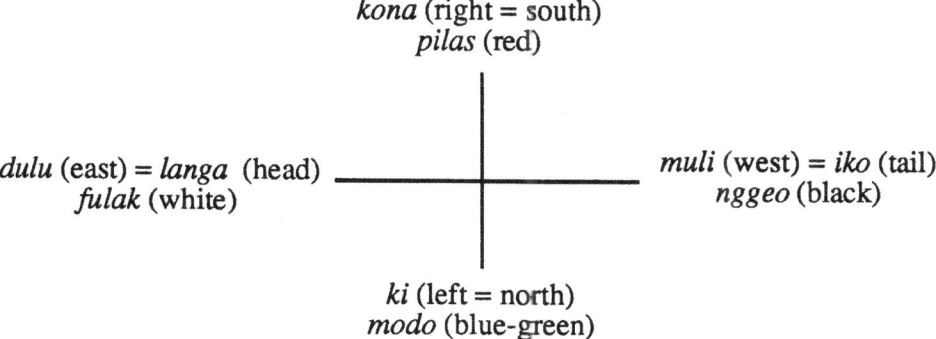

Figure 1. Directional coordinates and their symbolic associations

This orientation system is coherent, embedded in everyday speech as well as in ritual language, and consciously and sometimes explicitly articulated.

During my first fieldwork on Roti, after I had recorded, transcribed and begun to gather exegeses on the chant of the origin of the house, Mias Kiuk, the elder who had more or less adopted me as his son, in exasperation at my probing of what was obvious, got down on all fours and told me to look carefully at where his head, his ribs, his legs were. This, he felt, was sufficient to make clear the structure of the house.

The same model was once given explicit expression in the division of labour in the construction of the house. During fieldwork, I was informed only of a threefold division among the builders of the house based on the 'body' of the house: head, middle and hind-end or tail. Van de Wetering (1923), writing about the Rotinese house on the basis of his experiences in the early 1920s, reports a similar threefold division but a far more detailed subdivision of responsibilities (see Table 1). At that time a distinction was made between the master builder (*ndolu ina*) and his subordinates (*ndolu anak*). The master builder was always assigned to the 'head' of the house and was known as the 'builder of the head of the house'. A second builder was assigned to the middle of the house and, according to van de Wetering, had two assistants who were designated as the 'chest and upper back builders' and another two assistants assigned to work on the sections of the house on either side of the ladder. These assistants were called the 'shoulder builders'. Finally there was the builder assigned to work on the end of the house. He was referred to as either the 'tail' or the 'hind-end builder' and was assisted, in turn, by two workers who were the 'hind-leg builders'.

Table 1. Builders assigned to the construction of the house

I:	1. ndolu uma langgak (ndolu ina)	builder of the head of the house (master builder)
II:	2. ndolu tena dalek	builder of the inner middle
	3. ndolu tenek	builder of the chest
	4. ndolu nggoti-haik	builder of the upper back
	5/6. ndolu aluk	builders of the shoulders
III:	7. ndolu ikok (buik)	builder of the tail (hind-end)
	8/9. ndolu sakibolok	builders of the hind legs

This ninefold division of labour is an ideal schematic representation of the house as a body. On Roti, all such 'total representations' are supposed to consist of nine elements. Moreover, according to van de Wetering (1923:455–458), each builder received a corresponding division of meat of animals sacrificed for ritual purposes in the construction of the house.

With the knowledge of the Rotinese house as an oriented body and with an understanding of the associations of the Rotinese system of orientation, it is possible to consider, in more detail, the layout of the house.

The Internal Structure of the Rotinese House

From the outside, the traditional Rotinese house looks like an immense haystack (see Figure 2). A thatch of lontar leaves or alang grass extends downward to within a metre or so of the ground. Enclosed within this enveloping roof is a complex three-level structure. To enter, one must crouch beneath this thatch at its midpoint. Entry is only from the north or south, never from the east or west.

The question of the direction of entry to the house was in fact a contested, historical issue on Roti about which van de Wetering provides important information. Symbolically, in Rotinese conceptions, the south is unquestionably superior to the north and, for that reason, entrance to the house ought properly to be from the south. However, during the colonial period, entry was also permitted from the north since this was the quadrant of the Dutch whose power the Rotinese acknowledged. In explaining that entry was originally only from the south but later was also from the north, van de Wetering cites the Rotinese syllogism of the period: 'The north is the same as the south but the Company [originally the Dutch East India Company] comes from the north, therefore the north is greater than the south' (van de Wetering 1923:471–472; see also Jonker 1913:613). This acknowledgement of Dutch power did not effect a wholesale change in the direction of entry but at least allowed an alternative possibility in the system.

Figure 2. A traditional Rotinese house

Houses on Roti are classified according to the number of their main posts (*di*). Thus there are — or were — 'four-, six- and, in rare instances, eight-post houses' (*uma di-hak, di-nek* and *di-faluk*). These posts are the critical support structures of the house and they must preserve the same order as the trees from which they were cut with their bases (*huk*) planted in the ground. Similarly, house beams, and especially the ridge-pole, must be oriented with their bases at the tail of the house and their tips toward the head. This order is a fundamental requirement of auspicious construction practice.

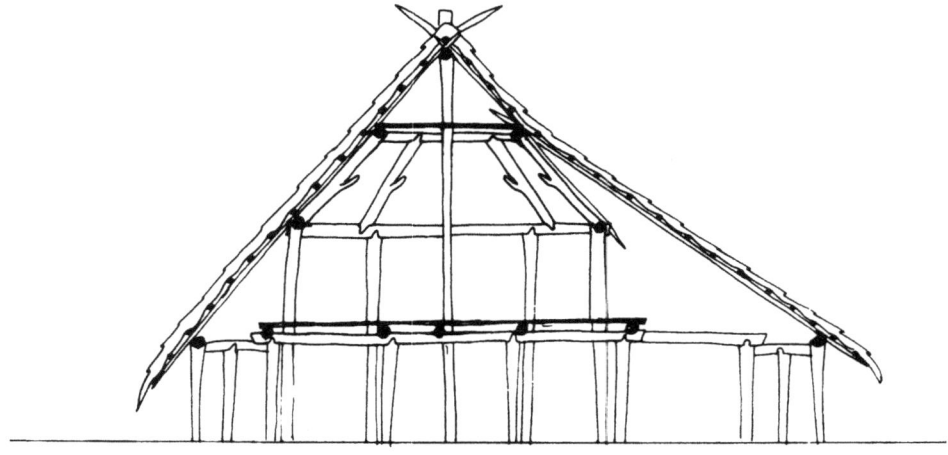

Schematic representation of the house (side view)

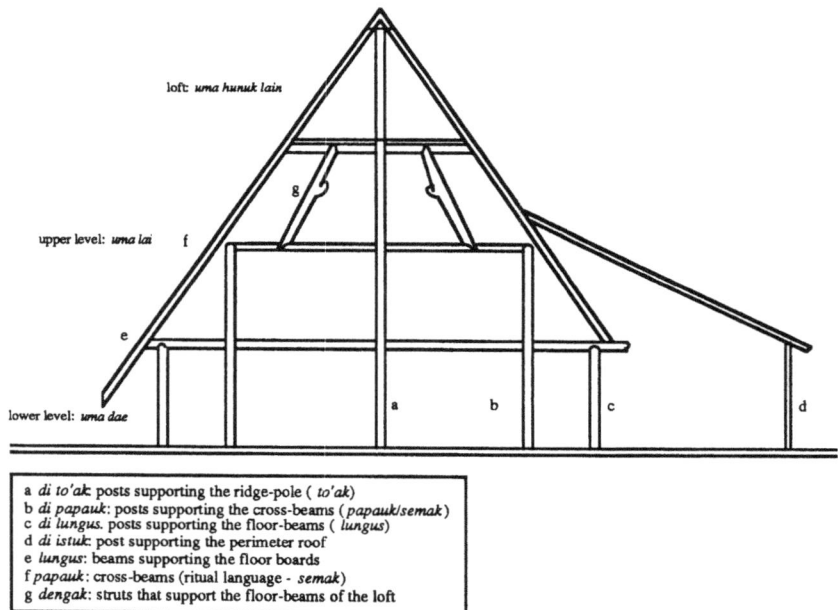

a *di to'ak*: posts supporting the ridge-pole (*to'ak*)
b *di papauk*: posts supporting the cross-beams (*papauk/semak*)
c *di lungus*: posts supporting the floor-beams (*lungus*)
d *di istuk*: post supporting the perimeter roof
e *lungus*: beams supporting the floor boards
f *papauk*: cross-beams (ritual language - *semak*)
g *dengak*: struts that support the floor-beams of the loft

Figure 3. The classification of levels of the Rotinese house

The basic minimal house structure is a 'four-post house'. The six-post house is essentially a four-post house with the addition of two more posts set at the western or tail end of the four-post structure. Larger houses are thus extensions on a basic form. All houses involve a science of construction (*ndolu*) based on proportions of an odd and even number of elements. Thus, for example, a 'six- or eight-post house' is not just a longer house but is also raised higher off the ground. The ladder must have an odd number of steps. For a four-post house, the ladder should have seven steps; for a six-post house, nine; and, for an eight-post house, eleven. Similarly, although the total number of roof spars must be odd, there must be an even number on the left side of the house and an odd number on the right side.

As with many Rotinese forms of classification, the levels of the house may be considered as either a dichotomy or as a trichotomy (see Figure 3). Conceived as a dichotomous structure, the house consists of a 'ground level' (*uma dae*) and a raised 'upper level' (*uma lai*). This division is based on coordinates, *dae*//*lai*, 'above'//'below' or 'earth'//'sky' and the entire raised portion of the house is regarded as a single unit. Conceived as a trichotomous structure, however, the 'upper level' is seen to contain the loft (*uma hunuk lain*) which can only be reached by an internal ladder from within the upper level itself. In this conception, the first raised level of the house forms a middle world between the loft and the ground.

Humans as well as animals, particularly dogs and pigs, occupy the space at the ground level of the house. This whole area is known as the *finga-eik*. A number of raised resting platforms (*loa-anak*) are set at this level and used for everyday activities. The head of the house occupies the 'head' or eastern-most platform and when guests visit, they align themselves in a rough order of precedence from east to west in relation to their host.

The organization of space at the first raised level of the house (see Figure 4) provides the major conceptual distinctions within the house. Here, again, classification is both a dichotomy and a trichotomy. Conceived as a dichotomy, the larger eastern half of the house is referred to as the 'outer house' (*uma deak*); the lesser western half of the house, separated from the 'outer house' by a partition, is called the 'inner house' (*uma dalek*). As a trichotomy, the 'outer house' is divided into 'head' (*uma langak*) at its far eastern end and 'inner middle' (*tena dalek*) or 'inner chest' (*tene dalek*) while the 'inner house' (*uma dalek*) remains conceptually undivided.

A ladder (*heda-huk*) is set on a flat stone base (*bata tatabuk*) under the roof and roughly in the middle of the house, facing the entrance (see Figure 5). It leads from the ground level up into the 'outer house'. The rules of proper order require that the first step from the ladder into the 'outer house' be with the right foot and the same rule for auspicious entry applies as one goes from the 'outer house' to the 'inner house'. The ladder itself can be drawn up and the entrance doors on either side of it can be closed to seal off this level from the ground. In

Inside Austronesian Houses

speaking of privacy, Rotinese remark that one does not know — nor does one inquire — what someone does inside a house when the ladder is drawn.

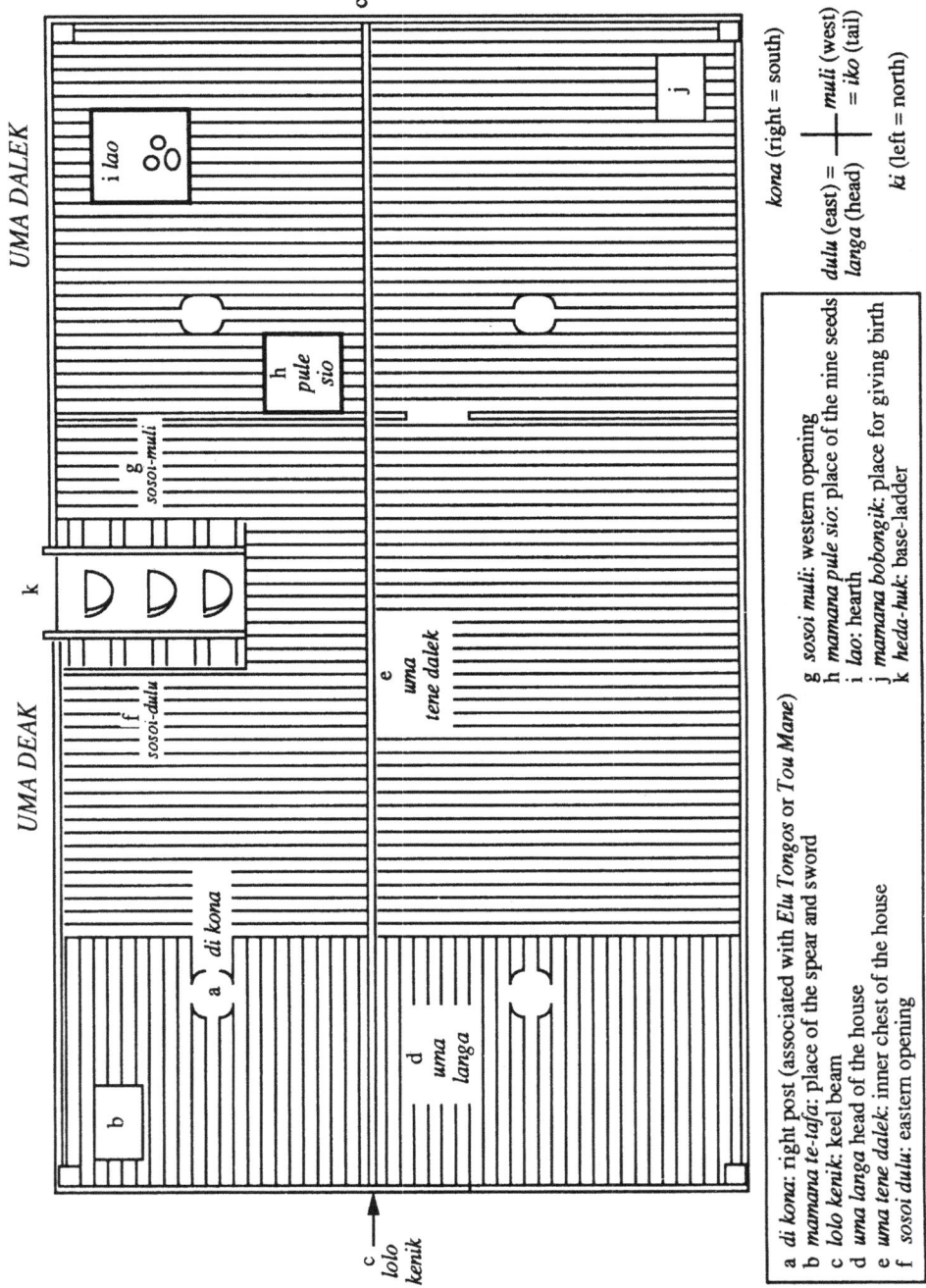

Figure 4. Plan of interior of a Rotinese house

The raised level of the house is a private area. Only family members, relatives and guests at certain rituals are allowed up into the house. The 'inner house' is an even more intimate precinct than the 'outer house'. In the 'inner house' is another ladder that leads up into the loft, which is the most closed and intimate section of the entire structure.

Figure 5. Sketch of the ladder (*heda-huk*) leading into the upper house (*uma lai*)

In marriage ceremonies, the close female relatives of the groom receive the bride when she is escorted to her husband's family house. There they wash her feet before she ascends the ladder into the house. The women then escort her into the 'inner house' and carefully place her hand on different objects in this part of the house. In traditional ceremonies, a marriage chamber was prepared for the couple in this inner precinct.

When a man has built a house for his wife and is able to move from his family house, he surrenders all access to the house to his wife. He can offer guests nothing if his wife is not present and he can only gain access to what is stored in the loft through his wife. By the same logic, if an unrelated man enters under the roof of a house when only the wife is present, he can be accused of adultery and heavily fined. When visiting a house, one must call out for permission to enter before stooping under the thatch.

The distinction between inner (*dalek*) and outer (*deak*) sections of the house is given marked gender associations. Although the house as a whole is conceived of as female and only one woman may have jurisdiction over it, the closed 'inner house' at the western end of the building has the strongest female associations. This precinct is reserved as the sleeping place for unmarried girls of the household. By contrast, adolescent boys should sleep in the 'outer' section of the house.

The gender associations between the 'inner' and 'outer' sections of the house imply a clear separation between brothers and sisters. Hence, when the children of a brother and sister marry, the marriage is described as a reunion of the two parts of the house. *Uma deak leo uma dalek, uma dalek leo uma deak*: 'the outer house goes to the inner house, the inner house goes to the outer house'.

In the inner house are located the cooking fire, a water jar, and a large sack-like basket (*soko*) of harvested rice which stands for the 'nine seeds' (*pule sio*) of the agricultural cult.[3] The close physical and symbolic association of rice, water and the hearth — all clustered in the female precinct of the house — is of critical importance since these elements serve to define the house as a commensal unit. A ladder leads from the 'inner house' into the loft which is a further, elevated extension of this inner sanctum, where more food and valuables are stored. Also located in the loft is a vat of lontar syrup, the 'great spirit jar' (*bou nitu inak*), which is never supposed to be empty. According to pre-Christian traditions, the spirits of the dead have their physical representations as specially shaped lontar leaves (*maik*) which are hung in the loft and are there given appropriate offerings. A house with such spirits is or was acknowledged as an *uma nitu*, a 'spirit house'. (Since the lastborn son inherits his parents' house, access to the spirits within the house passes to this youngest child, thus enhancing the strong associations — *muli/mulik* — of the last-born with the spirits of the west.) Births, however, are also arranged to take place in the 'inner house' in close proximity to the spirits, and women and children of the family who are seriously ill retreat to this part of the house to seek recovery.

A prerequisite for the well-being of a house is that it be inhabited by a cat. Such a cat is called the 'cat in the upper house' (*meo nai uma lai*). This cat is identified with the woman of the house in the same way as a man may be identified with his hunting dog. If a woman were to leave her husband, this can only be referred to, in polite conversation, as the departure of the 'cat in the upper house'. To retrieve his wife, a man must first ritually cleanse the ladder of his house before seeking to woo his wife to return.

The 'outer house', with its basic division into 'head' and 'inner middle', also contains other named locations. The most important ritual position in the 'outer house' is the post located at the south-eastern section of this precinct. This is called the *di kona*, the 'right/south post', the first and foremost foundation post of the house. It is dedicated to the Lord of Lightning and of the Rainbow who is known, in Rotinese, as Elu Tongos or, alternatively, as the Tou Mane, literally the 'Male-Man'. This post is believed to be the stabilizing point that secures the house to the earth. It is the first post that is set in the ground during construction and should be accompanied by offerings to the Earth and to Elu Tongos.[4] As the foremost post, this 'right/south post' marks the beginning and origin of the construction of the house. A red cloth is often wound around this post and a container of what is described as 'reddish' coconut oil is supposed to be hung on or near it and used to anoint the post at times of severe storms and typhoons. Formerly, sacrifices and divination by means of a spear were also carried out at this post.

The outer house holds male implements of various sorts. The spars offer convenient places to hang these implements; for example, the initial payment of bridewealth consisting of the spear and sword given by the groom's side to the bride's family. In the ceremonial presentation of these male tokens, the spear and sword are supposed to be carried into the outer house and hung from the spars in the south-eastern corner of the 'head of the house' near the right post.

There is a cryptic ritual language saying:

| *Ala lolo dulu no muli* | They lay the beams east and west |
| *Ma ala ba ki no kona.* | They lay the cross boards north and south. |

This saying is cited in reference to the planks in the 'inner middle of the house' which are supposed to run in a north-south direction in contrast to the other beams of the house, particularly those at the 'head of the house' which run east-west. One knowledgeable commentator referred to the north-south floor planks as *bak*, which in Rotinese can mean 'lungs' but could also be a technical term from the verb/adverb *-ba*, meaning 'to lay crosswise'. Interpretations based on folk etymologies and on basic terms of similar sound shape are recurrent features of local exegeses.

The inner middle of the house (*uma tena dalek*) is also referred to as the 'inner chest' of the house (*uma tene dalek*). The names of the lengthwise floor planks in this section of the house extend the body imagery of the house. On either side of the floor planks called the 'inner chest planks' (*papa tene dalek*) are the right and left 'rib planks' (*papa kaiusu ki/kona*). From this conceptual vantage point, the inside of the house is even more explicitly defined as the inside of a 'body'. (Figure 6 shows the ladder, levels and division within the house.)

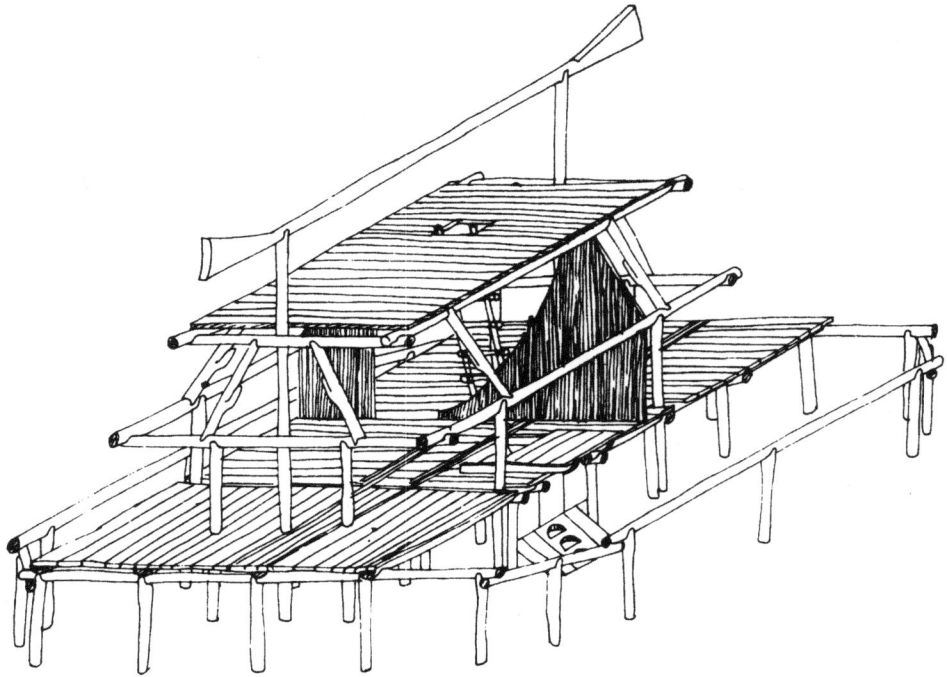

Figure 6. Schematic representation showing the ladder, levels and division within the Rotinese house

Not only is the house conceived of in terms of the physical categories of a 'body'; its internal structure also conforms to the major categories that define the 'person'. In Rotinese, *dale(k)* refers to the inner core of a person, the seat of both cognition and emotion. Thus serious thoughts, reflections and judgements are regarded as coming 'from inside' (*neme dale-na*) or as 'thought from within oneself' (*afi nai dale-na*). Similarly in Rotinese, there are numerous compound expressions for emotional states based on the category *dale-*: *dale-malole*, 'to be good hearted, friendly'; *dale-hi*, 'to desire intensely'; *nata-dale*, 'to be glad, overjoyed'. In contrast to this use of *dale* is the conscious, manipulative use of words (*dede'ak*) in which Rotinese delight. This verbal play is part of an external persona and does not belong to the inner core of the person (Fox 1973: 343–346). Like the 'inner house', the inner person is intimately distinguished from what is publicly expressed.

Internal Structures and the Performance of Rituals in the House

Running down the middle of the house beneath the floor planks is a supporting beam called the 'keel beam' (*lolo kenik*). According to the science of construction, there must always be an odd number of *lolo* with the *lolo kenik* as the middle beam of this set. Interpretation of the *kenik* introduces another set of metaphoric associations. Thus, for example, a common Rotinese saying asserts that the husband is the 'keel' of the house and the wife is its 'rudder' or 'steering oar' (*touk uma kenik ma inak uma uli*). Despite this notion of a 'keel', there is relatively little ship imagery applied to the house as a whole. However, the area demarcated by this 'keel beam' is reserved for the performance of the mortuary rituals. The principal ritual function of the 'keel beam' is to align the coffin within the house during the period of ritual mourning before burial (Fox 1973:359). In ritual chants, the coffin is described as the 'ship' of the dead and is pointed 'eastward' inside the house before it is taken out and lowered into the ground 'to sail' in a westward direction. A cloth given by the mother's brother to his deceased sister's child is supposed to represent the sail of this ship of the dead.

In mortuary rituals, the open coffin is laid out in line with the 'keel beam', and a covering cloth known as the *tema lalais*, the 'broad cloth of heaven', is hung above the coffin. The final ritual act of the mother's mother's brother for his deceased sister's daughter's child is to take down this cloth after the coffin has been carried out of the house and to throw it onto the outside thatch of the house, thus ending a life-giving relationship that began two generations before.

Ship imagery is confined chiefly to rituals that relate to the coffin. In the interpretation of the house based on the chant of its origin, the 'keel beam' is said to be the second '*to'ak*' or ridge-pole alluded to in the chant. This is an esoteric identification because the 'keel beam' does not bear the name '*to'ak*. A dialectic of gender oppositions is called into play here. In relation to the steering oar, the 'keel beam' is considered to be 'male' yet in relation to the ridge-pole, which is aligned directly above it, this beam is supposed to be 'female'. According to the science of construction, the wood for the ridge-pole should come from a male lontar palm whereas the wood for the 'keel beam' should come from a female lontar. This arrangement is consistent with the overall gender symbolism of the house and thus overrides the implications of the incidental symbolism of the ship.

On either side of the ladder that leads up into the 'inner middle' of the 'outer house' is a demarcated space known as the 'eastern opening' (*sosoik dulu*) and the 'western opening' (*sosoik muli*). These two 'openings' are actually platforms that constitute complementary positions within the house. They are not, however, of equal size since the western 'opening' is supposed to be wider than the eastern 'opening'. The two locations are a much used space within the house. Often during negotiations or discussions taking place at ground level, women of the house (who are not supposed to be formally present) sit at these 'openings', with their feet hanging down, and listen to what is being said by hosts and guests below them.

When the ladder is drawn up and the house is closed, these two 'openings' have another function. According to the traditions of the house, the husband sleeps on the 'eastern opening'. A wife is supposed to sleep on the 'western opening' and when they make love, the husband should move to the wife's 'opening'. Often, however, and certainly whenever there are visitors, the husband sleeps on the easternmost resting platform at ground level. According to the memories of older Rotinese, a young man who was considered a promising suitor was formerly invited into the house and allowed to spend the night on the 'western opening'. From there he could communicate with a daughter of the family who was separated by the partition dividing the 'inner house' from the 'outer house'.

In mortuary rituals, these places take on another function as ritual locations for the maternal affines (Fox 1971:241–243; 1988). The ritual position of the mother's brother (*to'o-huk*) is at the 'eastern opening' and that of the mother's mother's brother (*ba'i-huk*) at the 'western opening'. All guests who come up into the house must pass between these two affines to approach the coffin and mourn the deceased. Whether or not they are physically present at these positions for the duration of the ceremonies, the cooked food specifically given to these affines must be laid at these places within the house. Only when this cooked food has been placed at these locations, to feed these affines, can the funeral feast begin and other guests be fed.

Inside the house — roughly at mid-level height — on the first raised level of the house are the cross-beams (Termanu: *papauk*; ritual language: *semak*). These beams form a rectangular structure around the house. Struts (*dengak*) from these cross-beams support the floor of the loft. The long spars, to which the roof thatch is tied, extend down from the ridge-pole to roughly a metre from the ground. These spars, called *dodoik*, rest on the outer edge of the cross-beams. In terms of the imagery of the house as a body, these spars would appear to be ribs (see Figure 7). The spaces between them are called *latik*. These *latik* are conceived as different 'paths' (*enok*). They are aligned as an ordered set of pathways in relation to the internal structure of the house and each is given a name in association with a particular spar. In the non-Christian traditions of Roti, offerings are supposed to be made at the spars of these named paths to ensure the welfare of the creature or activity they preside over. The basic ordering of these 'paths' is similar throughout Roti but since houses may be of different lengths, and therefore may differ in the number of these 'paths', the actual arrangement of these paths may be more or less elaborate.

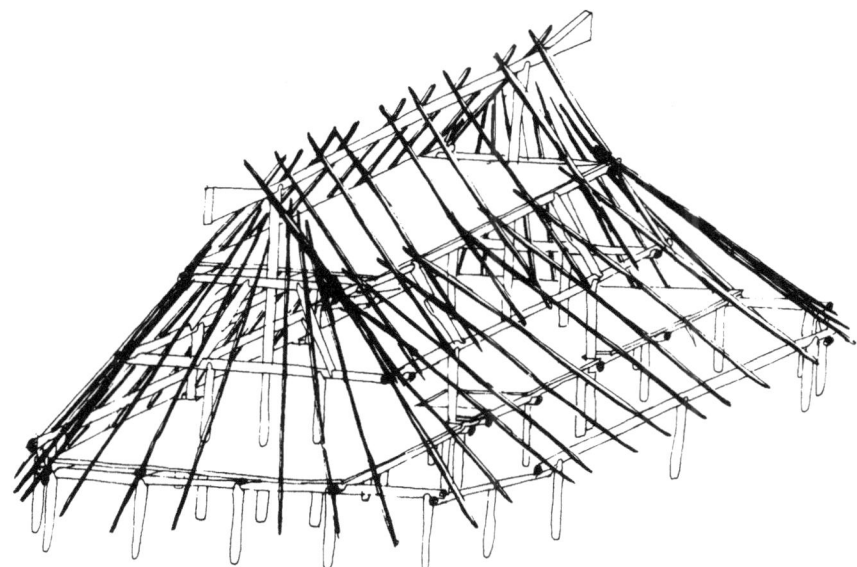

Figure 7. The spars of the traditional Rotinese house

Proceeding from the eastern end of the house, which constitutes the 'outer house', to the western end of the house, which forms the 'outer house', the ordered list of the names of these paths is as follows:

Path (*Enok/Latik*)	Gloss
lati Elu Tongos	path of Elu Tongos (Lord of Lightning)
lati touk	path of the man
lati kapa	path of the water-buffalo
lati ndala	path of the horse
lati bi'ik	path of the goat and sheep
lati sosoi dulu	path of the eastern opening
lati nusak (lelesu)	path of the domain (entrance)
lati sosoi muli	path of the western opening
lati bafi (bana)	path of the pig (animal)
lati pule sio (lakimola)	path of the nine seeds (*lakimola*)
lati ule oe	path of the water jar
lati lao	path of the hearth
lati ana fe'o	path of the daughters
lati bobongik	path of birth

The system is expandable or contractable. Paths may be designated by various alternative names. Thus, for example, the 'path of birth' and the 'path of the daughters' may form a single space. Similarly, while all houses should have a 'path of the nine seeds', some would argue that a house should also have a 'path of the water jar'. Together they may constitute one path. On the eastern side of the house, the 'path of the horse' and the 'path of the water-buffalo' may form a single 'animal path' as on the western side of the house. In theory, the horse and water-buffalo set could also be expanded to include a separate 'path' for goats and sheep (*bi'i*) as is the case in other domains (see Figure 8).

The system of the *latik* outlines an order to the house following a differentiation between female and male activities associated with the 'inner' and 'outer house'. At the western end of the house is the sleeping place of the daughters of the house, but it is also the place where a woman gives birth. To facilitate this birth, she is supposed to grip the two spars (*dodoik*) that frame the 'path of birth'. This location for giving birth is opposite to the hearth and, as is common throughout the region, it is here a woman must undergo a period of 'cooking' after giving birth. The hearth is a defining feature of the woman's side of the house.[5]

At the eastern end of the house is the 'path of the man'. It is located beside the 'path of Elu Tongos', the 'Male-Man' (Tou Manek), which is associated with the power of lightning, of storms and of the weapons of male prowess. Significantly, when a man becomes ill, he sleeps near the 'right post' in line with the 'path of the man'; when a woman is ill, she confines herself at the opposite corner of the house. Formerly, Rotinese insist, offerings for men were made at the south-east corner of the house and for women at the northwest corner.

The domestic animals are also assigned positions within this male and female space. The pig is assigned to the woman's side of the house whereas the horse and water-buffalo (as well as goats and sheep) are accorded one or more paths on the man's side of the house. This division parallels a distinction in affinal exchange gifts: water-buffalo, goats, sheep (and horses among high nobles) are defined as 'male' goods and given by wife-takers to wife-givers in exchange for pigs which are defined as 'female' goods (Fox 1980a:117–118). There are a variety of other reasons given for this assignment. Men spend considerable time caring for their herd animals and personally identify with their horses. Women, on the other hand, are charged with feeding household pigs and, therefore, the pig's feeding trough is supposed to be set in the courtyard in front of the west side of the house. The succinct and somewhat curious Rotinese expression that is cited to denote this relationship is: 'The pig [always] stomps on the woman's foot' (*Bafi molo ina ein*) implying that pigs are almost insatiable and, in their impatience for food, they invariably punish their feeder.

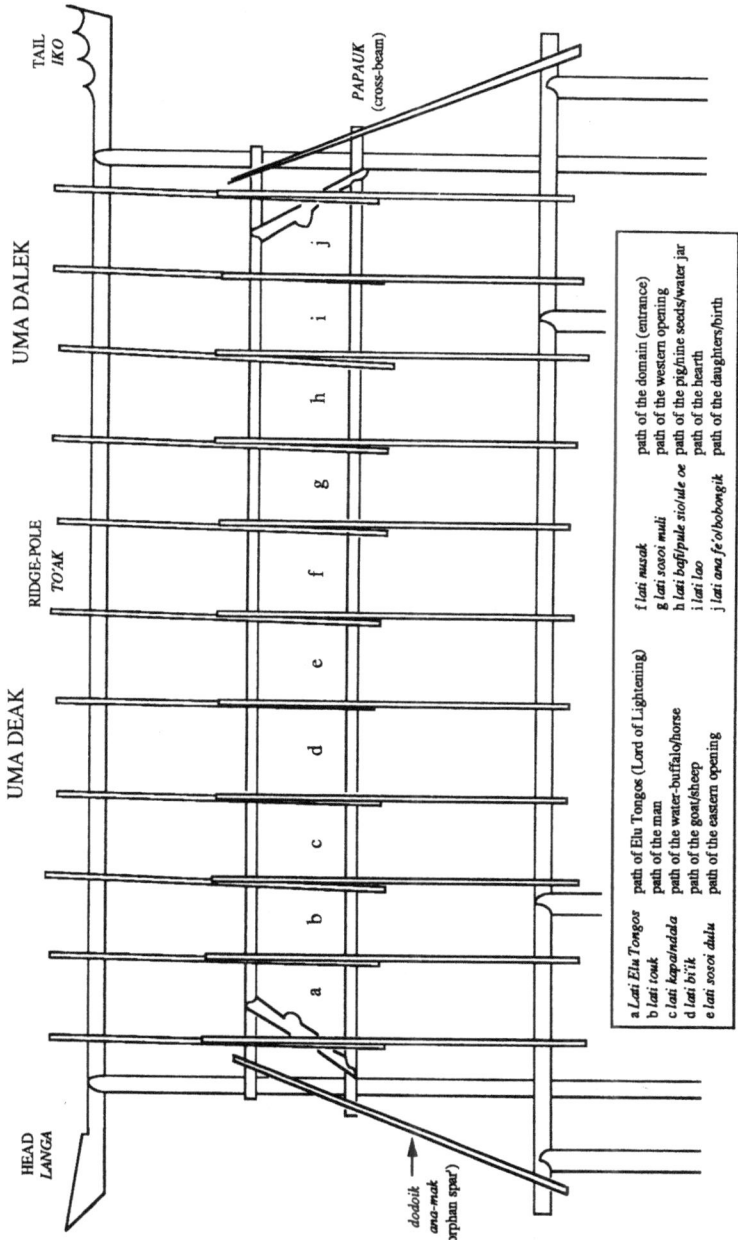

Figure 8. Schematic representation of the paths of the house

The cat also has a place in this system since the four spars at each corner of the house are called 'cat spars' and are associated with the 'cat in the upper house'. A close Rotinese friend, living as an elder bachelor after having been deserted by his wife, took me into his house to show me that one of the 'cat spars' of his house had been nailed where it should have been tied. He cited this improper construction as a cause of his marital difficulties. The dog, too, has its place. Dogs are opposed to cats in Rotinese complementary categorization. Dogs are 'male'; cats are 'female'. Unlike the cat, which is supposed to remain in the house, the dog is never allowed to mount the ladder into the house and is thus always confined to ground level.

At each end of the house, but especially at the front of the house where the roof extends outward, there is a spar that fills the corner gap. It extends only half the length of the other spars, fitting between them in the corner. This is called the 'orphan spar' (*dodoi ana-mak*), which is an apt description of its structural position. Interpretation of this spar does not, however, focus on its technical function in construction. The concept of 'widow and orphan' is metaphorically elaborated in Rotinese philosophy to stand for the conditions of bereavement, dependence and mortality (Fox 1988:184–185). As such, the 'orphan spar' is regarded as a necessary feature of the house and as a reminder of the human condition.

Just as the house has a 'head', 'tail', 'chest', 'ribs', and 'lungs', it also has a 'neck' (*botok*), the space just under the top of the roof. On top of this 'neck' are set an odd number of 'neck-braces' (*lange*), wooden cross-bars that are run along the crest of the roof to hold the thatch down. The same term, *lange*, is used to refer to the necklace that is sometimes given by the mother's brother for his sister's child thus 'purchasing' the child and averting life-threatening influences believed to follow the child's father's line. It is also used to refer to the neck-halters that are sometimes placed on the necks of goats or pigs to hamper their movements. Finally there is the term for 'elbow' that is used in reference to the house. The 'outside elbows of the house' (*uma si'u dea*) refers to the corners of the house at the outer edge of the roof.

The House as Oriented Structure and Inner Space

The house is a complex classificatory structure. It is also a coherent structure. Given its basic directional orientation, its levels, and the common associations linked to these coordinates, all points and parts of the house can be given a symbolic identification. At this level, however, classification is not confined to a single schema. The layout of the house and its levels may be considered either as a dichotomous or as a trichotomous structure.

According to the more general dichotomous structure of the house, all aspects of the house can be arrayed as a set of complementary pairs. The principal symbolic operators for this classification are the directional coordinates as well as the categories of 'outside' and 'inside'. On this basis, the layout of the house is so ordered that its 'eastern' half, which forms the 'head' of the house, is categorized as 'outside' in opposition to its 'western' half, which forms the 'tail' of the house, and is categorized as 'inside'. This complementary classification is asymmetric. The house is constructed to consist of unequal halves with the 'eastern' half being the larger structure. According to the rules of construction, the 'head' or 'outer house' must have an odd number of spars as opposed to the 'tail' or 'inner house', which must have an even number. Following the standard valorization or 'markedness' set by the directional coordinates (see Fox 1989), the categorical asymmetry of the house can be expressed in the following polarities:

Polarities of the House

(+)	(−)
East	West
Head	Tail
Outside	Inside
Odd	Even

This categorical asymmetry within the house represents one mode of classification. It conforms, to a considerable degree, to the representation of the house as a personified creature — crocodile, water-buffalo or human.

If, however, one focuses on the critical categories of outside/inside, another mode of classification emerges. Thus the Rotinese house may be seen as a progressive spatial delineation of the category of 'inside' (*dale-*), which is identified as 'female'. Thus all of the space under the low-hanging roof of the house is defined as 'inside', as indeed the house as a whole is associated with a woman. Similarly all of the space enclosed within the first raised level of the house is also considered 'inside' the house and is markedly so when the ladder is drawn up and this part of the house is closed to the outside. At this level, there is an important categorical division between the 'outer house' and the 'inner house' — a separation of precincts that is physically defined by a partition. Within the precinct defined as the 'outer house', however, there is a further dichotomy between the 'head' and 'inner middle' so that as one moves from east to west, one moves from the 'head', through the 'inner middle' of the house into the 'inner house'. If one follows this progression a step further, there is the ladder in the 'inner house' that leads up into the loft, the most sacred and restricted precinct 'inside' the house.

Herein lies the mystery of the Rotinese house: a reversal. By the conventions of the Rotinese directional coordinates, 'to go east' is 'to go up'. In the house, this structure is reversed: 'to go west' is 'to go up'. It involves going into an ever more circumscribed 'inner' space — a realm defined as 'female', a realm of the spirits, and a realm associated with the 'last-born' who retains the house and remains within it. It is also the realm associated with birth, with the cult of the 'nine seeds' and, most importantly, with the hearth, which is the symbolic focus of the house as a social unit.

There is a further implicit transformation in this symbolism of the house. In the origin narrative, the basic structures of the first house — its posts and beams — were the 'sinews and bones' of the Lord of the Sea, the crocodile, who is always represented as a male predator. This male structure, however, becomes a female whole. In Rotinese terms, the posts and beams of the house are 'erected' (*tetu*), but only when the house is roofed is it made whole (*tema*). This wholeness is what makes the house 'female' and its inner precincts the most vital of all female cultural spheres.

The Rotinese House as a Memory Palace

The Rotinese house is the locus for a complex symbolism and for the interpretation of this symbolism. Much of this interpretation depends on an esoteric knowledge of the origin of the house in the sacrifice of the Lord of the Sea, on clever exegesis of specific references in the chants, and on a mature understanding of the general postulates of Rotinese culture; all of which are represented as cultural knowledge (*lelak*) that anyone may gradually obtain and thus become a 'person of knowledge' (*hataholi malelak*). This valued knowledge exists apart from the house. The house is the physical means of its remembrance. In this sense, the Rotinese house is indeed a memory palace and the frequent injunction 'to remember and to bear in mind' is appropriate. From the perspective of a 'person of knowledge', the traditional house could disappear and the knowledge it is supposed to embody might continue. For others, the disappearance or radical transformation of the house would entail a fundamental alteration of a cultural understanding.

In 1965–66, at that time of my first fieldwork, an overwhelming majority of houses followed what was considered to be the traditional building pattern.[6] At that time, however, there were vigorous arguments about *which* houses followed this pattern closely and *which* houses had flaws in their construction. Flaws — the use of a nail where something should have been tied or the misplacement of a particular spar — were indicative of some misfortune that might befall members of the house. Most houses at the time used permanent stepped ladders rather than the tree-trunk ladders that could be pulled up into the house. This was acceptable and no longer courted disaster. On the whole, it could be said that most houses conformed to a recognized standard. A few houses were magnificent examples of this standard. Only the houses of schoolteachers and a minority of progressives, many of whom had lived on other islands, were built on the ground without reference to this standard.

By 1972 when I returned to Roti, a local government campaign had begun to tear down traditional houses on the would-be hygienic grounds that such houses were closed, sunless and unhealthy. The modernists who waged this campaign were mainly Rotinese intent on rapid and radical development. The house was rightly seen as the locus for traditional practice, but Christianity as well as health and development were invoked in an effort to replace the sloping-roofed 'haystack' houses with high-roofed, wide-windowed houses built on the ground. Sadly, the campaign was largely successful in Korbaffo and Termanu. Although the finest of the old structures need not have been targeted for destruction, it was inevitable that changes would have to occur in building techniques. The quality hardwood needed especially for posts, beams and the ridge-pole was becoming extremely scarce and the costs of building a solid traditional house were increasingly prohibitive.

During the 1970s, the transition to other building techniques began in earnest and was strongly encouraged by local officials. The increasing availability of relatively low cost cement and the lack of good timber prompted the building of some interesting and innovative cement and stone structures. Many traditional houses remained in various locations and by the 1980s, their potential as tourist attractions insured their preservation. Crucially, the fear that a flawed or altered house form might lead to disaster had receded but the argument over what constituted the essentials of a traditional house continued. If a house was built in proper east—west alignment, if it retained its four 'orphan spars' (or, in other words, was built in a rectangular form), if it preserved a relationship between 'outer' and 'inner' sections, and if it combined these features with a loft, did it not conform to a traditional pattern?

Certainly for the Rotinese, tradition is not some rigid framework that imposes itself on the present. It is rather a relationship with the past. If one reads the various Rotinese accounts recorded by the Dutch linguist J.C.G. Jonker at the turn of the century, one can already detect arguments over the nature of the 'traditional' house by reference to its contrary, the non-traditional house. This was a house built on the ground (*uma daek*) which was considered to be a European-style house (*uma filana*). By this time, however, a crucial change had already been imposed from above by the Dutch on the traditional Rotinese house. In the nineteenth century, the dead — or perhaps more correctly, the honoured dead — were buried underneath the house. The Dutch, for health reasons, forbad burial beneath the house and most burials were thereafter shifted to the courtyard in close proximity to the house. Thus the original Rotinese house was also a tomb. The spirits of the dead were represented by lontar leaves in the loft while their bones were buried in the earth below.[7] The symbolic operators, above (*lai*)/below (*dae*), had a greater significance in this house-and-tomb than they did after the dead were displaced from the ground below. Important aspects of the mortuary rituals had to be reinterpreted to accommodate these critical changes. One could argue therefore that the symbolic importance of a raised structure was already seriously undermined by forced changes in the nineteenth century. If such fundamental changes could be accommodated with a traditional understanding of the house, it is evident that the house has indeed served as a memory palace to transmit selectively certain ideas of the past. Despite the exhortation 'to remember and bear in mind', memories have altered with time.

COMPARATIVE POSTSCRIPT

Points of Comparison Between Houses on Roti and on Timor

In eastern Indonesia an understanding of the house embraces more than its physical structure and the symbolic significance attached to its parts. The house defines a fundamental social category. House structures are particular local representations of this wider conception. They define what is generally regarded as a 'descent group' but might more appropriately be referred to, in Austronesian terms, as an 'origin group'. This group is of a variable segmentary order (Fox 1980b:11). This variability is crucial to the concept of the house. It provides a sliding scale that may be associated with different physical structures depending on the development of the group, its conception of its origin and its relation to other groups, and the context within which it is considered. As a consequence, there can be no strict definition of the house as a social category since even within the same society the house embraces a range of possibilities.

Generally the societies of eastern Indonesia possess a category that identifies a social group larger than the house. On Roti this is the *leo*. Elsewhere, as for example among the Atoni Pah Meto of west Timor, it is the *kanaf*; among the Tetun of Wehali, the *fukun*; among the Ata Tana Ai of Flores, the *suku*; among the Savunese, the *udu*; throughout Sumba, it is the *kabisu* or *kabihu*. In the literature on the region this category is generally denoted by the term 'clan'.

'Houses' — often with specific ancestral names — make up units within the clan. Yet given the structural potential of the category 'house', in some instances a specific 'house' can claim to encompass, represent or head an entire clan. Thus at one level, and within a defined context, a 'house' can embrace the highest-level social unit of the society of which it is a part. More commonly, however, the 'house' refers to lesser social units. These houses may be identified in relation to some encompassing house — real or remembered — from which they originate. They may be referred to by their attributes or by their founding ancestors, or by the portion of the heirlooms and prerogatives that they have inherited from an earlier house. At a minimum, houses of this sort define social groups that are primarily, though not exclusively, involved in the arrangement of marriages and the performance of most rituals of the life cycle. At this level, houses are the basic units of society (Fox 1980b:10–12).

Houses, as physical entities, are supposed to manifest the characteristics of the social categories and groups that they represent. These, too, are variable structures. In the literature on eastern Indonesia, however, descriptions of the 'house' represent models of an idealized structure: a schematic order of the kind described for the Rotinese house. Even at this abstract level, it is difficult to compare one house with another because the descriptions of these houses portray elaborate structures that are overladen (over-determined, perhaps) with cultural significance. The variety of these structures and the different conceptions attached to them would seem to frustrate basic comparison. With such richness, it is difficult to know what elements ought to form the focus of comparison. The identification of a few common structures among closely related societies may, however, provide a clue to some of the important features of the house.

Here I would like to venture a number of comparisons based on the orientation of the house and on consideration of a limited set of its important named structures. These 'points of comparison' are intended to note both similarities and differences between related house structures. In an overall comparison, points of difference are as pertinent as points of similarity.

Because of the importance of the house in eastern Indonesia, the literature on these structures is extensive. For the purpose of comparison, I confine my consideration to the house structures of three distinct populations who are closely related, both linguistically and culturally. These populations are (1) the Rotinese, (2) the Atoni Pah Meto of west Timor and (3) the Ema of north central Timor.

My starting point is the orientation of these houses, which is fundamental. Thus, to be oriented at all, a house must have at least three axes, each of which constitutes one coordinate of the system. The first of these axes is the above/below, or up/down, axis. Since houses in eastern Indonesia are multilevel structures, this axis is important. As a coordinate, however, the up/down axis is virtually invariant among the societies of eastern Indonesia and is therefore less problematic than the other two axes whose identification may vary from society to society. Of these two axes, one appears to be primary in the sense that it is applied first and the other is applied in relation to it. As coordinates, these axes create a fourfold symbolic structure.

The Atoni Pah Meto of West Timor

Clark Cunningham (1973) has described the Atoni house of the domain of Amarasi in west Timor in an important article of exceptional clarity. Since the Rotinese and Atoni are related populations, the question of the relation of their houses to one another is pertinent. Although the Amarasi house (*ume*) has a beehive-like roof, it is in fact a four-post structure and therefore directly comparable to the basic four-post Rotinese house (*uma di hak*). In the Atoni language, these four posts are referred to as the 'mother posts' (*ni ainaf*). Note that *di* and *ni* are cognate terms, as are numerous other terms for similar items in the two houses.

The Amarasi house is also oriented in a similar fashion to the Rotinese house. (Compare Figure 4, p.156, with Figure 9 below.) The equivalent of the east/west (*dulu/muli*) or head/tail (*langa/iko*) axis of the Rotinese house is, among the Atoni, the axis of the sunrise/sunset (*neonsaen/neontes*). Similarly, as on Roti, right for the Atoni is south (*ne'u*) and left is north (*ali'*). The door of the Rotinese house may open to the north or the south; the door of the Amarasi house should be oriented to the south. This orientation produces a system of four corners referred to in Timorese as the 'great quarters' (*suku naek*). The colours associated with these quarters are also the same as on Roti: east is white, south is red, west is black and north is (green-)yellow. To this point, therefore, there is a virtual one-to-one correspondence of the orientation coordinates and their associations from one house to the other.

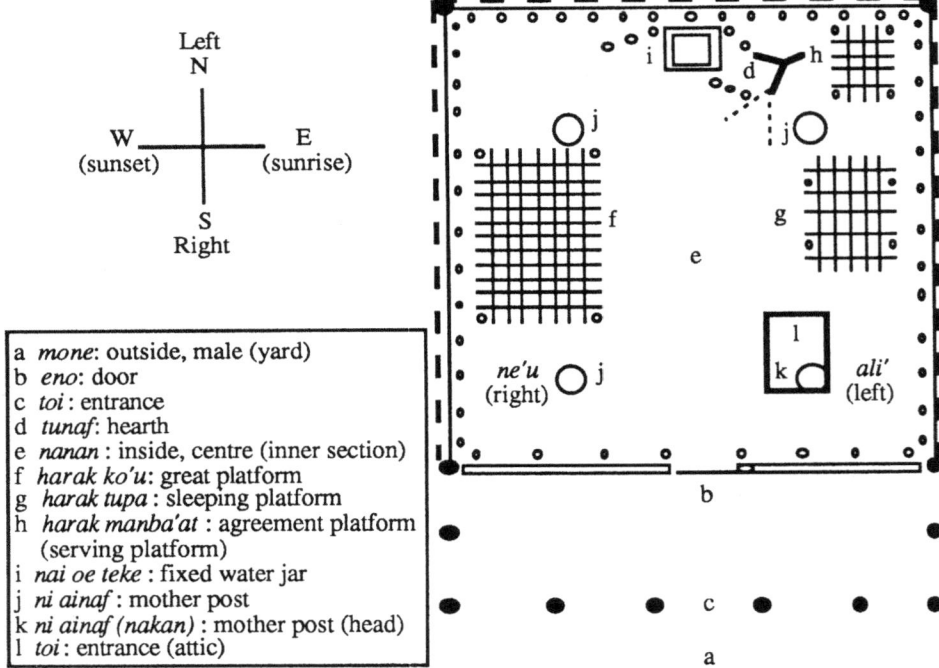

a *mone*: outside, male (yard)
b *eno*: door
c *toi*: entrance
d *tunaf*: hearth
e *nanan*: inside, centre (inner section)
f *harak ko'u*: great platform
g *harak tupa*: sleeping platform
h *harak manba'at*: agreement platform (serving platform)
i *nai oe teke*: fixed water jar
j *ni ainaf*: mother post
k *ni ainaf (nakan)*: mother post (head)
l *toi*: entrance (attic)

Figure 9. Floor plan of an Atoni house (adapted from Cunningham 1964:38)

There are, however, significant differences. Like the Rotinese, the Atoni make a distinction between 'inside' and 'outside'. This distinction also implies a distinction between 'female' and 'male' especially since the term *mone* among the Atoni means both 'male' and 'outside'. In relation to the Atoni house, the yard is referred to as *mone* while everything under the roof is the 'inside of the house' (*ume nanan*). There is, however, a further distinction made between the whole of this *ume nanan* and what is called simply the 'inside' (*nanan*). The 'elbow' (*si'u*) of the house under the roof has platforms for receiving affines and

Memories of Ridge-Poles and Cross-Beams: The categorical foundations of a Rotinese cultural design

guests but is separated by a partition from the 'inside' (*nanan*) precinct of the house which is reserved exclusively for members of the house and close agnatic relatives. All of this is functionally equivalent to the Rotinese distinction between the 'inner' and 'outer' sections of the house. Although cognate terms occur, such as the word *si'u* for 'elbow' in both languages, correspondences are different because the symbolic location of key objects and structures among the Atoni is entirely within the 'inside' house rather than being divided between 'inner' and 'outer' sections of the house among the Rotinese.

Orientation within the 'inside' house is crucial. For the Amarasi house, the right/left distinction is variably applied absolutely and relatively. Thus, as a directional coordinate, the right/left axis sets the basic orientation of the house. Within the house, however, the right/left distinction is applied relative to a person looking out the door of the 'inside' house. The superimposition of this interior distinction on the basic orientation system produces a situation where internally 'right' is on the 'sunset' side of the house and 'left' on the 'sunrise' side. Key objects and structures are positioned according to this second relative right/left orientation which is associated with an opposition between 'male' and 'female'. This produces a bifurcation through the house equivalent to the outer/male and inner/female opposition in the Rotinese house. Accordingly much of the right side of the house is taken up with a platform known as the 'great platform' (*harak ko'u*) on which tools, possessions, pounded corn and rice are kept. In the centre of the house — slightly to the left but never to the right — is the hearth (*tunaf*). The hearth may also be placed further back on the left side of the house near the 'fixed water jar' (*nai oe teke*) and what is called the 'agreement platform' (*harak manba'at*). This platform holds cooking utensils and cooked food, but it is also where a woman is placed when she gives birth and is later 'cooked' and bathed with hot water during a period of confinement. Also located on the left is a sleeping platform for the elder man and woman of the house.

Of the four principal posts of the Amarasi house, one post known as the 'head' (*nakaf*) is singled out for special ritual attention. This post has a flat stone altar at its base and sacred ancestral objects are tied to it. It is called the 'head' because there is a hatch next to it that leads up into the loft. In terms of the interior orientation of the house, this 'head' post is at the front and left, but in terms of the general orientation of the four quarters, this 'head' is at the south-east corner of the house and thus in exactly the same position as the 'right' post in a Rotinese house. From this perspective, the basic orientation of the two houses is retained; the difference is that the Rotinese house maintains a single systemic orientation, whereas the Atoni house has an internal orientation that overrides the 'external' Atoni orientation system. Access to the loft in the Atoni house is near the 'head' post whereas in the Rotinese house, it is at the 'tail'.

The Ema of North Central Timor

Brigitte Renard-Clamagirand (1980, 1982) has written with exceptional detail on the houses of the Ema of north central Timor. Particularly valuable is her discussion of the different categories of houses defined in relation to a core house, referred to as the 'house and hearth' (*uma no apir*) of the Ema descent group. Lesser houses within the group may either have specific functions such as the 'basketwork and enclosure house' (*uma taka no lia*) that has the task of caring for a sacred buffalo stone (*bena*) or the 'water and tree house' that must care for palm trees in irrigated gardens; or, they may simply be 'middle of the field houses' (*uma asa laran*) that are dependent on higher ranking houses for the sacred objects needed to perform their rituals (1980:136-138).

According to Renard-Clamagirand (1982:37-48), all houses (*uma*) are built on the same plan and differ only in their relative dimensions (see Figure 10). This plan defines a raised square structure with four walls and an open front veranda enclosed under a conical roof. The house is distinguished from the granary (*lako*) which consists of a relatively simple raised platform enclosed under a less extended conical roof. For the purposes of storage, the granary functions as the equivalent of the loft in the Rotinese house.

The orientation of the Ema house is remarkably similar to that of the Rotinese and Amarasi houses. The house is oriented on an east-west axis according to the directions of sunrise (*lelo saen*) and sunset (*lelo du*). Its veranda (*golin*), and the door (*nito*) that leads into the 'inner house' (*uma laran*), face to the south. On entering the house from the veranda, there is a basic dichotomy. The sunrise half of the house is called the 'great platform' (*soro boten*) and the sunset half the 'lesser platform' (*soro bi'in*). Ritual focus in this divided 'inner house' concentrates on two posts, categorized as 'male' and 'female' located at the sunrise and sunset ends of the house. The 'male head post' (*ri ulun mane*) defines the 'greater platform' as pre-eminently male, just as the 'female head post' (*ri ulun ine*) defines the 'lesser platform' as female. The other feature of the 'lesser platform' that defines it as female space is the presence of the hearth (*api matan*).

Memories of Ridge-Poles and Cross-Beams: The categorical foundations of a Rotinese cultural design

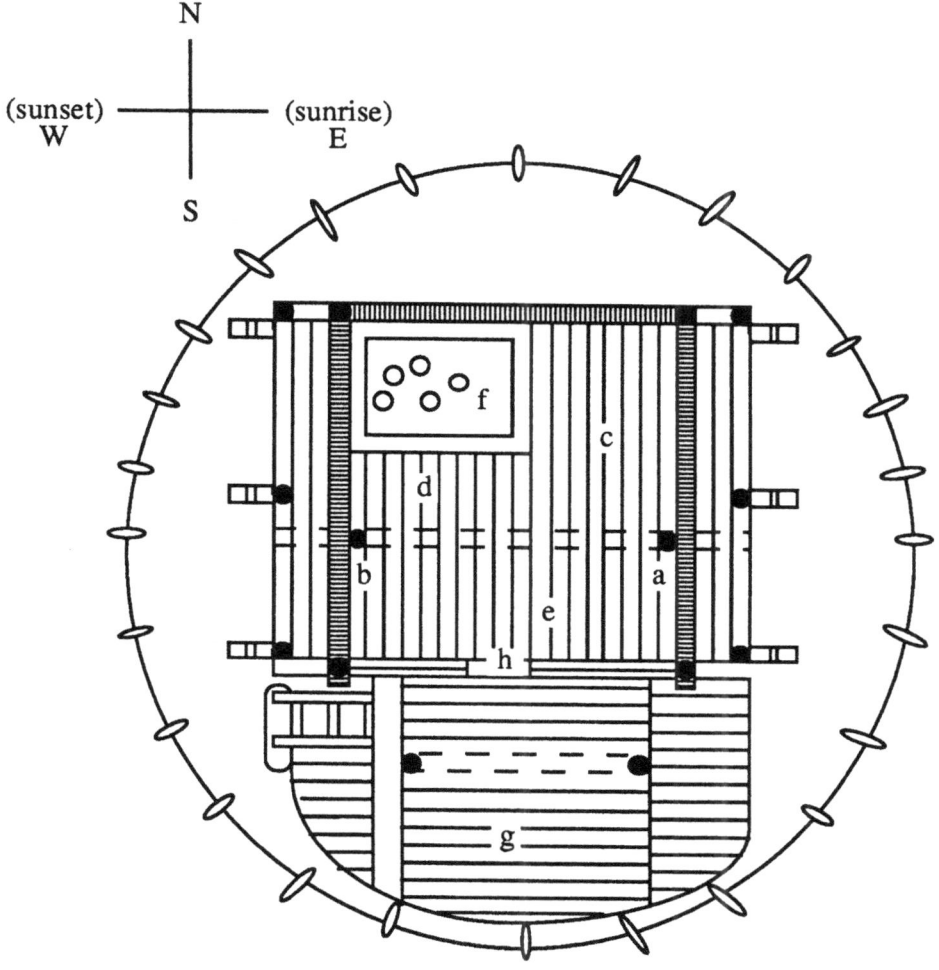

a *ri ulun mane* : 'male' post
b *ri ulun ine* : 'female' post
c *soro boten* : 'great platform'
d *soro bi'in*: 'lesser platform'
e *soro*: beam dividing 'great platform' from 'lesser platform'
f *api matan* : hearth
g *golin*: entrance platform
h *nito*: doorway

Figure 10. Floor plan of an Ema house (adapted from Renard-Clamagirand 1982:41)

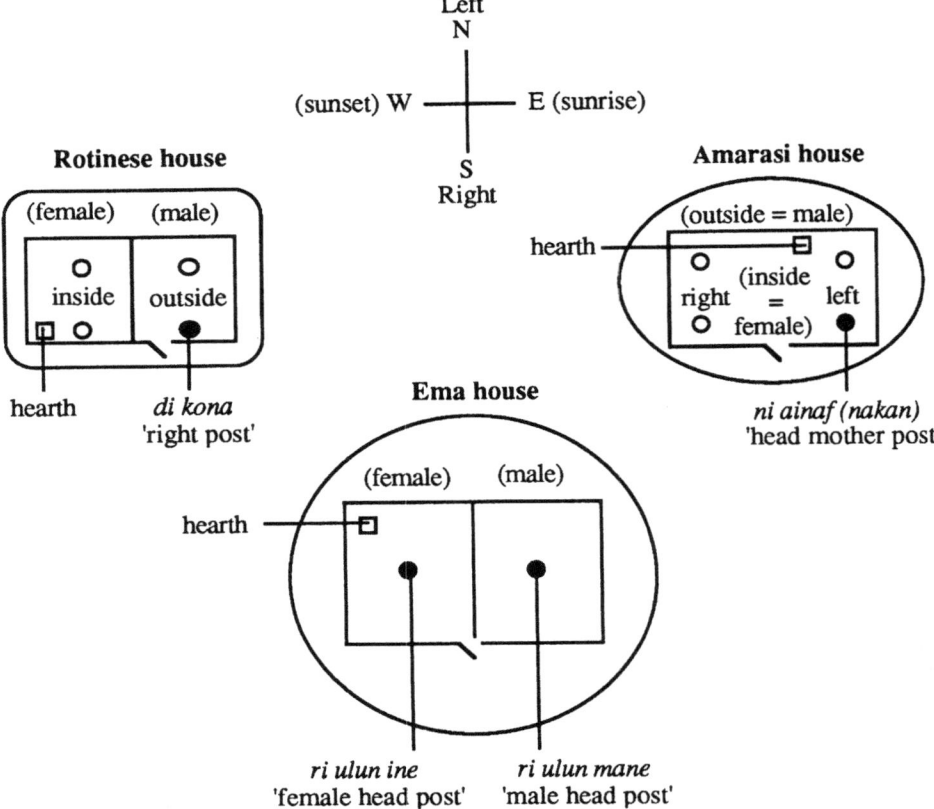

Figure 11. Comparison of the layouts of Rotinese, Atoni and Ema houses

In the Rotinese and Amarasi houses, ritual focus is on one of four posts; in the Ema house, it is divided between two posts that are considered as male and female. In general orientation and in the delineation of the 'inner' house, however, the Ema house resembles the houses of both the Rotinese and Timorese of Amarasi. Within the Rotinese house, the dichotomy is between 'inside' and 'outside'; in the Amarasi, it is between 'right' and 'left'; while in the Ema house, it is between 'male' and 'female'. Because of the relative application of 'right' and 'left' in the Amarasi house, the 'great platform' is located on the 'right' but at the sunset side of the house whereas in the Ema house, the 'great platform' is located in the 'male' half of the house which is on the sunrise side of the house. In all three houses, the chief post (post in Rotinese, *di*; Atoni, *ni*; Ema, *ri* from proto-Austronesian **SaDiRi*) — the principal ritual attractor of the house — is on the eastern or sunrise side. In the Rotinese and Amarasi, it is the south-eastern quadrant of the house. In all three houses, the hearth is given 'female' associations: for the Rotinese, it is 'inside'; for the Atoni, it is on the 'left'; and for the Ema, the hearth occupies a large segment of the 'female' half of the house.

It is interesting to note the shifting location of this hearth in relation to the main 'attractor' in the house. For the Rotinese, the hearth is in the south-west quadrant; for the Atoni, the north-east; and for the Ema, the north-west. Figure 11 provides a schematic representation of these various similarities and differences. One can begin, by means of this schematic representation, to discern how these structures may be related to one another.

References

Cunningham, C.E.

1973   Order in the Atoni house (revised version). In Rodney Needham (ed.) *Right and left: essays on dual symbolic classification*, pp.204–238. Chicago: The University of Chicago Press. (Orig. pub. 1964.)

Fox, James J.

1971 Sister's child as plant: metaphors in an idiom of consanguinity. In Rodney Needham (ed.) *Rethinking kinship and marriage*, pp.219–252. London: Tavistock.

1973 On bad death and the left hand: a study of Rotinese symbolic inversions. In Rodney Needham (ed.) *Right and left: essays on dual symbolic classification*, pp.342–368. Chicago: The University of Chicago Press.

1974 "Our ancestors spoke in pairs": Rotinese views of language, dialect and code. In Richard Bauman and Joel Sherzer (eds) *Explorations in the ethnography of speaking*, pp.65–85. Cambridge: Cambridge University Press.

1975 On binary categories and primary symbols: some Rotinese perspectives. In Roy Willis (ed.) *The interpretation of symbolism*, pp.99–132. London: Malaby Press.

1980a Obligation and alliance: state structure and moiety organization in Thie, Roti. In James J. Fox (ed.) *The flow of life: essays on eastern Indonesia*, pp.98–133. Cambridge, Mass.: Harvard University Press.

1980b   Introduction. In James J. Fox (ed.) *The flow of life: essays on eastern Indonesia*, pp.1–18. Cambridge, Mass.: Harvard University Press.

1988 "Chicken bones and buffalo sinews": verbal frames and the organization of Rotinese mortuary performances. In Henri J.M. Claessen and David Moyers (eds) *Time past, time present, time future: essays in honour of P.E. de Josselin de Jong* (Verhandelingen van het Koninklijk Instituut voor Taal-, Land- en Volkenkunde 131), pp.178–194. Dordrecht: Foris Publications.

1989 Category and complement: binary ideologies and the organization of dualism in eastern Indonesia. In David Maybury-Lewis and Uri Almagor (eds) *The attraction of opposites: thought and society in a dualistic mode*, pp.33–56. Ann Arbor: University of Michigan Press.

Jonker, J.C.G.

1913   Bijdragen tot de kennis der Rottineesche tongvallen. *Bijdragen tot de Taal-, Land- en Volkenkunde van Nederlandsch-Indië* 68:521–622.

Renard-Clamagirand, Brigitte

1980   The social organization of the Ema of Timor. In James J. Fox (ed.) *The flow of life: essays on eastern Indonesia*, pp.134–151. Cambridge, Mass.: Harvard University Press.

1982   *Marobo: une societé ema de Timor* (Langues et civilizations de l'Asie du Sud-Est et du monde insulindien No. 12). Paris: SELAF.

Spence, Jonathan D.

1984   *The memory palace of Matteo Ricci*. New York: Viking Penguin.

Wetering, F.H. van de

1923   Het Roteneesche huis. *Tijdschrift voor Indische Taal-, Land- en Volkenkunde* 62:452–495.

Yates, Frances A.

1966   *The art of memory*. London: Routledge & Kegan Paul.

1969   *Theatre of the world*. Chicago: The University of Chicago Press.

Notes

[1] It was this mnemonic art that Jesuits like Matteo Ricci are said to have introduced to Asia in the sixteenth century (Spence 1984).

[2] Frances Yates, in her book *Theatre of the world* (1969), has examined the development of the English public theatre, including the Globe, in relation to ideas that derive from the classical art of memory.

[3] These seeds are also identified as the 'nine children' of the figure known as Lakimola and thus the cult and the basket representing it are referred to simply as 'Lakimola'.

[4] Van de Wetering (1923:479–480) includes short prayers to both these figures in his description of the house rituals of Bilba.

[5] A good deal of everyday cooking may be done in a hut built outside the house. This kind of structure is generally located at the 'tail' of the main house. Such an arrangement does not diminish the symbolic importance of the hearth within the house.

[6] It is worth noting that when my wife and I took up residence in Ufa Len in Termanu we were offered accommodation in a non-traditional house built on the ground with a cement foundation, windows and a tin roof. The house was built by a man who lived in a traditional house and was the only house of its kind in a cluster of traditional houses. As far as I could determine, the house had been built — it was not quite finished when we arrived — as fancy but temporary accommodation that might attract a suitable high-status bride for the man's only son who would eventually inherit his father's house.

[7] In the 1970s it was still possible to find old houses where individuals remembered the location of specific relatives who were buried under the house. Until the early 1970s, this practice continued in a low key fashion in that the bodies of infants who lived for only a few days were often buried at the foot of the house ladder or at the threshold of the house in hope of their imminent return to the house.

Goodenough Island houses circa 1912[1]

[1] The top photograph is a print from a glass plate photograph taken by anthropologist Diamond Jenness in 1912. His caption reads, 'General view, Minafane village. Ballantyne boiling billy'. Minafane was a small village in the hills behind Bwaidoga in south-east Goodenough. Today the descendants of Minafane

people dwell on the coast. Andrew Ballantyne was Jenness' brother-in-law and the Methodist missionary at Bwaidoga from 1905 to 1915. The bottom photograph was also taken by Jenness in 1912. His caption reads, 'Two houses from gable end, Vatalumi, Goodenough Island; raised, leaf thatch, platform shielded by roof projection, notched log ladder. Two men on platform'. Vatalumi (today Wataluma) is in the north-east of the island. Both photographs are reproduced with the permission of the Pitt-Rivers Museum, Oxford.

Chapter 7. The Kalauna House of Secrets

Michael W. Young

The first government census patrol of the D'Entrecasteaux Islands in the Eastern Division of Papua was conducted in 1921, on foot and by boat, by a British officer named R.A. Vivian. He is commemorated in local legend as 'Misibibi', a colonial culture hero whose fantastic exploits, draconian laws and ruthless feats of social engineering have almost mythical status. He is credited with having transformed the social landscape, though I deduced that, on Goodenough Island at least, 'Misibibi' represents a telescoped series of government officers (Young 1971:31–32). One man alone could not possibly have done so much in so short a time that was so memorable — unless he was Ghengis Khan.

While Mr Vivian does not appear to have actually killed any of the people he travelled among (it would have been counterproductive for his census), he had the most virulent contempt for them. Contempt for their Papuan subjects was not uncommon among Resident Magistrates in the 1920s, but Mr Vivian was unusual for the skill with which he gave vent to it in the terse, schoolmasterly sarcasms of his patrol report (for example, 'I found it necessary to tell the people that dotting themselves over the landscape did not constitute a community'). Mr Vivian also expressed his contempt more directly by ordering the destruction of houses that were not up to his standards of adequacy. Disorder was his bane; unwholesome houses offended him deeply. His prejudices were confirmed in one Goodenough village where he had camped when a house with four occupants collapsed during the night. 'Nobody hurt but all shaken', he noted. 'This bears out my recent action in almost daily condemning ramshackle dwellings, very often bogus ones' (Vivian 1921).

What Vivian frequently referred to in his report as 'bogus houses' were the islanders' pathetic recourse to anti-colonial resistance. In an attempt to appease the all-powerful government (these islands had been pacified for a whole generation), yet to maintain their own preferred dwelling sites, people sometimes built false, dummy or 'bogus' houses on the 'healthier' (that is, more accessible) sites that they had been ordered to occupy. They only pretended to live in them, presumably once or twice a year when a government officer chanced to come by. It was these bogus houses in particular that Mr Vivian delighted in destroying.

As an ironic aside I might add that during World War II, when an immense airbase was constructed on the alluvial plain of northern Goodenough, Australian soldiers also built bogus houses, along with dummy gun emplacements and 'airplanes' made of painted sticks and paper. This elaborate exercise in deception was to fool Japanese spotter planes into reporting that the base was heavily armed and massively occupied.

The moral of this colonial tale is that houses in Goodenough Island may not be what they seem to be.

Architecturally, Goodenough houses (*manua*) were, and still are, very simple. The indigenous, pre-colonial design was described by Jenness and Ballantyne, writing of the early contact period of 1911–12:

> All houses, save an occasional widow's hut or a shelter for storing food, are erected on four poles forked at the top to hold the plates ... Two plates run horizontally from the front to the back posts of the house, and from them a series of poles and rafters lead up and support the ridge-pole. Everything is firmly lashed together with vines ... Thus the frame-work for the house is provided; for walls it is covered with overlapping layers of sago-leaf matting laid horizontally. Back and front are sometimes closed in the same way, but often the matting is here replaced by planks on which the native can display his artistic powers. The back wall is unbroken, but a gap is left in the front by which the inmates can enter; it can be closed at will by native mats. A platform is often built in front, usually as a mere extension of the floor, though sometimes a foot or so lower. This makes it easier to enter the hut, and at the same time offers a very convenient place to sit and gossip, especially when the roofs and sides are made to project as well and so ward off both sun and rain. Propped up against the platform, or lying on the ground below the house, will be found the ladder, which is simply the stem of a small tree with notches cut for steps at intervals of a few inches. The floor is made of transverse poles or rough boards resting on the plates, and is generally covered with mats of coco-nut leaves. The interior is sometimes divided into an inner and outer compartment, with a gap in the dividing wall similar to that in the front of the house. In some houses there is a low bench running along one side, for one of the inmates to sleep on, but this is not very common.

> All huts are built along these lines, though naturally there are slight differences in individual cases. The greatest variation, perhaps, is found in some of the larger huts, when the platform extends around one side and the door is made in one of the longer faces. A medium-sized hut that we measured had a front of 22 6 and a depth of 26 . The platform, which extended 6 outwards from the floor, was 5 above the ground, and the height of the room inside from floor to ridge-pole was only 4 8 . Sometimes a hut is first built upon the ground, then lifted entire and set

in place upon its posts; more often it is built up directly on the posts (1920:182–183).

In Kalauna the old style of house is called *manua mo'a* ('real' or 'true' house). Jenness and Ballantyne (1920:43), who appear to have visited Kalauna in 1912, estimated there were 150 houses. A decade later Vivian recorded 392 people living there. In 1967 I counted between 120 and 130 houses, though the population was then 470. I mentioned the discrepancy between Jenness and Ballantyne's count and my own to some Kalauna men, and they immediately suggested that there might well have been more houses in their grandfathers' time because many more men were polygamous in those days and required a house for each wife, and because many men would then have had separate yam houses (*bolu*).[1] Old men say that the *manua mo'a* houses kept out the rain better than the modern ones and lasted longer, probably because of the thicker thatch. They were warm and cosy, 'like a bird's nest', one man told me.

Figure 1. Kivina the architect, Kalauna 1968

An old man called Kivina taught many of his generation how to build in the modern style (see Figure 1). Others learnt from the Port Moresby region and on Misima Island, where men went to labour on copra plantations or in gold mines. When they returned to Kalauna, they experimented and pooled their new knowledge, but the new style was not adopted by everyone. It took a world war to make the new style fashionable in Kalauna and neighbouring villages. In 1942 the inhabitants of this area were evacuated to Fergusson Island, supposedly out of harm's way of anticipated Japanese airraids on the enormous allied airbase that was being constructed on the alluvial plain of Vivigani. Fergusson people, with government encouragement, had already adopted the new style of house. On their return to their own villages, Goodenough people began to build almost exclusively according to the new design, which they called *manua barak* after the 'barracks' or rest houses of patrolling government officers and their policemen.

The traditional design of *manua mo'a* had all but disappeared by the time of my first fieldwork in the late 1960s. Kalauna had only one such house, situated some distance from the main village, and although I photographed it, I neglected to measure it or inspect its construction before it was destroyed following the death of its owner's wife.[2]

Today houses in Kalauna are rectangular structures with an evenly gabled roof. The bush materials used are the same as before: walls of pandanus leaf or sago leaf mid-rib, floors of 'planks' of black palm or slats of areca palm, and roofs of woven sago leaves. Binding is still by means of the tough skin of a vine, though nails are also used, if available. Houses stand on piles 3 to 4 feet high and access is by a step or notched log through a single doorway. Small 'windows' or peepholes are cut in one or two of the walls. The houses of a hamlet are still clustered closely together, and most are less than 6 feet apart. Internally, houses are partitioned into two or more 'rooms', with a small annex sometimes forming a kitchen. Cooking is done on an open fire on a bed of sand and ashes, and vessels are supported by three hearth stones. A nuclear family usually sleeps together in the same room, and in a small house it is the one which is used to sit and eat in during the day.

A new Kalauna house with its walls of fresh and tightly-bound pandanus leaves looks like a large brown-paper parcel. In a matter of months the shiny brown walls fade to a dull fawn. After several years the sago roof turns black and threadbare and it leaks during rain; the floor slats become loose and treacherous. After about ten years the whole house may begin to tilt and fall apart.

House sites — rather than the impermanent houses themselves — are transmitted according to the normal rule of patrilineal inheritance: sons inherit the sites occupied during their father's lifetime, provided, that is, that they are in his natal (clan-owned) hamlet. Since deteriorating houses are replaced only over a period of several months, a man will build a new house on a different site to the old: perhaps closely adjacent to it, perhaps at the other end of the hamlet, perhaps in a new hamlet altogether. A house is usually abandoned once its owner has completed a new one. The old house is by that stage utterly derelict, having lost to the new dwelling its serviceable timbers, its nails and fittings, and even part of its black palm flooring.

Kalauna's settlement pattern, based on strongly patrilocal agnatic groups, reveals a systolic–diastolic movement over time (Young 1983:265–268). Offshoot hamlets are periodically founded outside the main village, often in the yam gardens where temporary garden huts (*vada*) are erected. These huts may form the basis of proper houses (*manua*). When these houses begin to decay, their occupants return to the parent hamlet once more. A twenty-year time-exposure photograph of the village would show its rhythmic expansion and contraction as families moved to the periphery to found new hamlets, then shifted back to the centre again. In addition to its houses, one or two other man-made structures can be found in every hamlet; these are the tidy piles of stone slabs, the sitting circles (*atuaha*) of the owners. They provide, far more so than do perishable houses, permanent lithic symbols of group identity and patrilineal continuity (Young 1971:22–24). To sit without invitation upon another's *atuaha* is a breach of good manners, though not as unforgivable as to enter a house without the owner's permission.

After the defeat of Japan the departing Australian army left behind a wealth of building material, and, even twenty-five years later, corrugated iron and 'marsden matting' were still being used in the construction of houses in eastern Goodenough. Typically, angled pieces of corrugated iron were placed along the apex of a roof; this both weighed down the sago thatch and sealed the ridge. Doors could also be fashioned easily from sheets of iron. The large heavy strips of 'marsden matting' (used by the soldiers to build bridges as well as to serve as airstrip matting) were used by villagers for pig fences and, when laid upon 44-gallon drums, they made admirable yam platforms for food exchanges. The same drums were in common use as house steps, and their severed tops, with three hearth stones set upon them, were still serving as fire trays in the kitchens of Kalauna as late as 1980. Heavy duty wire mesh (inexplicably called 'tiger wire' in Kalauna) makes an effective barbeque grill.

The new house design was approved by the colonial government, since it was believed to be an improvement on what were regarded as small, dark, pokey, flimsy and unhygienic dwellings. Although the houses that replaced them in Kalauna were lighter and possibly more hygienic, they were often also small, pokey and flimsy. (I have slept in houses that reminded me of Alice in Wonderland: with my head firmly against the back wall, my feet jutting into the 'kitchen', and every turn in my sleep shaking the entire house.) Few houses in Kalauna have more than two rooms, and since adolescent children often move out of the family home, there is no need for more than a single bedroom for a couple and their young children. Those adolescents who do remain make do with the kitchen-cum-dining room, and at night simply unroll their sleeping mats on the floor wherever there is space.

'Bachelor houses' (*manua tubulakata*), occupied by two or three adolescent boys, tend to be even smaller, flimsier (and with something like bravado) higher off the ground than the ordinary 'family' house. They resemble small tents on stilts. Since the boys do not cook for themselves but eat with their parents or married brothers (though they are expected to provision the hearths they eat at with food from their own gardens), the youths' houses can afford to be smaller, and they usually consist of one all-purpose room. They are singularly bereft of furnishings.

Furniture is minimal in a Kalauna house. In the 1960s one invariably sat on the floor (crisp new pandanus mats are always unrolled for visitors to sit upon); in the early 1980s there were a few chairs and tables to be found, usually hand-made by ill-equipped local 'carpenters'. Such chairs were precarious and often bedbug-ridden, so one's comfort was better served by declining them. Unless there was a chair or two, of course, a table was pointless; so Kalauna men who aspired to own a table had first to consider acquiring chairs. But I noted that people who did own tables and chairs rarely used them inside the house, since it was too small to accommodate them comfortably. For the same reason beds were also a rarity, though they are becoming more common in the present decade; again, a house owner would have to think about whether he wanted to build a bed before he planned his house.

So what do Kalauna houses house if not furniture? People certainly (nuclear families usually), but also their portable possessions, including tools, heirlooms, yams and, perhaps most important of all, magical paraphernalia.

The most remarkable thing — perhaps the only remarkable thing — about houses in Kalauna is the secrets they contain. I do not mean the personal or family secrets of their occupants (though of course they harbour their share of those), but rather the magical secrets of their owners.

A word first about magic and secrecy. With the unique exception of land, the most important heritable property in Kalauna is magic. This is so largely because its many kinds are held exclusively. Magic that is known to all is of no value; it is merely folklore (Young 1971:67). To Kalauna men magic is by definition something of intrinsic value; exclusive, secret and to be protected from appropriation by others. One's magic is one's skill for living, one's advantage in the endless skirmishes for status in an egalitarian but competitive milieu. I have elsewhere described this ethos of secrecy and the value of 'the hidden' in the following terms:

> When power is disguised and value is concealed, dissimulation becomes a way of life. That one does not know another's mind is a Melanesian axiom; that Papuans have white skins beneath their brown ones is common belief. The inside of a fruit, a tuber, a person, a house, a basket,

a tree, a mountain or a stone is where the true value of these things is to be found. Humanity itself came from inside the earth, emerging from a hole at the top of a mountain. Sorcerers and magicians contain their secret powers in bundles kept in baskets hung in dark recesses of their roofs. Everyone keeps their valuables in boxes or baskets likewise hidden away in their houses. To be 'showy' is a prerogative of rank — a transient attribute at best, temporarily accorded to feast-givers — or the privilege of marriageable youth. Display (of self, of wealth, of beauty) has its place, but the normal state of affairs is concealment, a studied modesty, and a cultivated shabbiness. There is a disregard for appearances, an indifference to aesthetics. But this belies the inward state. The diffidence is a cultural affectation, a display of non-display. That it is motivated is evident from the occasions when display is enjoined: at feasts, distributions, marriages, mortuary ceremonies, canoelaunchings and other inaugural occasions. Then men and women paint their faces, rub their skins with coconut oil, decorate their hair with the brightest flowers and feathers, adorn their limbs with scented leaves and shell valuables. To an outsider, the effect is dry land blooming after rain; the visual shock of the sudden flowering is all the greater for the unpromising aridity of the usual condition. People are revealed as aesthetes after all, beautiful beneath the skin (Young 1987:249-250).

Interiority is synonymous with secrecy, and both are synonymous with magic. Indeed, English 'secret' (*sikeleti*) has passed into the vernacular as a generic term for magic. Indigenously the closest to a generic term was *yiba*, though strictly speaking this refers to the material paraphernalia or 'stuff' of magic: small stones, dried roots or plants, greenstone axe heads, bone relics, red ochre, ancient limesticks, the teeth of dogs and flying foxes, and many other things worthy of a medieval alchemist. *Yiba*, then, is used metonymically. There were generic terms also for the various *classes* of magic: for love, for war, for the infliction of illness, for weather, for crops, for controlling hunger, and so forth. All of these varieties of magic, which are believed to control human destinies, have their associated paraphernalia or *yiba*.

The house, *manua*, is thus the repository of its owner's magical paraphernalia, just as the owner's mind, *nua* (variously located in the skull or the belly), is the repository of his magical incantations (*kweli*). The lexical correspondence of *manua* and *nua* is doubtless coincidental (*nua* is not the root of *manua*), but this does not prevent one from appreciating the pun of the conceptual complementarity given by the formula:

nua	:	*kweli*	::	*manua*	:	*yiba*
mind	:	spell	::	house	:	paraphernalia

In other words, the house contains the material appurtenances of the human mind's magical knowledge. Fancifully, insofar as it contains the tools of his trade, the Kalauna magician's house might be likened to the Western scholar's library of rare and valuable books.

The typical Kalauna house shape, traditional or modern, signifies nothing but itself. It does not imitate, reflect or resemble a boat, a canoe, a temple, or even a human body. Insofar as the house is a symbol, therefore, it is basic and underivative, like the Platonic 'house' which a Western child draws (typically on a smaller scale to Mummy and Daddy). Neither are the named, constituent parts of the Kalauna house metaphors of other structures, and they do not reflect other symbolic domains. The Kalauna house has no particular orientation, no symbolically salient 'sides' or halves, no interior demarcations which the sexes must observe, and no conceptually significant oppositions such as above and below, high and low.

In short, the social space encompassed by the house is relatively unmarked and undifferentiated.[3] Nevertheless, the house's interior (*vetawana*) is symbolically salient in itself: as concealed interiority, a domain of *nafone*, 'inside' or 'within-ness'.

As a social space, then, the house's interior is its most important feature. It contains, minimally, a cooking hearth, a storage area for yams, and a shelf or platform (*ubudoka*) in the roof at the back of the house (usually above the 'bedroom'). The shelf or platform is typically the place for the secrets: the locked boxes containing shell valuables and other heirlooms; the baskets containing bone relics, yam stones and the paraphernalia (*yiba*) of magic and sorcery, all placed well out of the way of children's questing fingers and visitors' prying eyes.

Among the secrets of any house in Kalauna are fist-sized black stones that lie in some dark recess. A man bequeaths to his married sons one or more such stones. They are 'inhabited' by ancestral spirits, *inainala*, which guard the house and protect its contents from theft. *Inainala* are the undifferentiated spirits of dead patrilineal ancestors, and a Kalauna man would be hard put to say which particular ancestor dwelt in which particular stone. (Some say that certain key components of the house — the ridge-pole, and even the walls — may be 'occupied' by *inainala* too.)

What matters is the pragmatic belief that the stones 'protect' the house, rather like a burglar alarm, or more accurately perhaps, a couple of guard dogs. Unauthorized persons entering the premises (as our own warning notices have it) are at risk of being 'hit' by the *inainala* associated with the stones. To be 'hit' (*kwava*) by a spirit means either to be physically struck down (people literally fall out of houses) or to become crazed, deranged and even run amok. Typically, a man who is *kwava* behaves like one posssessed, and some people entertain the vague belief that the striking *inainala* does enter the victim's body. The victim can be cured most readily by the house owner himself, who bids the *inainala* leave the intruder alone. When strangers are invited to enter a house the owner should announce them by name to reassure the *inainala* that their presence is no threat. It occasionally happens that even friends and distant kinsmen are struck when they enter a house; they suffer nightmares, delirium or worse, and deduce that the guardian *inainala* had not recognized them. So one approaches unfamiliar houses warily — rather as if savage dogs were kept inside. The presumption that dwelling houses contain their owners' *inainala* spirits is the only sense in which Kalauna people believe that houses are animated or 'alive'.

Despite the fact that the house doorway (*awana*) also means 'mouth', and that windows are called 'eyes' (*matana*), the house as an analogy of the human body is not systematically developed. I once tried to get my Kalauna friends to concede that the back of the house where yams are stored was 'like' the human belly (*kamona*). They were perplexed. For a start, they pointed out, the *vetawana* is the place of *sisikwana*, the magic of appetite suppression. 'Yes', I urged, 'like the belly!'. But, they reminded me, the whole purpose of *sisikwana* is to permit *lokona* (prestigeous abstention). Now the human belly, on the other hand, is precisely the place where they do *not* want their yams to go, for to consume them is to waste them! So my literalism was defeated by their more devious logic of secret *sisikwana* in the service of food conservation and the prestige of the *tolokona*, the man-who-abstains.

A big-man's house is generally no larger than anyone else's; the size of the man is not indicated by the size of his house. Sometimes quite the contrary, for Kalauna leaders play a dissimulating game of affected humility. They wear old clothes. They deny their gardens are big; they keep their pig herds small. They practise penury quite deliberately to avoid the charge of *yakaikai* (hubris) or *kasisi* (swank or showiness), both of which imply an unseemly pride that challenges the social worth of others. The egalitarian ethos justifies resentment of such behaviour and instigates sorcery attacks or accusations to cut the ostentatious down to size.

Traditionally, it was the custom for a big-man to deflect personal status onto his eldest son and heir by building him a more imposing house than his own. It would serve as a dwelling for the unmarried youths (*tubulakata*) of the hamlet. More importantly, however, it would serve as a repository for crop wealth. The *manua tubulakata* would be painted with the clan or sub-clan design (*naba*), and inside the house the centrepost would be specially doctored with powerful *sisikwana* magic to 'guard' and preserve the largest yams of the hamlet. That is to say, the men of the clan or sub-clan would, on their leader's instruction, put their biggest and best yams in the *manua tubulakata*, arranging them neatly around the centrepost. There they would stay, the secret pride of the hamlet, until they hardened and rotted or were given away coercively in competitive exchange (*abutu*). The magic was believed to make them inedible, even poisonous. So strong was this *sisikwana* that women and children were forbidden to enter the house. (It is due to this inconvenience, this danger, that men say they discontinued the practice of building *naba*-decorated boys' houses.) *Sisikwana* is believed to stunt a child's growth and dry up the milk of a lactating woman; it can even render her infertile. *Sisikwana* represents a principle of self-denial and abstention, as manifested in shrunken stomachs and shrivelled yams, and it is therefore antithetical to sex, fecundity and growth.

The most important set of rituals in Kalauna is sometimes loosely referred to as 'big' *sisikwana*. This ceremony is performed periodically by the magicians of the dominant clan of Lulauvile, the *toitavealata* or 'guardians' of the village. The ceremony concerns communal prosperity and is called *manumanua*, a reduplication of the word for house. Figuratively *manua* can also mean 'clan' or 'village', hence *manumanua* can be glossed as 'staying at home' or 'remaining in the village'. Indeed, sitting still is a performative act of the magicians who conduct *manumanua*: the ceremony which is designed to banish famine and anchor food in the community. In its broadest sense *manumanua* refers to any rite (or myth) concerned with creating or maintaining prosperity.

I have described *manumanua* at length elsewhere (Young 1983), so I say little about it here except to stress that the symbolic weight it derives from *manua*, house, is precisely that of something fixed, secured or anchored. With the occasional exception of special feasting platforms (which are also magically 'anchored'), the house represents the largest and most solid, the most static and immovable manufactured object within the competence of local technology.[4]

The fact that the house is a *human* creation is also important, for Kalauna people believe their creations to be vitalized by ancestral powers (*inainala*) of their own, human, kind: *kaliva mo'a* ('real people'). Large trees and rocks, on the other hand, although seemingly symbolically apt for the purposes of *manumanua*, are more ambiguously animated by non-ancestral spirits, *tubuvagata* ('eternal ones'). It would be inappropriate and even dangerous to attempt to summon their powers. In the *manumanua* ceremonies the static or immobile properties of the house are magically transfered to garden produce, and both people and their crops are ritually enjoined to stay, to remain in place. Conversely, *manumanua* ritually countermands the 'wandering' (of both people and crops) associated with famine. Thus does 'house', redolent of hearth and home fixed in space, symbolize the dominant idea of *manumanua*.

There is another form of magic, called *bakibaki*, which increases the stasis of the house and induces contentment in its occupants. When a new house is built, certain leaves (and sometimes a small stone) are bespelled and placed at the bottom of one of the post holes. *Bakibaki* may also be performed by rubbing the post itself before it is planted in the ground. This magic is intended not only to 'anchor' the house in the hamlet but to keep its occupants dwelling there, by making them homesick whenever they leave it. *Bakibaki* is thus a quotidian complement to *manumanua* in that it promotes 'sitting still' and discourages 'wandering'. This anchoring magic is also performed whenever a new stone sitting circle (*atuaha*) is built; in this instance a ritual specialist places the bespelled leaves (or stone) beneath the main backrest of the circle.

It is to be expected, given this scheme of values, that the housepost — particularly the *owola*, or centrepost — is a symbol of anchored strength and endurance. The centrepost is a synecdoche of the house, as the big-man is a synecdoche of his hamlet. Hence, the centrepost is to the house as the leader is to his hamlet or clan. Lulauvile men also argue that since their leaders — the *toitavealata* — 'guard' and 'look after' the entire community, they are entitled to be regarded as the *owola* of the village: in English idiom, too, we speak of 'the pillars of the community'.

Figure 2. Moving house in Kalauna 1968

I might add that Lulauvile clan used to be known as *manua u'una*, the 'head' or ruling 'house'. Its traditional *naba* design, as I have described elsewhere (1983:266–267), is based on a zigzag motif which symbolizes the mythical snake-man hero, Honoyeta. Lulauvile's most awesome magical secrets are concerned with the control of the sun through stones and spells bequeathed by Honoyeta. (One of the Lulauvile magicians had a special hole in the roof of his house through which the sun's rays entered to warm his sunstone, and it was believed to be within his power to activate drought at any time. People were understandably wary of displeasing him.)

Every house has an exterior and an interior, and in many societies the exterior of a dwelling is an important indication of the status of its owner(s). I have argued here that in Kalauna it is the interior of the house that is more important (another blow to Western visualism?). Traditionally, it is true, some exterior house-boards in Kalauna were painted with esoteric clan or sub-clan designs (*naba*), which non-owners copied on pain of illness or death. Such designs were a visual clue to the owner's identity and the range of his magical competences. But as I have also noted, it was more usual for a leader's unmarried son to display the *naba* on the front of his bachelor house. Nowadays *naba* decorations have disappeared entirely and the great majority of Kalauna houses are drably undistinguished and uniformly anonymous. The meanest hovel may be occupied by the most respected leader or the most highly ranked magician. But it is what he keeps *inside* his house that signifies his reputation.

The dissemblance of power is a fine art in the ostensibly egalitarian society of Kalauna. Insofar as the house is a site of concealment and the innermost locus of secrets, it represents, too, the principle of least exposure by which power is disguised in Kalauna. This principle is the very antithesis of the principle of simulated aggrandizement manifested in large façades, in bogus houses with empty interiors — the very buildings, in fact, erected by Australian soldiers in 1942 to bluff the Japanese.

References

Jenness, D. and Ballantyne, A.

1920   *The northern D'Entrecasteaux*. Oxford: Clarendon Press.

Vivian, R.A.

1921 Report of a census patrol to Goodenough Island. Canberra: Commonwealth Archives.

Young, Michael W.

1971 *Fighting with food: leadership, values and social control in a Massim society*. Cambridge: Cambridge University Press.

1983   *Magicians of manumanua: living myth in Kalauna*. Berkeley: University of California Press.

1987   The tusk, the flute and the serpent: disguise and revelation in Goodenough mythology. In Marilyn Strathern (ed.) *Dealing with inequality: analysing gender relations in Melanesia and beyond*, pp.229–254. Cambridge: Cambridge University Press.

Notes

[1] Jenness and Ballantyne worked on the assumption that the houses contained on average only two or three occupants. The average is higher than that today: between three and four was my estimate in 1967. These early authors also acknowledged that house counts were an unreliable guide to population numbers:

> Usually there are one or two ruinous uninhabited structures in each hamlet, since it is customary, when an inmate dies, for the rest of the family to abandon their old home and build a new house close by. It is, therefore, impossible to estimate from the number of houses the approximate population of any hamlet, unless one first inquires as to the number of the houses that are uninhabited (1920:47).

[2] On my most recent visit to Kalauna (June 1989) I was surprised to find three houses of the old design. Their owners said they had built them with the express purpose of preserving the knowledge of their construction, 'so that the custom would not be lost'. The newest and best of these houses was built by a classificatory son of Kivina, from whom he learnt the technique. It was too small to live in, however, and resembled a yam house in size (12 foot long, 5 foot wide and 7 foot high). The owner was using it as a store house for his clay pots, tools and yam seeds, and for sitting in during the heat of the day. The pleasing visual lines of the superstructure were starkly incongruous with the four squat and rusty 44-gallon drums on which it sat. This did not trouble the owner; he said he would not bother to replace them with wooden posts.

[3] This is just as well in view of its physically cramped dimensions; if as Douglas Lewis has said, the Tana Ai house is 'a machine for the suppression of time', the Kalauna house is for me a machine for the suppression of space.

[4] Notwithstanding the notion of stasis associated with the concept *manua*, houses are sometimes moved lock, stock and barrel. A large group of men lift it bodily off its posts and carry it to another part of the village (see Figure 2), where they set it down on another set of posts. (See also plate 4 in Young 1971, showing men of Mulina clan shouldering a medium-sized house down an incline. They were bringing it from a garden site into the village.)

A view of the meeting-house at Maketu Marae, Kawhia

Chapter 8. Maori Meeting-Houses in and Over Time

Toon van Meijl

The landscape of New Zealand is remarkably European in character. Its folding surface is dyed with the verdant leaf of pastureland. Meadows are often marked out by hedgerows so typical of England. The grazing pastoral animals were all introduced from the northern hemisphere less than 200 years ago. Only the omnipresent Maori *marae* (ceremonial centres) remind travellers from overseas that they are, in fact, exploring a country in the South Pacific.

Marae are distinguished from ordinary localities scattered over the countryside by a meeting-house used by Maori people for various ceremonies and community assembly. Meeting-houses are the most outstanding indigenous feature of the landscape in New Zealand. As such they are often thought to antedate the advent of James Cook in 1769. However, there is no evidence to support this popular belief widely held among both Maori and Pakeha, the overall term for non-Maori.[1] Neither Cook nor any other explorers of New Zealand in the late eighteenth century and early nineteenth century reported the existence of houses of a size significantly larger than average and belonging to the surrounding community at large. Moreover, the sometimes elaborately carved meeting-houses of the twentieth century bear little resemblance to the pre-European dwellings excavated by archaeologists.

In this paper I first describe contemporary meeting-houses, how and why they are built, and the symbolism that is embodied in their construction. Subsequently, I reflect upon standard anthropological analyses of the spatial orientation of meeting-houses, before analysing the temporal dimensions involved in the use of the house. I explain how various notions of time collapse into a conception of timelessness during ceremonies performed in the house. Furthermore, I argue that the sense of timelessness evoked during ceremonial gatherings must not be extended to the construction of meeting-houses themselves. To put it simply, the symbolism of meeting-houses may involve timelessness in some respects, yet the houses themselves have been and are subject to historical changes. An account of the development of meeting-houses over time is presented in the penultimate section, and I conclude with some notes on ongoing development in the future. I argue that in spite of the dramatic transformations of meeting-houses and their importance, they continue as the focal point of many Maori communities in both rural and urban areas.

The *Marae*

Before I examine the fascinating symbolism of meeting-houses, I must first explain the concept of *marae*. Nowadays the term *marae* evokes two related meanings. In the first place, *marae* is used to denote an open space, a clearing or plaza in front of a meeting-house, reserved and used for Maori assembly, particularly ceremonies of welcome. This narrow meaning of the term *marae* is often distinguished as *marae aatea* or *marae* 'proper' (see Figure 1). In the second place, the concept of *marae* is used in the broader sense for the combination of the *marae* proper, the courtyard, with a set of communal buildings which normally include a meeting-house, a dining hall and some showers and toilets (Metge 1976:227). *Marae* are often regarded as the final sanctuary of Maori culture (Walker 1977).

Figure 1. A view of the *marae* proper and the meeting-house Taane-i-ti-Pupuke at Waahi Pa, Huntly

In the 1980s only 10 per cent of the Maori population was based in rural communities. As a consequence *marae* are few and far between in the isolated villages scattered over the countryside. Generally *marae* are surrounded by only a couple of houses. Wherever they live, Maori people now occupy ordinary family houses of European design, each with its own modern conveniences. As a result, the *marae* is no longer used regularly as an extension to the private dwellings. Instead, *marae* are used only for ceremonial gatherings on occasions of life crises or especially to entertain guests. Under these circumstances the houses, that in pre-European days seem to have belonged to chiefs and their extended family only, have been enlarged and their ornamentation has often been refined as well. In addition, *marae* have been provided with a kitchen and a dining hall, with lavatories and shower facilities, all able to cope with large numbers of visitors.

Meeting-houses and *marae* are seen as 'going together' in more than one way (Metge 1976:230). Visiting orators commence their ceremonial speeches by greeting them both: *Te whare e tuu nei, teena koe; te marae e takoto nei, teena koe* (House standing here, I greet you; *marae* lying here, I greet you). Not only spatially, but also functionally, the meeting-house and the *marae* proper are complementary (Metge 1976:230). The *marae* is used for speech-making and welcoming guests during the daytime and in dry weather; the meeting-house is used to accommodate guests and for speech-making after dusk or on rainy days.

The complementary relationship between *marae* and meeting-house is often expressed by analogy with the gods of war and peace. Traditionally, so it was said, the *marae* was the area of Tuu-matauenga, the god and father of war, whereas the meeting-house was associated with Rongo-ma-tane, the ancestor of the *kuumara* (sweet potato) and the god of all other cultivated food as well as the god of peace:

> *Ko Tuu a waho; ko Rongo a roto*
>
> Tuu outside, Rongo inside (Metge 1976:231).

A contemporary rephrasing of the old saying I noted was voiced by a *kaumaatua* (respected elder), who explained to a group of young people that

> the *marae* is the area of the good, the bad, and the ugly. The meeting-house, on the other hand, is the realm of Jesus Christ and the Kingdom of Heaven.

The elder intended to indicate that disputes are expressed and settled in the *marae* during the exchange of ceremonial speeches, while the conversation in the meeting-house after the welcoming of guests is not supposed to be about contentious issues. However, practice often proves otherwise.

The Meeting-House Described

A meeting-house is usually the dominant feature of any *marae* complex. It is a large rectangular building with a gabled roof and a front veranda, often, but certainly not always, marked by embellishments of carving, curvilinear rafter patterns (*koowhaiwhai*) painted in black, red and white with lattice-work panels (*tukutuku*) on the wall. Houses range in length from approximately 12 or 13 metres to nearly 30 metres. Both the size and the degree of ornamentation of a house say something about the *mana* (prestige) of its owner group. In myths there is evidence to be found that the size of a meeting-house adds to the prestige of the ones who built it (Salmond 1975:36). The size of a house also varies with the magnitude of the owner group. The house of a *whaanau* (extended family) will be smaller than the house serving a *hapuu* (sub-tribe). The other feature to be mentioned is the degree of decoration, particularly carvings, and here, too, prestige is at stake. However, it is important to point out that not all meeting-houses are necessarily carved. Only in some areas, particularly the east coast of the North Island, are most meeting-houses carved, whereas in the Waikato area where I did my fieldwork, for example, carved meeting-houses are extremely rare. Carving only came into fashion from the mid-nineteenth century on, and in that period of history, after the wars and confiscations of vast areas of land, few tribes had the means, let alone the morale, to become artistic.

Generally a meeting-house is built of modern materials. The foundations are embedded in concrete, the walls are made of weatherboarded timber and the roof is covered with sheets of corrugated iron. The front of the house is extended in the form of a porch or *maahau* up to 4 metres deep. When a meeting-house is richly embellished, this intermediate veranda, linking the *marae* proper with the interior of the house, is decorated the most with intricate carvings. An outstanding figure (*tekoteko*) is normally carved at the apex of the meeting-house. Some wood surfaces may be carved into ancestors or motifs derived from mythology, such as the infamous *taniwha* ((sea-)demons). The veranda rafters may be painted with the curvilinear *koowhaiwhai* patterns in white and black, and in some areas mixed with red. The doorway is to the right of centre,[2] with the name of the house and often also the date on which it was formally opened, marked on a small panel fixed above it. Not infrequently the only window is in the front wall and to the left of centre. Along the walls of the veranda one might find wooden benches to accommodate visitors during *hui*, community gatherings for any purpose.

Inside the meeting-house old portraits of ancestors hang on the walls. Often the rafters rising from each side-panel to the ridge-pole are painted with *koowhaiwhai* designs, and under the roof there may be lattice-work panels between the rafters. The ridge-pole is supported by one or two freestanding heart-posts (the *poutokomanawa*), which, contrary to what Salmond reports (1975:37), are rarely carved into human figures, as, according to one informant of chiefly descent — an elderly woman of the Ngaati Porau tribe — Maori people do not recognize chiefs. 'This *backbone* of the house is not carved, because we don't recognize chiefs. We all carry the canoe together.'

In some houses there is a platform at the rear. The floor is usually covered with flax mats (*whariki*) or a carpet. Mattresses are stored against the walls or in a separate shed, and they are rolled out if the house is in use during *hui*.

Visitors who stay the night in a meeting-house are provided with clean sheets and pillows.

Social and Political Aspects

The Maori name for a meeting-house varies according to its function at a particular moment: *whare tupuna* (ancestral house), *whare runanga* (council house), *whare hui* (meeting-house), *whare puni* (sleeping house), *whare manuhiri* (guest house), and sometimes *whare tapere* (house of amusement). As some meeting-houses have become increasingly ornamented with carvings since the last century, they may be referred to as *whare whakairo* (carved house) as well, but in my experience this term is rarely used, except perhaps when visitors or tourists are shown around. The primary function of the meeting-houses is one of shelter in case of rain or darkness. In addition it provides a community with the facility to accommodate up to 200 people. Greeting-ceremonies (*mihimihi*) and religious services (*karakia*) may be conducted in the house during formal *hui*. Oratory may be performed in the house during the evenings, followed by some entertainment before the lights are turned off and everybody goes to sleep. Apart from activities associated with guests at a *marae*, the meeting-houses are regularly used as a venue for meetings of the *marae komiti* (committee) or other community groupings.

In the meeting-houses owner groups, usually subtribes, symbolize their unity and their distinction from other subtribes. In that sense the meeting-houses were often built as a political counter (Salmond 1975:38). When a new subtribe emerged, when extended families bickered or community factions arose, the meeting-houses were erected to symbolize the newly developing social structure of a group. Many such cases have been reported, not all of them historical. I once visited adjacent *marae* of two relatively recent subtribes that used to constitute one united subtribe before World War II. Each *marae* had its own dining hall, but the two subtribes still shared one meeting-house. However, in contradistinction with normal etiquette, each group predominantly occupied one side of the house. For example, their dead were put either on the left or on the right side. Members of either *marae* mowed the lawns in front of the house only up to a symbolic boundary extending from the ridge-pole of the house. Children often played around the house, but when they accidentally crossed the invisible boundary they were smacked. Intermarriage between members of the two subtribes was not uncommon but definitely not encouraged either. Members of the two *marae* met only once a year, during the annual *poukai*, a 'loyalty gathering' of the Maori King Movement. On this day they attempted to outdo their rival group in offering the most lavish meal to the visitors, pledging loyalty to the Maori queen. Indeed, in this extremely rare case one wonders just when one of the two subtribes will decide to build a meeting-house solely for itself.

The house as a symbol of solidarity of the kinship group is not new and may well antedate European settlement (Johansen 1954:27). More interesting, however, is the fact that the meeting-houses continue to be a most powerful symbol for newly emerging kinship groupings, which themselves are the result of an increasing disintegration of the kinship structure. In New Zealand, for example, there are clusters of several closely related, extended families scattered over the countryside. The core of these kin communities is formed by those who are descended, through either male or female lines, from a patriarchal head of no more than two or three generations ago. In some cases he may still be alive. The colloquial term for these kin communities is 'families', but in order to distinguish them from nuclear and ordinary extended families, Metge labelled them 'large-families' (1976:136–138). Since many large-families have erected a meeting-house to symbolize their autonomous status, they could also be called 'houses', to use the concept recently added to the anthropological kinship terminology by Lévi-Strauss (1982:163–187; 1987:151–152). Although he did not mention a link with meeting-houses, Lévi-Strauss (1987:178–184) applied the term to the Maori *hapuu* (subtribe) as well. However, in his theoretical consideration he pointed out that 'houses' are not equivalent to extended families, lineages (or in Maori society, subtribes) and clans (or tribes) (1987:151). Instead Lévi-Strauss argued that 'houses' take an intermediate position. He defined the house as

> possessing a domain, perpetuated by transmission of its name, wealth and titles through a real or fictitious descent line which is recognized as legitimate as long as the continuity can be expressed in the language of descent or alliance or, most often, of both together (1987:152).

Lévi-Strauss added that in order to perpetuate themselves, houses make extensive use of fictive kinship, in terms of both alliance and adoption. Likewise, large-families or houses in Maori society were distinguished from subtribes because for practical purposes they included spouses and adopted children attached to the group. Nonetheless, large-families remained strictly limited in size and depth.

Lévi-Strauss (1982) also suggested houses may be a fairly recent phenomenon in the history of societies traditionally organized along kinship lines, but now 'in a situation where political and economic interest, on the verge of invading the social field, have not yet overstepped the "old ties of blood" ' (p. 186). In New Zealand the Maori houses emerged relatively recently as well, and, as yet, the dynamics of their development does not seem to have come to an end. After World War II large-families began building ancestral meeting-houses which in the past were invariably subtribally based. In the situation of the New Zealand Maori the meaning of Lévi-Strauss' concept of house is thus being enriched by the erection of meeting-houses to symbolize and reinforce the unity of the groups associated with them. The construction of meeting-houses by, and for, large-families or houses originated on the east coast of the North Island but is spreading across all areas of New Zealand.

Symbolic Representation

That meeting-houses are the most powerful symbol a group may possess is apparent from the meaning embodied in their form. They represent reverence for the past and deference to the ancestors of the subtribe or large-family concerned. Meeting-houses offer a statement that the ancestors are present when groups assemble at a *marae*. I will explore this symbolism on the three levels distinguished by Ann Salmond (1975) in her monograph *Hui: a study of Maori ceremonial gatherings*. While I follow Salmond's account closely, I often disagree with her analysis. Although ethnographically quite accurate, even brilliant at times, Salmond creates an ideal-typical view of what meeting-houses represent and the meaning she reads into them also represents her logical construction as anthropologist. There is too much evidence available to dispute the commonly accepted notion that meeting-houses represent ancestors, but, on the other hand, it is a fact that nowadays few Maori people are aware of all the symbolic conceptions that, according to anthropologists, are embodied in a meeting-house. Often I met Maori people reading books such as Salmond's classic work, and it would therefore be interesting to explore the question: to what extent have etic interpretations of meeting-houses been incorporated in emic discourse?

At the most general level, a remote but famous ancestor is represented in the meeting-house, after whom it is usually named. Salmond (1975:39) mentions that such an ancestor may have been, among others, an inhabitant of the mythological homeland Hawaiki. This was what the people at the *marae* where I lived told me as well. However, nobody knew anything about him. In my attempts to find out who Taane-i-te-Pupuke had been, I was initially unsuccessful until one of the more senior elders told me the ancestor after whom the meeting-house was named had been a paramount chief in Hawaiki. He added that he had not been able to tell me about him beforehand, because anything coming from Hawaiki was highly *tapu* (sacred; see pp.203–207).[3]

Meeting-houses are not only named after an ancestor. Their structure represents the body of an eponymous ancestor too. The *koruru* at the junction of the eaves of the veranda represents his face. The porch itself is regarded as his brain (*roro*). The barge-boards (*maihi*) are his arms, while the extensions of the barge-boards, called *raparapa*, represent his fingers, as carvings sometimes suggest. The front window is seen as his eye (*mataaho*). The interior of the meeting-house is the chest (*poho*) of the ancestor. The ridge-pole (*taahuhu*) is regarded as his spine representing the main line of descent from the apex of the (sub)tribe's genealogy. The rafters (*heke*) are his ribs representing junior descent lines derived from the senior line (*taahuhu*). *Heke* means literally 'descend' or 'diminution', but in the meeting-house it bears connotations of 'my line as distinguished from your line' (Webster 1975:140). The structure of the meeting-house evokes the concept of welcome according to Salmond (1975:40). She interprets the eaves as arms 'held out in welcome', and she argues that it also explains why the door is always left open during gatherings. However, since the early 1980s the door of a meeting-house is no longer left open unless a Maori warden is available to keep an eye on the house when the visiting crowd is in the dining hall; otherwise the house, with all the belongings of the visitors, would be ransacked by children and youngsters playing around the *marae*.

At the second level, within the house the *poupou* (slabs) from which the *heke* extend, ideally represent junior ancestors descended from the founder. Salmond (1975:40) automatically assumes that slabs are carved and that they are 'ancestors within the ancestor'. She argues that the slabs constitute a genealogy around the walls. However, in many meeting-houses slabs have not been carved and I am not sure whether in that case they are still associated with a particular ancestor. I suspect they are not. When the slabs are carved, though, they often represent ancestors directly related to the group. In some cases they may symbolize the patriarchal heads of the extended families associated with the subtribal *marae*, and the number of slabs should ideally accord with the number of extended families. In older meeting-houses the carved ancestor on each slab may be recognized by a distinctive feature that portrays his character, but nowadays few people know enough history or mythology to interpret these without controversy. Hence, in more recent meeting-houses the name of the ancestor is marked on the slab. Not all the figures depicted in the *poupou* relate to the genealogy of the subtribe (Kernot 1983:191; Neich 1984:7–9). In Te Awamutu I visited a brand new meeting-house in which a number of Pakeha historic figures were carved, including a military officer, General Cameron; a colonial official, Sir John Eldon Gorst; and the first Anglican bishop, Selwyn; all of whom had played a significant yet not necessarily positive role in colonial history. This is a telling example of how Maori people have accommodated foreign elements in their traditions and changed these according to circumstance.

Finally, ancestors are represented in Maori meeting-houses by photographs hanging on the walls, particularly the front wall. These portraits constitute the representation of the most recent forebears. In the past, Salmond (1975:41) reports, photographs were put in order by the *kaumaatua* (elders) of the *marae*, who arranged them according to family affiliations. The people portrayed in the house are invariably of superior rank or status. Usually a portrait is taken into the house for the first time after a person's death. During the *tangihanga* (the funeral wake) photographs of the deceased are placed at the end of the coffin and around it, along with those of male and female ancestors as well as of other close relatives and friends who have died. After the *tangi* they may be taken back to the dwelling where the deceased used to live until the unveiling of the tombstone, normally one year later. On this occasion the portrait of the deceased replaces the open coffin. It is placed on flax mats spread out on the veranda. The family and visitors assemble in the porch of the meeting-house for a memorial service. They weep over the picture as they had done over the coffin a year before. Subsequently they move on to the cemetery to unveil the stone.

In summary, the portraits, like the carved slabs and, at the most general level, the structure of the meeting-house itself, can be regarded as substitutes for the forebears they represent. During ceremonies in and around the meeting-house the most recent, the more remote, as well as the most remote ancestors are present in both spiritual and physical form (Salmond 1975:41).

Spatial Orientation

Cross-cutting the symbolism of ancestors in meeting-houses and the different temporal dimensions involved in this representation is a spatial orientation which has more effect on the practical use of meeting-houses. This is the complementary distinction of various parts of the meeting-house into *tapu* (sacred) and *noa* (common) dimensions. *Tapu* and *noa* are obviously exceedingly complex concepts with which anthropologists could not come to grips for a long time, but since the brilliant analysis by Michael Shirres (1982) it is beyond doubt that the greatest contrast is not between *tapu* and *noa* but between 'intrinsic' *tapu* and 'extensions' of *tapu*, or simply between more and less *tapu*. An exhaustive application of this pioneering insight is beyond the scope of this paper, although a preliminary attempt is made to explore the consequences of Shirres' conceptualization of *tapu* for the analysis of the meeting-house. However, since the concepts of *tapu* and *noa* are essential to the understanding of most aspects of *marae* layout and usage, I will first explain their relevance in general.

As a whole, the *marae* complex is regarded as *tapu* in relation to the outside world (Metge 1976:232). When a group of visitors arrive at a *marae*, they will wait at the gate entrance (*tomokanga*) until called to enter. In the shrill high-pitched call of welcome (*karanga*) always recited by a woman, often words that mean 'come up' rather than 'come in' are used: *piki mai, kake mai, eke mai* (climb, ascend, rise; Figure 2 shows a group of people doing a *powhiri*, a part of the welcoming ceremony immediately after the *karanga*). Although in former days Maori *paa* (strongholds) were often located on top of a hill, nowadays most *marae* are flat, and therefore it is obvious, as Metge (1976:232) points out, that the climbing is a symbolic movement.

Figure 2. Welcoming a group of visitors in front of the meeting-house Taana-i-te-Pupuke at Waahi Pa Marae in Huntly

Within the boundaries of the *marae* complex a number of complementary domains are distinguished. Between these domains there is some tension that originates in the distinction between more *tapu*, less *tapu* and, to some extent, *noa*. Thus the *marae aatea*, or *marae* proper, and the meeting-house are often distinguished as the *tapu* sector compared to the dining hall and kitchen which are regarded as *noa*. At the same time, however, each is internally differentiated into complementary parts representing intrinsic *tapu*, the extensions of *tapu* and/or *noa* qualities. Without doubt the most *tapu* part of the *marae* complex is the central part of the *marae* proper, the area on which the ceremonies of welcome are performed and where orators make their speeches. It is one of the most serious violations of *marae* protocol and of *tapu* to walk across this area during a ceremony or speech. Even when the *marae* proper is not in use it should be treated with the utmost respect, although this is no longer obvious to Maori youths. Where I lived old people could not get the boys to understand that it was disrespectful to play football on the *marae* proper. By the same token, I remember some old people nearly having heart attacks when a Pakeha social worker laid down to sunbathe on a *marae* proper during a bicultural gathering. By comparison the meeting-house as well as the areas surrounding the *marae* proper, where people take up a position to listen to the speeches, are less *tapu* than the *marae* proper. However, they can never be *noa* because they are allegedly opposed to the intrinsically *tapu* courtyard, as Metge (1976:232) would like us to believe.⁴ *Tapu* and *noa* do not constitute a complementary opposition. They are surely complementary, but merely as distinctions mediated by extensions of *tapu*.

In regard to the meeting-house itself there are a number of practices that exemplify its intrinsic *tapu* qualities. The meeting-house is most *tapu* while it is being built, and in the course of its construction neither women nor food, which are far from intrinsically *tapu* — even *noa* under certain circumstances — are allowed entry. Even after the meeting-house is opened, food is never to be taken inside.

Within the meeting-house the first distinction that can be drawn is between the *mahau* (the open-air veranda) and the interior (Salmond 1975:45). Since the veranda marks the transition between the *marae* proper and the meeting-house, it is used in a distinctive manner. Salmond reports that at a funeral wake (*tangihanga*), the coffin, which is one of the most *tapu* objects one can think of, used to be placed in a small shed or marquee to the left of the entrance to the house in order to avoid contaminating the building. Nowadays, however, the coffin is either put on the veranda under the window or taken inside the house. In some areas people still seem to be reluctant to take the coffin inside and this may indicate a fundamental difference between the veranda and the interior. The veranda could be more *tapu* for some reason or another.⁵

The passage from veranda to interior is made through the door by the living, and, in some more traditionally oriented areas, through the window by the dead (Salmond 1975:46). In the Urewera district, where the Tuhoe Maori people reside, the window is regarded as highly *tapu* and therefore the coffin, if it is taken inside the house at all during a funeral wake, is passed through the window. The door is said to be less *tapu* and it is not believed to present a risk to the living, who may pass through it without hindrance.

When entering the house, even in museums where visitors are still expected to revere the meeting-house, one custom is widely practised: the practice of removing shoes at the door and entering with bare feet or socks. This is said to reflect the *tapu* state of the house, and Salmond (1975) quotes an informant as saying that people should take off their shoes because 'your boots have been walking outside, into the *whare kai* [dining hall] and all sorts' (p.46). However, it is more likely to reflect concern for the flax mats or the carpet on the floor of the meeting-house than to have something to do with *tapu*. I recall a well-respected woman who told me when I was hanging about a meeting-house: 'Hey, Pakeha, you take your shoes off in the house of the *horis*,⁶ hey'. Subsequently she proceeded to enter the house with her shoes on.

Inside, the meeting-house is also divided into two separate yet complementary domains: the *tara whaanui* (the 'big' side) and the *tara iti* (the 'little' side), which are related as more and less *tapu*. The boundary between the big side and the little side extends from the doorway which is generally to the right-hand side of the house. Consequently, the *tara whaanui*, or big side, lies to the left of a person, and the *tara iti*, or little side, to the right. When guests are accommodated in the meeting-house, they are placed along the left wall and across the *tara whaanui*, the more *tapu* side, which is reserved for visitors. The local people (*tangata whenua*), the 'people of the land' or the 'hosts', sleep on the *tara iti* to the right (Metge 1976:232).

Surprisingly, Salmond (1975:47) does not mention the distinction between the big side and the little side, although she reads a whole range of other symbols in the obvious distinction between left and right sides inside the meeting-house. She writes that at some places the doorway lintel is surmounted with a carved panel representing a female ancestor (*pare*), which leads her to conclude that the right side of the house is *noa* and associated with the living (p.47). The fact that the carving, as she wrote on the previous page in another context, usually represents the goddess of death, Hine-nui-te-Poo, does not appear to her as contradictory (cf. Jackson 1972:40-60). Further, Salmond writes that the window, being the entrance to the house on the left side, is said to be *tapu* and dedicated to the use of the dead (p.48). This holds true in the case of funeral wakes. Coffins are placed on the porch to the left of the house under the window, or if taken inside they are laid down somewhere on the left side of the house (depending on the tribal area) either under the window, at the window end of the left wall, or just in the middle. The intrinsically *tapu* body always stays on the more *tapu* side.

Within the spatial orientation of meeting-houses special places of honour were allocated to people of highest rank. It was, but no longer is, a rule, as Salmond (1975:48-49) has it, that the most distinguished guests at a *hui* were placed to sleep under the front window. The position was referred to as *iho nui:iho* having connotations of 'essence', 'strength' or an 'object of reliance'; *nui* meaning 'big' or 'large'. The local chiefs lay down to sleep to the right-hand side of the front door, which was called the *kopa iti* position: *kopa* evoking associations with 'weak' or 'numbed'; *iti* meaning 'small' or 'unimportant'. However, nowadays the more prominent visitors do not necessarily sleep at the former positions of honour up front. Metge (1976:234) mentions that people of highest rank are now usually placed under the recently introduced windows at the rear, away from traffic in and out during the night. However, at the *marae* where I was based, the door to the nearest lavatories was in the rear wall as well. There chiefs usually just slept somewhere in the centre of the house.

In the meeting-house the placement of a coffin, of visitors and locals, of prominent visitors and local chiefs, and, in some contexts, of men and women, was generally no accident. It did and, up to a point still does, relate to a scheme of spatial orientation characteristic of the *marae* which distinguishes between intrinsic *tapu*, extensions of *tapu*, and *noa* domains. However, it is important to point out that the principles of spatial structure are now expressed only by a few expert elders and a number of anthropologists.

Temporal Implications of Spatial Orientation

In a more recent consideration of semantic associations of some key concepts in the Maori world-view, Salmond (1978:9–11) discovered a link between the temporal and spatial orientation of the meeting-house. She noted a contrasting opposition between the meanings of 'front, past time, sacred place, seniority of birth' and the meanings of 'hind part, rear, future time, *noa* (unrestricted, profane) place and cooked food, junior birth, north and death' (p. 10). In the Maori language the past was described as *ngaa raa o mua*, 'the days in front', whereas the future was 'behind', *kei muri* (Metge 1976:70). Maori people moved, as it were, into the future with their back to the front while facing the past. The spatial orientation of the Maori concept of time concurs with Salmond's interpretation (see pp. 10–14) of the symbolism of the meeting-house as a progressive time sequence from the remote past — with the house itself representing the eponymous ancestor, who ideally stands at the apex of the subtribe's genealogy — through the intermediate stage of the ancestor's descendants represented in the carved slabs along the interior walls, to the stage of portraits figuratively depicting recently deceased kin members. In addition, the place of the sacred seniors (past) in the front and the more junior (future) towards the rear of the house, corresponds with the temporal succession from remote past to more recent past, toward the future.

The linear progression over time that takes place when entering the meeting-house may, to some extent, be condensed to a contrast between a mythological past outside of the meeting-house and a more historical past in the interior of the house (Neich 1984:34). The transition from the world of myth to the world of history was marked by the doorway which was recognized as a *tapu* boundary. In fully carved meeting-houses the threshold was marked with a carved slab, or *pare*, over the door (Jackson 1972:40–60). Many *pare* depicted a female figure with her legs outstretched, often representing the goddess of death Hine-nui-te-Po.[7] The *pare* indicated its function of lifting the *tapu* of anyone entering the house (Salmond 1975:46). Nowadays the *pare* has been replaced by a small sign with the name of the house painted on it.

Interestingly, the linear progression from the mythical world of the ancestors in front of the meeting-house to the historical past inside, leading toward the future at the rear of the house, is an inversion of the symbolic implications of the movement into the house as a transition into the timeless, ever-present world of the ancestors. The spatial orientation of the meeting-house with the remote past outside, to the more recent past inside and the future towards the rear, seems to be reversed in the metaphor of the movement into the house as an apparent regression in the past. After all, the future (*kei muri*, rear) was behind the people moving into the house, pushing them forward into the past (*mua*, front). When moving into the house the future was, thus, resolved in a meta-historical past, while the past repeated itself in the future.

The inversion of the temporal implications of the spatial orientation of the meeting-house when entering the house, signifying the spiritual realm of the ever-present ancestors, can only be understood in relation to the Maori conception of time and their view of history (see Neich 1984:32). In the Maori world-view time was intimately linked up with natural events and processes. Time was not yet hypostatized into generalized, quantifiable periods independent of human action. Time was relative rather than absolute, concrete rather than abstract. By the same token, the Maori view of history was characterized not by a quest for abstract continuity in an infinite stream of events, but by an appraisal of concrete events in their own right:

> to us the event — apart from picturesque aspects — is of no value until it stands as an expression of the forces of history and their conflicts; to the Maori the event in itself is so significant that history obtains a full meaning simply by consisting of events (Johansen 1954:151).

Thus, separate historical events acquired a meaning fundamentally different from the meaning they have in Western conceptions of history: 'We find it quite obvious that when an event has happened, it never returns; but this is exactly what happens' (Johansen 1954:161). Consequently, in the Maori world-view history unfolded as a return of the same experiences: 'We cannot underline the literal meaning too much when we say that the Maori relives history' (Johansen 1954:161).

The continuous regeneration of historical events explains the relevance of ancestors. They were still present to support and guide their descendants. Hence they were spoken of in the present tense as well (Metge 1976:70). Ancestors lived on in the history of kinship groups and as such their lives were the same as those of the living (Johansen 1954:163). Ancestors reappeared in the living as history emerged and was actualized.

In the recurrent manifestation of the same events and experiences, different conceptions of time collapsed. The point may be illustrated by an analysis of the act of entering the meeting-house. As pointed out above, the doorway of meeting-houses was highly *tapu*. In old meeting-houses the boundary was marked by a carved *pare* (lintel) over the door to signify the linear transition from the timeless world of myth to the historical world of ancestors. However, the same movement symbolized a return to the eternal past of ancestors. In other words, the movement into the house paralleled a progression in linear time, but the arrival in the historical world of the ancestors involved a constant regeneration and ceremonial recapitulation of their legendary past. The Maori attempted to resolve the present in the past while simultaneously calling upon the ancestors for guidance and spiritual support to make the future accord with their heroic past. Ultimately, in the ideal model of the cosmos, the past, the present and the future collapsed. In the meeting-house all time was made one (see Jackson 1972:61).

Thus the Maori material offers some evidence for the hypothesis formulated by Maurice Bloch (1977) in a brilliant article on the relation between a cyclical notion of time in ceremonies and rituals, and linear time in practical activity. The practical act of entering the house was associated with a linear progression from myth to history, whereas the ceremonies in the house involved a (cyclical) recurrence of the spiritual past in order to invoke a dimension of timelessness. In so far as the present is a mere recapitulation of the past to make it channel the course into the future, in the Maori world-view different notions of time were collapsed.

Transformation of the Meeting-House Over Time[8]

The meaning of timelessness as generated during gatherings in the meeting-house is often extended to the house itself. At a funeral wake a respected elder (*kaumaatua*) formally welcomed the anthropologist and apologized for the noisy children running around playing with dogs. 'But', he said, 'it is like the house, it is part of our life-style and will never change'. The elder implied that meeting-houses had been in existence from time immemorial expressing a popular belief widely entertained in New Zealand.[9]

However, although meeting-houses invoke a cosmic timelessness through a collapse of the past into the present to assure the continuation of the past through the present into the future, the construction of meeting-houses itself clearly follows a non-timeless, historical transformation. Archaeological evidence reveals that large carved meeting-houses as described by explorers from the 1830s onward did not exist before the arrival of Europeans. The type of house most common in prehistoric times was generally of a significantly smaller size. However, a difference in size between pre-European Maori dwellings was reported as early as 1769. James Cook noted that some houses were twice the size of others and suggested that

> this depends upon the largeness of the Family they are to contain, for I believe few familys are without such a House as these, altho' they do not always live in them, especially in the summer season, when many of them live dispers'd up and down in little Temporary Hutts, that are not sufficient to shelter them from the weather (1968:223).

Cook's account conveys the impression that the main difference between houses was the range in size. Other explorers, however, described some ornamentation with carving as an additional feature of the houses that were larger than average (see Groube 1964:89). These houses were identified as chief's houses. In addition, the early records suggest they were used as sleeping-houses (*whare puni*) for the chief's family, and to some extent also for community gatherings.

The *whare puni* appear to have a long history. In the early 1970s the New Zealand archaeologist Nigel Prickett (1987) excavated the oldest specimen of this type of house yet found. The dwelling excavated in the Moikau Valley in south Wairarapa dates back to the twelfth century. It was rectangular in plan with a partly enclosed front porch and the door left of centre, thus indicating that spatial orientations of the Maori may have been in existence six or seven centuries ago (Davidson 1984:153). This type of house clearly resembles the *whare puni* of later ethnographic accounts by, for example, Elsdon Best (1941, II:558–592) and Raymond Firth (1926).

However, Firth began his article entitled '*Wharepuni*: a few remaining Maori dwellings of the old style' by pointing out the difference between the *whare puni* and the modern meeting-house, the carved house (*whare whakairo*), as described by Williams (1896). Firth (1926:54) denoted the latter as 'the property only of a man of rank'. The *whare puni* was instead owned by 'common people' or 'plebs'. Firth made a clear distinction between the *whare puni* and *whare whakairo*, which he linked to a difference in social status between the people to whom they belonged. He also indicated that the *whare whakairo* were of recent origin, but he did not place the distinction in an historical context. Since Firth wrote his essay on the *whare puni*, however, times have changed.

At present it is widely accepted that (carved) meeting-houses (*whare whakairo*), although they roughly follow the plan of *whare puni* on a larger scale, are a post-European development. The architectural design of modern meeting-houses may originate in the pre-European era, but the really large and elaborately carved meeting-houses, as distinct from the chief's dwelling or *whare puni*, became a dominant feature of Maori settlements only under the new conditions of the nineteenth century (Davidson 1984:151–160).

In his pioneering MA thesis, the New Zealand archaeologist Leslie Groube (1964) formulated the hypothesis

> that much of the change in Maori material culture which has been assumed to be prehistoric may in fact have taken place in the protohistoric period from the stimulus given to Maori culture by the arrival of European ideas and technology (p.16–17).

Groube substantiated his proposition, among other things, with an analysis of the development of meeting-houses in the early nineteenth century. He compared and contrasted accounts of the first missionary, who arrived in 1814, with reports written in the 1830s, and noted a significant increase in size as well as in ornamentation. While original chiefs' houses were rather plain and were used primarily as domestic dwellings, the houses built in the 1830s were more elaborately carved and they served in the first place to accommodate guests, particularly white explorers, traders and whalers (Groube 1964:120). Soon after the missionaries arrived the chief's house acquired new functions, and from the specialized use of the *whare puni*, the much larger, often fully carved *whare whakairo* developed. Thus the meeting-house emerged from the domestic level of an extended family of superior rank to the level of the community.

The modern style meeting-house was first developed in the Bay of Islands in the far north of the North Island, where colonial trade and settlement commenced. The increase in size and also the more detailed elaboration of carving designs were probably the result of better wood-working tools introduced by the Europeans (Groube 1964:118). The fact that they did not spread to southern regions until after 1835 (Groube 1964:122) offers some evidence for the hypothesis that they most likely were built to persuade missionaries and other Europeans to settle among them.

The Influence of Pakeha Patronage

In the course of the nineteenth century the *whare whakairo* gradually replaced the *whare puni*. It received more artistic attention and acquired novel functions in the swiftly changing dimensions of religion and politics. However, during the late 1800s the number of large, carved meeting-houses being built markedly declined. The size of the Maori population approached an absolute low through loss of land following the New Zealand wars of the 1860s, through famine and raging epidemics, and through a fundamental dislocation of the Maori morale. It was commonly believed that the Maori people as a 'race' were doomed to extinction in the near future. The general despondency marking this period generated a special interest in Maori art among European art collectors. If the Maori people were dying out, so they believed, Maori culture must soon die out as well. This stimulated them to make an effort to preserve Maori art and culture. The extent to which these European patrons had a direct impact on the further transformation of the *whare whakairo* is a most interesting issue.

In his analysis of changing carving styles in the centre of the North Island, Roger Neich (1983) argued that around the turn of the century in Rotorua a rather 'orthodox doctrine' about traditional Maori art was formulated by two European art collectors: C.E. Nelson, the manager of a tourist hotel in Rotorua, and Augustus Hamilton, the director of the Colonial Museum in Wellington. In order to salvage traditional Maori culture, these two men employed a number of Maori carvers to build and ornament meeting-houses for display and tourist use. Their commissions were rather detailed, including particular instructions with regard to certain carved items. If these were not to their satisfaction, they did not hesitate to correct the carvers. Thus figures with heeled boots as introduced after contact were removed as inauthentic and carved with the more genuine feet and toes (Neich 1983:257–259). Celebrated characters from super-tribal mythology replaced the tribal ancestors to make the carvings easier for tourists to understand (Neich 1983:259). Both Nelson and Hamilton obviously held strong views as to what genuine Maori culture had looked like in the past, and as patrons of the Maori carvers they specifically requested them to carve in what was supposed to be the most traditional way. Nelson even liked to be known as the 'white *tohunga*' ('expert'). One journalist characterized him as 'more Maori than the Maori' (see Neich 1983:255).

The basic assumption in Nelson's and Hamilton's quest for the authentic was that traditional Maori culture had remained unchanged since the time of discovery and settlement of Aotearoa, the land of 'the long white cloud' as the Maori allegedly named New Zealand when they first set foot ashore between 1000 and 1500 years ago. From their point of view change had only commenced with the advent of European missionaries and settlers in the early nineteenth century. As a result of European contact Maori culture had fallen into decay, which in the second half of the nineteenth century was increasingly explained by Darwin's theory of evolution (Howe 1977:140, 142). The vanishing of the Maori was an inevitable result of natural selection following the advance of European civilization.

Interestingly, however, the meeting-houses built under the guidance of Nelson and Hamilton, and particularly the accompanying carvings, displayed some innovative features that have become firmly entrenched in the carving tradition since then. The orthodox doctrine, as developed by Europeans committed to the preservation of the putatively pre-European Maori culture and art, ironically enough, entailed a new style of carving to portray Maori culture in its most traditional, authentic form. The link between form and content was finally disconnected. Aspective representation was gradually substituted by perspective representation. And the artist became more self-conscious regarding the transformation of his vision of the world in an art-object (see Neich 1983:260).

Over the years the style of carving used in the meeting-houses that were erected under the supervision of Nelson and Hamilton has become the prototype of traditional Maori art.[10] Thus emic models of Maori tradition have been affected by etic interpretations. Contemporary Maori art and craft has been fundamentally influenced by Pakeha conceptualizations of pure Maori culture that developed around the turn of the century. The influence of etic models, however, was not restricted to the domain of art, but rather originated in an emerging theory of the whence and whither of the Maori (Sorrenson 1979). Implicit in the new ideas about the voyage of the Maori from mythological Hawaiki to Aotearoa was the assumption that from the moment of settlement no change had taken place. Maori culture was portrayed as static. Now, by replicating traditional items of carving and building meeting-houses in the ancient style, Maori culture had to be transformed into a timeless culture, so that the past would never disappear in the future.

The conceptions of time involved in this discourse about the Maori past have proved tenacious. The tenets of this mode of thought have haunted not only views of art and carving but overall discourse on Maori culture as essentially comprising relics of a distant yet eternal past. Even though Maori culture may seem to have been superseded by modern civilization, it is conceived of as unchangeable, as timeless. Meeting-houses are just one, albeit one of the most conspicuous, of the elements of this ideology.

Concluding Remarks

The fact that the tradition of building and carving meeting-houses was given a crucial impetus by a number of European art lovers, who as tourist entrepreneurs and museum directors had a vested interest in the continuation of Maori material culture, should not lead to the conclusion that meeting-houses are any less important. Only when meeting-houses are seen as 'inauthentic', could it be argued that they are insignificant. However, the notion of inauthenticity proves highly problematic when a long-term perspective of change is taken into account. Archaeological evidence suggests that meeting-houses developed out of pre-European sleeping-houses of chiefs and which were, among other things, to tempt Europeans to settle in a Maori community. At the time they replaced the war canoe as a focus of group pride (Neich 1983:247).

In spite of the transformation of meeting-houses over time, the spatial orientation of their structures and their temporal implications persist. Even the distinction between intrinsically *tapu* domains, their extensions and their *noa* counterparts continues to play a role in contemporary Maori people's lives. Since contact, *tapu* observances may have been progressively phased out of people's daily lives. Today, too, *tapu* and *noa* may be unknown as concepts to many Maori youngsters. However, many people, including young people, still follow *tapu* rules in their homes, although they are often unaware of the implications of their own practices. I will never forget the moment I was admonished by a little Maori boy, barely five years of age who told me I should not wash my hands in the kitchen sink, but who could not tell me why. By the same token, many people are still reluctant to wash teatowels in the same machine as they use to wash underwear. Children playing in meeting-houses are still taught never to sit on pillows on which you put your head, since the head is considered to be the most *tapu* part of the human body. Little girls know from an early age that they may never step over someone lying on the floor in the meeting-house, not even over the legs. Thus *tapu* is far from insignificant in day-to-day interaction, but it is no longer legitimized in traditional Maori terms.

To the extent that *tapu* and *noa* are still consciously present, they are, like a great deal of Maoritanga, increasingly relegated to the *marae*. The *marae* is the place where tradition is respected and relived. People who can no longer relate to their traditional roots feel alienated from a *marae* environment and will never go there, while those who find it a model for contemporary reality might prefer to stay there. They might regard the *marae* as the final refuge of Maori culture.

Within the *marae* complex it is the meeting-house which is the focus of activity. As the *marae* has changed over the years, so too has the meeting-house; it is being changed in contemporary constructions of new meeting-houses (Kernot 1983), and it will continue to change in the future. Hence the notion of timelessness, so important in contemporary experiences of the meeting-house, should not be extended to the construction nor even to the symbolism of the house itself. As mentioned before, not only is the erection of carved meeting-houses a post-European development, the interpretation of the meeting-house as a representation of an ancestor and the entire ancestor cult may also be of recent origin. And, of course, not only will the architectural design of meeting-houses continue to change in the future but also the interpretation of their symbolic representations.

I was given a foretaste of a possible change of direction in the symbolic interpretation of the meeting-house by the following event. I overheard a respected elder explaining the meaning of a meeting-house to a group of senior European (Pakeha) managers on an introductory course in Maoritanga or Maori culture. He told them the structure of meeting-houses was based on a canoe turned upside-down. The elder added that the canoe constituted one of the most spiritual concepts of the Maori people because they had travelled by canoes from mythological Hawaiki to New Zealand, and, he said, 'we still refer to people from other tribes as the descendants of the crew of a particular canoe. It is a living thing, you know. It is not within you. You are it yourself'.

To make sense of his rather unconventional explanation of meeting-houses, I ought to inform the reader that the narrator was trying to organize the descendants of the crews of all the 'canoes' (*waka*, currently a 'confederation of tribes') that had migrated to New Zealand to build another canoe at a site in Auckland that would be accessible to tourists during the period of construction and carving. The canoes were to be built over the six months preceding 6 February 1990 when they would embark on a voyage to Waitangi in the far north of the North Island to commemorate the 150th anniversary of the signing of the Treaty between Maori and Pakeha. With the blessings of the Maori queen the Maori elder was trying, symbolically, to reunite the various Maori (super-)tribes or canoes in opposition to the Europeans. His mind was preoccupied by canoes, which caused him to invent a new way of looking at meeting-houses. It indicates that the representation of ancestors possibly could be replaced by the original focus of group pride, the symbol of the canoe, or, at least, that the canoe may reacquire a prominent position as a rallying symbol for Maori tribes.

References

Best, Elsdon

1941 *The Maori* (2 volumes)(Memoirs of the Polynesian Society, Vol. 5). Wellington: The Polynesian Society. (Orig. 1924.)

Bloch, Maurice

1977 The past and the present in the present. *Man* 12:278–292.

Cook, James

1968 A journal of the proceedings of His Majesty's bark 'Endeavour', on a voyage round the world, by Lieut. James Cook, Commander, commencing the 25th May, 1768. In Captain W.J.L. Wharton (ed.), *Captain Cook's journal during his first voyage round the world made in H.M. bark 'Endeavour' 1768–71: a literal transcription of the original MSS*, pp.129–230. Adelaide: Libraries Board of South Australia. (Orig. 1893.)

Davidson, Janet

1984 *The prehistory of New Zealand*. Auckland: Longman Paul.

Firth, Raymond

1926 *Wharepuni*: a few remaining Maori dwellings of the old style. *Man* 26(30):54–59.

Goldsmith, Michael

1985 Transformations of the meeting-house in Tuvalu. In Antony Hooper and Judith Huntsman (eds) *Transformations of Polynesian culture* (Memoirs of the Polynesian Society, No. 45), pp.151–175. Auckland: The Polynesian Society.

Grey, George

1971 *Nga Mahi a Nga Tupuna*. Wellington: Reed. (Orig. 1854.)

Groube, L.M.

1964 Settlement patterns in prehistoric New Zealand. Unpublished MA thesis, Auckland University.

Howe, K.R.

1977 The fate of the 'savage' in Pacific historiography. *The New Zealand Journal of History* 11:137–154.

Jackson, Michael

1972   Aspects of symbolism and composition in Maori art. *Bijdragen tot de Taal-, Land- en Volkenkunde* 128(1):33–80.

Johansen, J. Prytz

1954   *The Maori and his religion in its non-ritualistic aspects.* Copenhagen: Ejnar Munksgaard.

Kernot, Bernie

1983   The meeting house in contemporary New Zealand. In Sidney M. Mead and Bernie Kernot (eds) *Art and artists of Oceania*, pp.181–197. Palmerston North: Dunmore.

Lévi-Strauss, Claude

1982   *The way of the masks* (translated by Sylvia Modelski). Seattle: University of Washington Press. (Orig. pub. Paris, 1979.)

1987   *Anthropology and myth: lectures, 1951–1982* (translated by Roy Willis). Oxford: Basil Blackwell. (Orig. pub. Paris, 1984.)

Mead, Sidney M.

1976   The production of native art and craft objects in contemporary New Zealand society. In Nelson H.H. Graburn (ed.) *Ethnic and tourist arts: cultural expressions from the fourth world*, pp.285–298. Berkeley: University of California Press.

Metge, Joan

1976 *The Maoris of New Zealand: Rautahi* (Revised edition). London: Routledge & Kegan Paul. (Orig. pub. 1967.)

Neich, Roger

1983   The veil of orthodoxy: *Rotorua Ngati Tarawhai* woodcarving in a changing context. In Sidney M. Mead and Bernie Kernot (eds) *Art and artists of Oceania*, pp.244–265. Palmerston North: Dunmore.

1984   The complementarity of history and art in T tāmare meeting-house, marumutu Marae, p tiki. *The Journal of the Polynesian Society* 93:5–37.

Prickett, Nigel

1987   Shelter and security: houses and settlements. In John Wilson (ed.) *From the beginning: the archaeology of the Maori*, pp.95–108. Auckland: Penguin in association with the New Zealand Historic Places Trust.

Salmond, Anne

1975   *Hui: a study of Maori ceremonial gatherings.* Wellington: Reed.

1978   *Te Ao Tawhito*: a semantic approach to the traditional Maori cosmos. *The Journal of the Polynesian Society* 87:5–28.

Shirres, Michael P.

1982   *Tapu. The Journal of the Polynesian Society* 91:29–51.

Sorrenson, M.P.K.

1979 *Maori origins and migrations: the genesis of some Pakeha myths and legends.* Auckland: Auckland University Press.

Walker, Ranginui

1977   Marae: a place to stand. In Michael King (ed.) *Te Ao Hurihuri, the world moves on: aspects of Maoritanga*, pp.21–34. Wellington: Hicks Smith & Sons. (Orig. pub. 1975.)

Webster, Steven

1975   Cognatic descent groups and the contemporary Maori: a preliminary reassessment. *The Journal of the Polynesian Society* 84:121–152.

Williams, H.W.

1896   The Maori *whare*: notes on the construction of a Maori house. *The Journal of the Polynesian Society* 5:145–154.

Notes

I thank Aletta Biersack, James J. Fox and Michael Reilly for comments on an earlier version of this paper.

[1] In its quest for a distinctive national image the New Zealand population as a whole eagerly embraces Maori art and craft (Mead 1976).

[2] Throughout this paper when I refer to locations on the right-hand and left-hand side of the meeting house, I am positioned inside the building facing towards the front wall.

[3] I was convinced, however, that it had just taken him a couple of days to think of a satisfactory answer.

[4] Metge (1976:232–235) conceived of *tapu* and *noa* as a complementary opposition, on the basis of which she described, for example, the meeting-house as *noa* in contrast to the *marae aatea*, whereas both the meeting-house and the *marae aatea* were *tapu* in contrast to the dining hall. However, in my opinion, a meeting-house can never be *noa*, not even after the *tapu* has been lifted. It may be less *tapu* than the *marae aatea*, but it can never be *noa* under any circumstances.

[5] In Tainui, where I did my fieldwork, however, coffins were routinely taken inside the meeting-house, except on sunny days, so I cannot really address that question.

[6] 'Hori', a Maori transliteration of 'George', is a New Zealand colloquialism used as a derogatory term for Maori people.

[7] Relevant in this context is the myth of the demi-god Maui, who attempted to procure immortality for humanity by beguiling Hine-nui-te-Po (Great-lady-of-the-Night), the goddess of death. While she was asleep Maui wanted to enter her vagina and emerge by her mouth after cutting out her heart on the way through. However, Hine-nui-te-Po awoke, brought her thighs together and Maui was strangled. Since then death has remained in the world (Grey 1971:21–23).

[8] For a comparative overview of the transformation of the meeting-house in Tuvalu, see Goldsmith (1985). Goldsmith, however, situates his analysis in a broader theoretical perspective.

[9] This belief may have misled anthropologists like Anne Salmond, who insufficiently situated her analysis of the meeting-house in an historical perspective. She wrote about the meeting-house as a static edifice that invoked timelessness during ceremonies performed within it. However, she neglected to examine the implications of the historical fact that the meeting-house itself was a post-European development. In a later publication, *Te Ao Tawhito* ('The ancient Maori world'), she mentioned in passing that the interpretation of the meeting-house as the representation of an ancestor may have been introduced only recently (Salmond 1978:24). However, she failed to explore the consequences of that statement, which she only made to explain the contradictions in the otherwise consistent model of the Maori cosmos she claimed to have discovered. Whether the logic of the model Salmond expounded was Maori logic remains to be seen (Shirres 1982:49).

[10] For a more detailed analysis of the changes in style of carving, see Neich (1983).

The renowned Toraja *tongkonan* (origin-house) of Nonongan, hung with precious heirlooms for a ceremony to celebrate completion of its rebuilding (Tana Toraja, Sulawesi, 1983)

Chapter 9. Houses and the Built Environment in Island South-East Asia: Tracing some shared themes in the uses of space

Roxana Waterson

The place of architecture in people's lives is a subject which anthropologists have, to a surprising degree, been guilty of neglecting. The extent of this neglect was highlighted recently by Caroline Humphrey (1988) in a review of Paul Oliver's (1987) *Dwellings: the house across the world*. Oliver is one writer who has consistently and creatively crossed the boundary between architecture and anthropology, and his work should inspire greater efforts to make good the many areas of neglect still existing in the anthropology of architecture. The Austronesian world provides one of the richest fields for enquiry into this topic, and one which promises to yield new insights into other aspects of social life and organization.

Architectural styles can change rapidly — but they can also maintain continuity over surprisingly long periods. The antiquity of some aspects of architectural style in the Austronesian world is undoubted. Elements such as pile building and the saddle roof with its extended ridge line are first to be seen on the bronze drums of the Dong Son era, but to judge from their appearance in regions as distant from the mainland as Micronesia and New Guinea, it is reasonable to assume that they are much older than their earliest surviving pictorial representations: in other words, that this style is a genuinely Austronesian invention. What is intriguing about the pursuit of meaning in Austronesian built form, however, is what it reveals to us about the continual recurrence and re-use, not just of material forms but of more abstract themes and ideas.[1] Such themes mould the way that people live in the buildings they create and their relations to each other. Ultimately they concern ideas as fundamental as the nature of life processes themselves. This paper attempts to summarize briefly some of these themes, as I have come to perceive them over five years of research into the vernacular building traditions of South-East Asia; a fuller treatment of them is to be found in Waterson (1990).

Structures and Functions

Dutch visitors to Indonesia often recorded disparaging impressions of the buildings they saw. Not only did these buildings strike an unfamiliar note aesthetically since they often lacked walls and windows, being dominated instead by roof, but in addition their interiors were perceived as dark, smoky, overcrowded, dirty and insect-ridden. It was rarely noted that the inhabitants spent little time in these buildings during the day; the principle function of the house being as the origin-site, and storage-place for heirlooms, of a group of kin. In fact, a number of structures in the island South-East Asian world have been designed to complement the enclosed form of the house itself and provide shady open spaces for daytime use: from the *tagakal*-roofed platforms of the Yami of Lanyü Island, through the pavilions of the Balinese house courtyard, to the platform underneath the granaries of the Toraja of Sulawesi and the Ema of Timor. Understanding built form thus requires, among other things, a consideration of the relations between different types of structure and the distribution of functions between them. In addition, we need to study the motivations behind the buildings, which in island South-East Asia would appear to have a great deal to do with the interweaving of kinship structure, rank and ritual.

The function of the house as dwelling is relatively insignificant in some of these societies. One finds numerous examples, from Madagascar to Timor, of houses or origin-villages left empty save for important ritual occasions. It is their importance as origin-places which causes those who trace ties to them to spend sometimes large amounts of money on their upkeep, and to return to them from great distances for the celebration of rites. Occasionally, as among the Merina of Madagascar (Bloch 1971:131) or the Nuaulu of Seram, houses are continually in process of construction, but rarely ever finished. For the Nuaulu, says Ellen (1986), 'there is a notion of an ideal house which is only temporarily realized, but which people are always striving toward' (p.26). For the Toraja, rebuilding is the process which transforms an ordinary dwelling into an origin-house, and the more times it is repeated, the greater the house becomes. It is because of this fusing of habitation and ritual site that some houses come to have the nature of temples, and to be referred to as such in the literature. In most of the indigenous religions of the region, we find an absence of permanent buildings set aside for sacred purposes, but the house itself is charged with the power of the ancestors and of the sacred heirlooms stored within it. Granaries too may serve sacred as well as practical functions, for rice is typically treated with great deference. House, granary and sacred site may even be fused into a single structure, as among the Ifugao, Donggo or Alorese.

The same ambiguity or fusing of functions pertains to 'public' buildings. Such structures, again, are absent in many South-East Asian societies. Borneo longhouses combine public and private spaces within a single structure; among the Toraja, the platforms of privately owned rice barns are utilized for public functions, as sitting-places for guests at ceremonies or for elders hearing a village dispute. Structures called *bale*, or variants thereof, though extremely widespread throughout the archipelago, are by no means uniform in their appearance and function. Two predominant meanings of the word appear to be 'an unwalled building' and 'a meeting-hall', but in some instances *bale* refers to a dwelling, and the range of referents which has developed in eastern Austronesia is very wide. Certainly it seems illegitimate to generalize, as Rassers (1959) did, that 'public' buildings are 'men's houses'; this is actually a rare institution in Indonesia. Where public buildings do exist, their use may articulate a distinction not simply between men and women but between the married and the unmarried. Most communal structures are used as sleeping-places for *unmarried* males, and one can find one or two unusual instances of structures built especially for unmarried girls or boys. On Siberut, according to Kis-Jovak (1980:26), Sakuddei boys sometimes build themselves a special house in adolescence, while Loeb (1935:56) reported the existence of communal girls' houses among the 'southern Batak', where girls spent the night with an older woman as chaperone, and were allowed to receive their suitors for conversation and an exchange of betel-nut. The *kusali* of Tanimbar is a curious instance (which may have existed only in myth) of a structure in which a very high-ranking girl might be secluded, surrounded by 'female' valuables, for a period before her marriage (McKinnon 1983:28).

Houses, then, rather than public buildings, must be viewed as the dominant structures in the organization of the community. In many instances there is something of a continuum between 'public' and 'private' buildings, 'temple' and 'house', while the significance of dimensions such as sacred/profane, male/female and married/unmarried requires critical examination in each instance. Rather than a too hasty categorizing of structures themselves, a close consideration of the distribution of functions proves a better way of understanding the interrelation of built forms.

The House as an Animate Entity

The house commonly forms a microcosm; its layout and decoration reflecting images of society and cosmos. Attitudes toward houses themselves are an integral part of peoples' world-views and need to be understood in this wider context. A fundamental feature of the indigenous 'animist' religions of South-East Asia is the belief that the universe is suffused with a vital force which may attach itself in differing concentrations to people and things. Humans thus participate in the cosmos on much the same terms as everything else; this results in a particular attitude towards the world, in which objects as well as some quite abstract categories can be considered as subjective entities with whom communication is possible (Endicott 1970; Benjamin 1979). Frequently, though not invariably, this vital force or some aspect of it, is known by the term *semangat* or its cognates. These ideas are elaborated to greater or lesser degrees through the archipelago, and without wishing to over-systematize their variety, it is impossible to ignore the frequency with which ethnographers record ideas that the house itself has a 'soul' or vital force: Malay, *semangat rumah*; Buginese, *sumange'* or *pangngonroang bola* (a house's vital force or 'spirit warden'); Sakuddei, *simagere*; Savunese, *hemanga*; and Atoni, *smanaf*, provide a few notable examples (Endicott 1970:51; Errington 1983; Pelras 1975; Schefold 1982; Kana 1980:229, n.7; Schulte Nordholt 1971:137–138).

Howe (1983) writes of Bali that 'all buildings are considered to be "alive"', a fact 'whose omission from the literature is quite remarkable' (p.139). In what exact sense buildings are regarded as alive is not easy to describe. A number of elements may be involved in the process by which life is thought to enter a building: the conversion of forest trees (which have their own vital force) into timbers, the construction process itself, the carving or decoration of the timbers and, perhaps most significantly, the rituals carried out during house building. Moreover, the elaboration of body symbolism and anthropomorphic (or zoomorphic) imagery in speaking about the house is so detailed and explicit in many cases as to reinforce strongly the idea of the house as a 'living' thing (see, for example, Howe 1983:149 on Bali; Forth 1981:29 on Sumba; Hicks 1976:56–66 on the Tetum of Timor). Finally, rituals held to deal with the destruction or 'death' of a house may vividly highlight the fact that it is viewed as an animate entity. In my own fieldwork in Tana Toraja I had occasion to witness such rites performed after a fire destroyed most of a village along with two old noble origin-houses or *tongkonan*. Some villagers described the rites as a 'funeral' for the 'dead' houses; the small buffalo sacrificed on this occasion being intended, they said, to accompany the soul of the oldest origin-house to the afterlife. Others stressed that an origin-house should never disappear, and viewed the rites rather as a means of declaring the continuing existence of the houses until such time as they could be given physical form once again through rebuilding.

Houses as Units of Kinship

This leads to the observation that a 'house', in South-East Asia, constitutes not just a physical structure but also the group of people who claim membership in it. Fox (1980), for example, has noted in the eastern Indonesian context that 'house' is one of the most fundamental and salient categories used by people in talking about social groupings, though it is 'remarkably flexible in its range of applications' (p.12). The relation between houses and kinship groupings, and the manner in which people trace their ties to and through houses, I believe, provides us with the real key to the understanding of the house in South-East Asian societies. At the same time it proffers the chance of advancing our understanding of kinship systems which themselves have never fitted comfortably into more conventional anthropological categories. Lévi-Strauss' (1983) fertile concept of 'house societies' provides a useful and thought-provoking starting point for examining this question. However, the vagueness of his formulations in some crucial respects means that their application is still a matter for testing and debate (see, for example, the essays in Macdonald 1987). It is unclear, for example, how many of the wide range of Borneo or Philippine societies, which include both very egalitarian and strongly hierarchical groups, may usefully be defined as 'house societies', or whether it is only the hierarchical ones which exhibit all the features which Lévi-Strauss defines as characteristic of the phenomenon. Again, where longhouse arrangements are concerned, there is some ambiguity about whether the 'house' as a unit should be deemed to consist of the whole longhouse, or the apartments which make it up. The characteristics of the 'house', as Lévi-Strauss describes them, may in some instances be split between the two (Sellato 1987; Guerreiro 1987). Further testing of Lévi-Strauss' concept in the societies of island South-East Asia promises to provide some fresh understandings of the kinship systems of the region.

Social Relationships and the Uses of Space

How do people order their daily activities and interactions within the built forms that they have created? Rules about the uses of space oblige people to *act out* their relationships to each other in a particularly immediate and personal way, and they provide one of the most important means by which the built environment is imbued with meaning. Bourdieu (1977:90) describes the house as a 'book' which children learn to read with the body, and from which they learn their vision of the world. This 'em-bodying of the structures of the world' becomes a powerful tool for the reproduction of culture precisely because the principles thus transmitted in condensed, symbolic form are simultaneously placed beyond the grasp of consciousness (Bourdieu 1977:94). They thus remain unchallengeable. But where in Berber society, as Bourdieu describes it, the symbolic system revolves around the all important division between male and female, 'public' and 'domestic', South-East Asian views of the world typically begin from different premises. Here, as Errington (1984) has expressed it, 'the system of gender may include notions of a difference, but it is not the difference that makes a difference, the fundamental difference on which other differences are predicated' (p.2). On the contrary, other dimensions of organization, such as rank, may cut right across gender divisions. Most societies of western Indonesia appear to pay remarkably little symbolic attention to distinctions of gender; in eastern Indonesian societies, where they *are* highly elaborated, the predominant theme is not separation and opposition, but rather the complementarity of male and female and their bringing together in fertile fusion.

A second possible dimension of spatial and social arrangements which demands particularly careful scrutiny in the South-East Asian context is that between the 'public' and the 'domestic'. This division, and the attempt to relegate women to the 'domestic' world, has frequently been identified as a prominent feature of the development of industrial capitalist economies during the last century. Within this economy, production and paid labour take place outside the household, which becomes the locus merely of consumption and of the unpaid labour of women in reproducing the workforce. Power, whether economic, political or religious, resides outside the domestic domain, so that the latter inevitably becomes identified as the place where power is not. Those confined to the domestic domain thus find themselves trapped in a dependent and marginalized position, cut off from 'cultural' activity in general and at risk even of being regarded as less than complete persons.

The sphere of the 'domestic', by contrast, is closely associated with the function of reproduction, which is deemed to be 'natural' to women. Ortner (1974) and others have argued that this structure of ideas can be used more universally to explain the subordination of women cross-culturally. But since they really derive from a Western framework of ideas, we cannot uncritically assume that they will apply in other cultures too. In response to Ortner, a number of anthropologists have been prompted to develop much closer analyses of the variable patterns linking male and female, nature and culture, and the public and domestic spheres in different societies. It has consequently been demonstrated that the content of all these oppositions (where they can be said to exist at all) may in fact fail quite markedly to coincide with our own (Tiffany 1978; Weiner 1978; MacCormack and Strathern 1980; Strathern 1984). The 'domestic' is a culturally relative concept, and in other societies, even where it exists as a category, we cannot simply assume that the political, ritual or economic action is taking place elsewhere. Tiffany (1978), for example, notes the lack of consensus in anthropology over what constitutes 'politics', and particularly the tendency to dismiss or overlook informal processes. Weiner (1978) argues that for the matrilineal Trobrianders, women's reproductive powers are not merely 'natural' but cultural; through childbirth (and their roles in ceremonies and wealth exchanges) they ensure the continuity of the matrilineal kin group or *dala*, and thus perpetuate social groups and identities (p.175). And La Fontaine (1981) reminds us that the domestic group, far from being the irreducible 'building block' of society, is itself the product of wider social relations. Its isolation is only apparent, for its very existence is predicated upon the existence of other similar units.

In non-industrial economies, the economic demands placed upon the household usually involve production for wider ends than mere subsistence: bridewealth, feasting or prestations of different kinds. She concludes that: 'The division into domestic and public which is made in some, but not all, societies is not a description of structural cleavages but a symbolic statement whose meaning we must interpret in each instance where we find it' (La Fontaine 1981:346).

In the South-East Asian world, too, the concept of domesticity would appear to be of limited relevance in explaining the meanings associated with the house and its space. Firstly, the economy itself is typically organized around the household as the basic unit of production as well as consumption, with women playing substantial roles in agriculture and the control of household produce. Given the importance of house units in traditional kinship and ritual systems, as well as political processes, it would be unwise to regard the house as being 'outside' any of these spheres. Frequently, too, as among the Northern Thai, Acehnese, Minangkabau or Toraja, rather than woman belonging to the home, it is the home which belongs to her. In examining uses of space and their symbolic implications, then, it is essential to avoid any preformed conclusions about the hierarchical implications of associations with gender. The kitchen or hearth, for example, although closely associated with women in their nurturing capacities, was often centrally located (as in older Toraja houses). Rather than a division between 'back' and 'front' portions of the house, in a number of cases the more meaningful contrast would appear to be between 'inner' and 'outer' parts, women often being associated with the womb-like 'inner' portion of the house — the source of life, fertility and nourishment.

One type of rule about the uses of space which serves particularly clearly to define social relationships is that which prohibits particular individuals from entering a certain space. This imposes on them a kind of vigilance about their own movements and forces them to be aware of the status distinction embodied by the rule. In the asymmetric alliance systems of eastern Indonesia we can find a number of examples where in-marrying women are excluded from certain areas of the house. For example, among the Atoni of western Timor a wife, as an in-marrying affine, has access to the inner section of her husband's parents' house only after she has been initiated into his descent group ritual (Cunningham 1964:39). This temporary restriction thus marks the process of her acceptance by the husband's kin group (though in practice a considerable proportion of Atoni marriages are uxorilocal). Cunningham describes the use of the inner (or back) section of the house principally by women and the outer (or front) by men as being co-ordinate with Atoni ideas of subordination and superordination respectively. But he goes on to draw a comparison with traditional political arrangements, and it is precisely at this point that we encounter Atoni ideas of sacredness and the 'still centre' of the kingdom, a palace where a sacral ruler, actually a man but characterized as 'female' (*feto*), ideally should remain motionless. The rest of the kingdom was divided into four 'great quarters', each headed by a secular lord called *monef-atonif* ('male-man'). (Note the symbolic relativity of gender here.) It becomes a nice point whether it is the periphery or the centre which should be considered superior. In some contexts, the 'inner', left or 'female' section of the house is treated as if it were subordinate. Yet it is the left which is most closely associated with ritual, in which the 'female', and women themselves, play a pivotal role. They, after all, form the mediating category between wife-givers and wife-takers. Furthermore Cunningham

(1964:60) states that ritual or spiritual matters, far from being associated with a 'subordinate' sphere, are actually considered superior to secular affairs.

Among the Ema of Central Timor, studied by Clamagirand (1975), the house floor is divided into two unequal parts, a 'male' and 'female' side, called the 'great' and 'small' platforms. The great platform is used for the storage of heirlooms and the performance of rituals. In earlier times, an in-marrying woman, for whom bridewealth payments and counter-exchanges had not been completed, was not allowed to set foot on the great platform. A very similar division of floor space, with the same restriction on women for whom bridewealth payments had not been completed, exists among the inhabitants of Rindi in eastern Sumba (Forth 1981:38), while in Tanimbar it is the bride's home village, rather than a part of the spouse's house, which becomes temporarily off-limits to her. This is the case, according to McKinnon (1983:250), where a high-ranking woman is married in an alliance which aims to repeat an already-established affinal link with another high-ranking house. She then cannot return to her village at just any time, but must wait until her husband and the wife-taking group of his house are ready to make another major prestation to their wife-givers.

In all these cases we are dealing with alliance systems which tend to conceptualize marriage in terms of the transfer of women between houses. In all of them, kinship ideology tends toward the patrilineal, even though actual marriage and residence patterns may be highly flexible. Not surprisingly, this kind of spatial rule is unlikely to occur in societies with bilateral kinship systems, such as the Toraja. Here, house membership for the individual is much less exclusive, and the apparent contradiction posed by the arrival of a new member presents less of a conceptual problem. What, however, of peoples like the Acehnese, whose kinship systems show distinct matrilineal bias combined with rules of uxorilocal residence? Might such rules occur in inverse form where it is men who are the newcomers in their wives' houses? (See paper by Cecilia Ng in this volume.)

An interesting analysis by Dall (1982) of the uses of space within the Acehnese house suggests the need for caution in making any assumption about the 'inferiority' of rear parts of the house, which are particularly the domain of women. In some ways these are better seen as 'inner', in relation to the front part of the house, used by men, which is 'outer'. Alternatively, one can view the central bedroom as the most important and 'inmost' part of the house, in relation to which both male and female ends are 'outer'. It is in the bedroom, where procreation takes place, that the uniting of male and female principles is symbolically represented by the two main posts, called 'prince' and 'princess', against which the bridegroom and bride are seated on their wedding day. Dall (1982) states that his male informants regarded the carved and decorated front balcony as the most important part of the house. He apparently was not in a position to collect female informants' views of their homes, but given that women are actually the house owners, he cannot avoid wondering whether the decoration is not perhaps intended to 'keep the guests happy'. He echoes the impressions of previous writers, such as Snouck Hurgronje (1906) and Siegel (1969:55), that the house remains essentially the domain of the woman, and that the man, in spite of the respect accorded to him while at home, remains little more than a guest (Dall 1982:53). The same pattern is, if anything, even more pronounced among the Minangkabau, where the position of an in-marrying son-in-law is notoriously tenuous. And a final, striking example comes from the Rejang, as described by Jaspan (1964), where in *ssemendo* marriages (involving bride service and a much reduced bridewealth payment), the uxorilocally residing husband was confined like a guest to the veranda and the front room. Putting all these examples together, what we see is not a simple division between 'male' and 'female' spaces, or between 'front' and 'back' as superior/inferior, but the expression of a relation between affines, involving the gradual incorporation of an in-marrying member into the house. In the latter instances, rather than women being 'confined' to the back of the house, it is men who are 'confined' to the front — a dubious honour at best.

In a number of other cases, such as Sunda (Wessing 1978) and south central Java (Tjahjono 1988), 'inner' parts of the house are used for the storage of rice, which itself is intimately associated with women — as evidenced in its widespread personification as a goddess (Dewi Sri in Java and Bali, Lady Koosok in Thailand, and other variants in different parts of the island South-East Asian world). Frequently, whether granaries are separate structures or incorporated into the house, it is the woman who has sole access to the rice store (see, for example, Wessing 1978:55 on Sunda; Hitchcock 1986:26 on the Dou Wawo of Sumbawa; and Barnes 1974:76 on Kedang). In Tana Toraja, too, though men are not prohibited from entering the granary, it is women who customarily control the rice store and remove rice for daily consumption. In Savu, where we again find a marked division of the house into a 'male' and a 'female' side, it is the enclosed and 'female' side which is the place of storage (and cooking) of grain (Kana 1980). The Savu house, like so many houses of the archipelago, is windowless, dominated by its enormous roof. Its enclosed part is symbolically womb-like, in Kana's words, 'dark, female and hidden'. The profound symbolic tie between women and grain in all these cases is a reflection not just of the important economic and productive roles played by women but of a deeper association between agricultural and female fertility, between the nurturing capacities of women as child-bearers and as farmers. Respect for this creative power is echoed in the spatial rules surrounding the rice store.

Trunk and Tip, Centre and Periphery: Images of Growth and Power

A recurring chain of associations appears to exist in many Indonesian societies between the idea of centres, navels, and root/trunk ends of plants, forming a complex of ideas, which resonate with deep significance throughout the archipelago. Given their widespread occurrence and the fact that the origins of some of the key terms involved are Austronesian, it appears to be a strong possibility that this is a distinctively Austronesian set of ideas. Centres, navels and roots are all metaphoric sources of vitality; the botanic metaphors of 'trunk' and 'tip' occur not just in rules about the correct 'planting' of house posts but as ways of talking about kinship, for example: women, wife-givers, or senior houses are all in particular Indonesian societies contrasted with men, wife-takers, or junior houses, as 'trunk' to 'tip' (see for example Forth 1981:201 on Sumba; Lewis 1983:36 on the Ata Tana Ai of Flores; and Schulte Nordholt 1980:241 on the Atoni). Immobility and fertility seem frequently to be associated with the centre; the idea of rulers or ritual specialists 'staying put', often actually in a house, recurs with noticeable regularity. Immobility, again, is a prominent feature in wedding ceremonies (as among the Malays, Bugis and Minangkabau) at which the bride and groom, dressed as 'king' and 'queen' for the day, must sit motionless for hours at a time. Immobility thus is utilized as a way of representing a concentration of creative, supernatural or political power.

Since in some cases there appears to be a clear association between 'male' mobility and 'female' immobility, it might be tempting to equate the former with independence, freedom and power, and the latter with dependence and confinement. But I would argue that here especially interpretative caution is required. For, as we see, immobility is frequently used in a ritual context to signal high status and concentration of power. Moreover, whether the 'still centre' is identified as male or female may in fact vary according to context. In any case, symbolic oppositions such as these do not necessarily translate into any literal confinement of women within the house such as Bourdieu describes for the Berber. On the contrary, women play active roles in economic, ritual and, at times, political life.

That this immobility is in fact frequently matched symbolically with the female principle, and the idea of the mother as source, is nowhere more dramatically demonstrated than among the Tetum of Timor, described by Hicks (1976:31). Here, the house is conceptualized as a body, the main room being called the 'house womb'. This is the centre both of domestic and ritual activity, containing the hearth and the ritual ancestral pillar. Here, a woman gives birth, aided by a midwife who, after delivering the baby, fastens a pouch containing the afterbirth to the ritual pillar, and drops the soiled birth cloths onto the ancestral altar. This act (which would be an unthinkable desecration in any culture where the categories of 'male' and 'female' are polarized as 'sacred' and 'profane') perhaps demonstrates more dramatically than any other example the extremely positive associations of female reproductive powers in the South-East Asian world.

It is in this light that we must view the recurrence of the idea of the house as womb, implicit in some cases but quite explicit in others. What difference is there, if any, between the womb-house of the Tetum or the Savunese and that of the Berber as described by Bourdieu? Are we faced here simply with a form of universal symbolism, so fundamental that it will tend to present itself to house dwellers anywhere in the world? I would argue that this is not the case, for it is by very different routes that peoples may arrive at such equations. In a patriarchal society, the dependence upon women for the furtherance of life may come to seem an uncomfortable anomaly. Rather than celebrating biological life processes as being the very stuff of religion, these are associated instead with sin, corruption and mortality. In the world religions they are viewed as intrinsically opposed to the life of the spirit, to which men claim privileged access. But in the house-based societies of Indonesia, instead of a realm of the 'sacred' being sharply defined in opposition to the 'profane' world, there is rather a sort of continuity of sacredness, which makes sense in terms of the monistic world view, in which everything in the cosmos is imbued with vital force. Thus the fact of the womb as life-source serves here only as the starting-point for a wide-reaching web of ideas about life processes and the reproduction of social groupings, which themselves are intimately identified with the house.

References

Barnes, R.H.

1974 *Kédang: a study of the collective thought of an eastern Indonesian people*. Oxford: Clarendon.

1977 *Mata* in Austronesia. *Oceania* 47(4):300–319.

Benjamin, Geoffrey

1979 Indigenous religious systems of the Malay peninsula. In A.L. Becker and Aram A. Yengoyan (eds) *The imagination of reality: essays in Southeast Asian coherence systems*, pp.9–27. Norwood, NJ: Ablex.

Bloch, Maurice

1971 *Placing the dead: tombs, ancestral villages, and kinship organization in Madagascar*. London: Seminar Press.

Bourdieu, Pierre

1977   *Outline of a theory of practice* (translated by Richard Nice). Cambridge: Cambridge University Press.

Clamagirand, Brigitte

1975   La maison Ema (Timor Portugais). *Asie du Sud-Est et Monde Insulindien* 6(2–3):35–60.

Cunningham, Clark E.

1964   Order in the Atoni house. *Bijdragen tot de Taal-, Land- en Volkenkunde* 120:34–68.

Dall, G.

1982   The traditional Acehnese house. In J. Maxwell (ed.) *The Malay-Islamic world of Sumatra: studies in politics and culture*, pp.34–61. Melbourne: Monash University Centre of South-East Asian Studies.

Ellen, Roy

1986   Microcosm, macrocosm and the Nuaulu house: concerning the reductionist fallacy as applied to metaphorical levels. *Bijdragen tot de Taal-, Land- en Volkenkunde* 142:2–30.

Endicott, Kirk

1970   *An analysis of Malay magic*. London: Cambridge University Press.

Errington, Shelley

1983   Embodied sumangé in Luwu. *Journal of Asian Studies* 42:545–570.

1984   The construction of gender in Southeast Asia: a call for papers. Unpublished paper.

Esterik, Penny van

1984   Continuities and transformations in Southeast Asian symbolism: a case study from Thailand. *Bijdragen tot de Taal-, Land- en Volkenkunde* 140:77–91.

Forth, Gregory L.

1981   *Rindi: an ethnographic study of a traditional domain in eastern Sumba*. The Hague: Nijhoff.

Fox, James J. (ed.)

1980   *The flow of life: essays on eastern Indonesia*. Cambridge, Mass.: Harvard University Press.

Guerreiro, Antonio

1987 "Longue maison" et "grande maison": considérations sur l'ordre social dans le centre de Bornéo. In Charles Macdonald (ed.) *De la hutte au palais: sociétiés "àmaison" en Asie du Sud-Est insulaire*, pp.45–66. Paris: CNRS.

Hicks, David

1976 *Tetum ghosts and kin: fieldwork in an Indonesian community*. Palo Alto: Mayfield.

Hitchcock, Michael J.

1986 Basket makers of the highlands: the Dou Wawo of Bima, Sumbawa. *Expedition* 28(1):22–28.

Horridge, G.A.

1986 A summary of Indonesian canoe and Prahu ceremonies. *Indonesia Circle* 39:3–17.

Howe, L.E.A.

1983 An introduction to the cultural study of traditional Balinese architecture. *Archipel* 25:137–158.

Humphrey, Caroline

1988 No place like home in anthropology: the neglect of architecture. *Anthropology Today* 4(1):16–18.

Jaspar, M.

1964 From patriliny to matriliny: structural changes among the Redjong of southwest Sumatra. PhD thesis, The Australian National University, Canberra.

Kana, N.L.

1980 The order and significance of the Savunese house. In James J. Fox (ed.) *The flow of life: essays on eastern Indonesia*, pp.221–230. Cambridge, Mass.: Harvard University Press.

King, V.T.

1985 Symbolism and material culture: some footnotes for Penny van Esterik. *Bijdragen tot de Taal-, Land- en Volkenkunde* 141:142–147.

Kis-Jovak, J.

1980 *Autochthone Architektur auf Siberut*. Zürich: Eidgenössische Technische Hochschule.

La Fontaine, J.S.

1981 The domestication of the savage male. *Man* 16:333–349.

Lévi-Strauss, Claude

1983   *The way of the masks.* London: Cape.

Lewis, E. Douglas

1983   Opposition, classification and social reproduction: gender as operator in Tana Ai thought. Working paper presented to the research seminar on Gender, Ideology and Social Reproduction, Canberra: Department of Anthropology, Research School of Pacific Studies, The Australian National University, August 1983.

Loeb, Edwin M.

1935   *Sumatra: its history and people.* Vienna: University of Vienna Institut für Völkerkunde.

MacCormack, Carol P. and Marilyn Strathern (eds)

1980   *Nature, culture and gender.* Cambridge: Cambridge University Press.

Macdonald, Charles (ed.)

1987   *De la hutte au palais: sociétés "àmaison" en Asie du Sud-Est insulaire.* Paris: CNRS.

McKinnon, S.

1983   Hierarchy, alliance and exchange in the Tanimbar islands. PhD thesis, University of Chicago.

Manguin, P.

1986   Shipshape societies: boat symbolism and political systems in insular Southeast Asia. In David G. Marr and A.C. Milner (eds) *Southeast Asia in the 9th to 14th centuries*, pp.187–213. Singapore and Canberra: Institute of Southeast Asian Studies, Research School of Pacific Studies, The Australian National University.

Oliver, Paul

1987   *Dwellings: the house across the world.* London: Phaidon.

Ortner, Sherry B.

1974   Is female to male as nature is to culture? In Michelle Zimbalist Rosaldo and Louise Lamphere (eds) *Woman, culture and society*, pp.67–88. Stanford: Stanford University Press.

Pelras, Christian

1975   La maison Bugis: formes, structures et fonctions. *Asie du Sud-Est et Monde Insulindien* 6(2–3):61–100.

Rassers, W.H.

1959   *Pañji, the culture hero: a structural study of religion in Java.* The Hague: Martinus Nijhoff.

Schefold, Reimer

1982   The efficacious symbol. In P. Erik de Josselin de Jong and E. Schwimmer (eds) *Symbolic anthropology in the Netherlands*, pp.125–142. The Hague: Martinus Nijhoff.

Schulte Nordholt, H.G.

1971   *The political system of the Atoni of Timor*. The Hague: Martinus Nijhoff.

1980   The symbolic classification of the Atoni of Timor. In James J. Fox (ed.) *The flow of life: essays on eastern Indonesia*, pp.231–247. Cambridge, Mass.: Harvard University Press.

Sellato, Bernard

1987   Note préliminaire sur les sociétés "àmaison" àBornéo. In Charles Macdonald (ed.) *De la hutte au palais: sociétés "àmaison" en Asie du Sud-Est insulaire*, pp.15–44. Paris: CNRS.

Siegel, James T.

1969   *The rope of God*. Berkeley: University of California Press.

Snouck Hurgronje, C.

1906   *The Acehnese* (2 volumes). Leiden: E.J. Brill.

Strathern, Marilyn

1984   Domesticity and the denigration of women. In Denise O'Brien and Sharon W. Tiffany (eds) *Rethinking women's roles: perspectives from the Pacific*, pp.13–31. Berkeley: University of California Press.

Tiffany, Sharon W.

1978   Models and the social anthropology of women: a preliminary assessment. *Man* 13:34–51.

Tjahjono, Gunawan

1988   Center and duality in Javanese dwellings. Paper presented to International Symposium on Traditional Dwellings and Settlements in a Comparative Perspective, University of California, Berkeley, April 1988.

Waterson, Roxana

1990   *The living house: an anthropology of architecture in South-East Asia*. Kuala Lumpur: Oxford University Press.

Weiner, Annette B.

1978   The reproductive model in Trobriand society. *Mankind* 11:175–186.

Wessing, Robert

1978   *Cosmology and social behavior in a West Javanese settlement* (Southeast Asia Series No. 47). Athens, Ohio: Ohio University Center for International Studies.

Notes

[1] For analyses of some other examples of recurring symbolic themes and associations in Austronesia see Barnes (1977), Esterik (1984), King (1985), Horridge (1986) and Manguin (1986).

Contributors

Jennifer Alexander

(PhD, University of Sydney, 1985.) Australian Research Fellow, Department of Anthropology, The University of Sydney, Sydney, NSW, Australia.

James J. Fox

(PhD, Oxford, 1968.) Professor, Department of Anthropology, Research School of Pacific Studies, The Australian National University, Canberra, ACT, Australia. (Convener of the Comparative Austronesian Project.)

Christine Helliwell

(PhD, The Australian National University, 1990.) Lecturer in Anthropology and Comparative Sociology in the School of Behavioural Sciences, Macquarie University, Sydney, Australia.

Toon Van Meijl

(PhD, The Australian National University, 1991.) Post-doctoral Research Fellow of the Royal Netherlands Academy of Arts and Sciences, and Manager of the Centre for Pacific Studies, Department of Anthropology, University of Nijmegen, Nijmegen, The Netherlands.

Cecilia Ng

(PhD, The Australian National University, 1988.) Director of Campaigns and Education, Australian Council for Overseas Aid, Canberra, ACT, Australia.

Clifford Sather

(PhD, Harvard, 1971.) Southeast Asian Studies Program, University of Oregon, Eugene, Oregon, USA. Fulbright Fellow 1993–94, Department of Anthropology and Sociology, University of Malaya, Kuala Lumpur, Malaysia.

Roxana Waterson

(PhD, Cambridge, 1981.) Senior Lecturer, Department of Sociology, National University of Singapore, Singapore.

Michael W. Young

(PhD, The Australian National University, 1969.) Senior Fellow in the Department of Anthropology, Research School of Pacific Studies, The Australian National University, Canberra, ACT, Australia.

www.ingramcontent.com/pod-product-compliance
Lightning Source LLC
Chambersburg PA
CBHW060903090426
42735CB00033B/3490